Privatization and
Foreign Investmen
in Eastern Europ

PRIVATIZATION AND FOREIGN INVESTMENTS IN EASTERN EUROPE

Edited by *Iliana Zloch-Christy*

PRAEGER

Westport, Connecticut
London

Library of Congress Cataloging-in-Publication Data

Privatization and foreign investments in Eastern Europe / edited by
   Iliana Zloch-Christy ; [contributors, Gabor Bakos . . . et al.].
        p.   cm.
   Includes bibliographical references and index.
   ISBN 0–275–95212–6 (alk. paper)
        1. Privatization—Europe, Eastern.   2. Investments, Foreign—
   Europe, Eastern.   3. Eastern Europe—Economic policy—1989–
   I. Zloch-Christy, Iliana.   II. Bakos, Gabor.
   HD4140.7.P752   1995
   338.947—dc20   95–6942

British Library Cataloguing in Publication Data is available.

Library of Congress Catalog Card Number: 95–6942
ISBN: 0–275–95212–6

First published in 1995

Praeger Publishers, 88 Post Road West, Westport, CT 06881
An imprint of Greenwood Publishing Group, Inc.

Printed in the United States of America

The paper used in this book complies with the
Permanent Paper Standard issued by the National
Information Standards Organization (Z39.48–1984).

10 9 8 7 6 5 4 3 2 1

*To the fellow economists
in post-communist Europe*

Contents

PART II. PRIVATIZATION AND FOREIGN INVESTMENTS: WESTERN PERSPECTIVES

PART III. CONCLUSION

Tables and Figures

TABLES

FIGURES

Abbreviations

BIS	Bank for International Settlements
CEFTA	Central European Free Trade Association
CIS	Commonwealth of Independent States
CMEA	Council for Mutual Economic Assistance
CPE	centrally planned economies
DME	developed market economies
EBRD	European Bank for Reconstruction and Development
EC	European Community
EFTA	European Free Trade Association
EIB	European Investment Bank
EU	European Union
FDI	foreign direct investment
FNPs	Funds of National Property
GATT	General Agreement on Tariffs and Trade
GDP	gross domestic product
GNP	gross national product
IBRD	International Bank for Reconstruction and Development
IFC	International Finance Corporation
IMF	International Monetary Fund
IPFs	Investment Privatization Funds

IPO	initial public offering
LDC	less developed country
LIBOR	London interbank offered rate
NIC	newly industrialized country
NIFs	National Investment Funds
NMP	net material product
OECD	Organization for Economic Cooperation and Development
OPEC	Organization of Petroleum Exporting Countries
SOEs	state-owned enterprises
UFE	Union of Food Exchanges
UN	United Nations
UNCTAD	United Nations Conference on Trade and Development

Acknowledgments

This book is based on a selection of papers presented at the International Studies Association (ISA) Annual Meeting in Acapulco, Mexico, in March 1993 by the panel on "Systemic Transformation in Eastern Europe" chaired by Dr. Gabor Bakos, Hungarian Academy of Sciences, as well as on invited papers. The contributors to the volume represent a wide range of views and a large number of nationalities from Eastern Europe, Western Europe, the United States, and Japan. Hence gratitude should be expressed to the authors and to the active participants in the conference.

I would like to acknowledge the intellectual support of Professor R. N. Cooper, Department of Economics, Harvard University, who provided encouragement and inspiration for my work during my faculty fellowship. My participation at the ISA conference in Acapulco was financed by the Austrian Forschungsgemeinschaft, Vienna. The Theador Koerner (Vienna) Prize for Scholarly Work is also gratefully acknowledged. Bank Austria AG provided technical support in preparing the volume. I have benefited from discussions and the papers by Lowell M. Dicke and Leonid Grigoriev. The final work on the study was completed at St. Antony's College in Oxford and Hoover Institution in Stanford, whose fascinating intellectual atmospheres are gratefully acknowledged. J. Hanns Pichler has generously supported my scholarly work. Franklin P. Johnson Jr. shared with me his experience as a pioneer American investor in Eastern Europe. Last but not least, special thanks should be expressed to the editors at Praeger who encouraged my work: James Ice, Marcy Weiner, Catherine Lyons, and Andrea Mastor.

Editing proceedings of a conference for style is apt to be a notably difficult task. Each of the authors is responsible for the printed contributions, and where I have added or substracted from the delivered manuscript, regardless of the many people who contributed to the production of this study, I bear responsibility for any remaining errors.

Privatization and
Foreign Investments
in Eastern Europe

Introduction: Foreign Investments and the Transition in Post-Communist Europe

Iliana Zloch-Christy

When the panel proposal for the forthcoming International Studies Association Annual Meeting in Acapulco, Mexico, was conceived in late 1991, it was obvious that one of the important economic and political issues in the transformation process in post-communist Europe would be the privatization issue and the foreign investment flows to the region.[1] These two topics were of great interest for both Eastern European and Western scholars and politicians. Privatization is one of the main pillars of the transformation of the economic structure and political philosophy in the countries of Central and Eastern Europe. It was also clear that foreign investments would be of great importance for these countries, which had been centrally planned economies isolated from the world market and had scarce capital resources, in order in the first place to provide the organic links to the world economy, and also to bring in capital, to save jobs and open new jobs, and to bring in innovative management, new technology, and modern production techniques.

Foreign investments can contribute to the efforts of the Eastern European countries to meet the challenges of the transformation. These challenges are too many to be successfully resolved in a decade or even in a generation. Institution building has to be carried out. The capital stock of the Eastern European economies is obsolete and has to be rebuilt through large investments. Human capital has to be adjusted through retraining the workforce and through reallocation. Infrastructure capital must be improved and restructured. The spatial structure of the economy and the environment, much of which was destroyed by the central planners, will also have to be restored and adjusted.

In the first years after 1989, a wave of interest in inward foreign investments was observed in Eastern Europe. A new legal framework as well as institutions and agencies to encourage and regulate these flows were established. Business reports suggest that almost two-thirds of multinational companies have been interested in investing directly in the region. For the foreign investors, the newly opened Eastern European economies have been regarded as attractive locations because of the following three major reasons: historical, cultural, and geographical proximity to European markets; skilled and relatively (to Western Europe) cheap labor; and natural resource endowments (raw materials, e.g., the large oil and gas endowments in Russia).

The stock and the flow of foreign direct investments rose particularly rapidly in 1990–1993. Germany, the United States, France, the United Kingdom, Italy, and Austria were the leading countries investing in the region. Before presenting some data on these total investments, I would like to mention some problems regarding their assessment at present. There are difficulties in estimating the flows and stocks both for the region and for the individual Eastern European countries, the main reason being the absence of well-established recording and publication procedures and consequently the lack of reliable statistical data in these countries and in the international agencies (United Nations [UN], International Monetary Fund [IMF], the International and the European Banks for Reconstruction and Development [IBRD and EBRD]). This is, of course, not surprising, given the rapid economic and political changes in the region. Some of the problems in estimating data on foreign investments in post-communist Europe are associated, for example, with the lack of reliable balance of payments statistics, which represent only cash transfers through the banking system of these countries. These statistics may underestimate the actual flow of foreign investment (and of other flows, e.g., capital flight). Since foreign investments can also be transferred in kind, the problem of their assessment becomes even more complicated; obviously it is difficult to record such investments. Other problems are associated with the reporting of foreign investments: there are differences (which can be considerable) between the values of these investments based on protocols of intent and values of actual transfers. In these cases, the flow and stocks of foreign investments may be overestimated, for example, protocol values of foreign capital invested in joint ventures in most of the Eastern European countries (and particularly in Russia) greatly exceed the share of capital in joint ventures that are in operation.

Although there are difficulties in estimating the flow and stock of foreign investments, some recent surveys and analyses suggest that the data for 1992 are $5.23 billion and $13.57 billion respectively.[2] Hungary, Poland, and former Czechoslovakia were able to attract the bigger share of Western stock and flow in the recent three years, followed by Bulgaria, Romania, and Russia. Data on these countries are presented in Table 1.1 and Table 1.2.[3] It should be mentioned here, however, that these data refer to foreign direct investments only. Control over an Eastern European entity distinguishes such investments from foreign portfolio investments (e.g., using financial instruments as government bonds or stock). There are almost no available statistics on such investments in Eastern Europe. However, foreign portfolio investments are gradually increasing in im-

Table 1.1
Estimated Stock of FDI in Central and Eastern Europe (US$ millions)

Country	1991	1992
Bulgaria	350	570
Czechoslovakia	1200	2750
Hungary	2900	5400
Poland	770	1450
Romania	270	600
USSR	1550/4900	–
Russia	1300/2100	1500/3000

Notes: Ranges for USSR and Russia reflect data on capitalization of both operational and registered investment projects (see explanation in text). Lower capital figures (operational investments) are more comparable to those given for other countries.

Sources: Estimates based on McMillan (1993) and various reports of United Nations.

portance in some post-communist countries in the region, for example, Poland, Hungary, and in the Czech Republic.

The data from Tables 1.1 and 1.2 show that foreign direct investments are still at relatively low levels. At the same time, they clearly indicate a radical shift of the strategy of the Eastern European countries towards attracting foreign capital in their economies as compared to the pre-1989 period. I would like to mention here a few points about this period as a basis for our future discussion. As is well known, foreign direct investments were de facto restricted (prohibited) in the domestic economies of the Eastern European centrally planned economies until the late 1970s. They were marginal in form, scope, and effect. Among the communist countries in Europe, in 1967 Yugoslavia became the first to take legislative steps to allow foreign direct investments in its economy, followed by Romania and Hungary in 1972. The other countries in the region proceeded with such legislation in the late 1970s and, mostly, during the 1980s. Foreign investment was de facto restricted in the Council for Mutual Economic Assistance (CMEA) region first of all for ideological reasons, and also for political and economic reasons. On the economic side, such investment was seen as a destabilizing and at some point disruptive factor in the centrally planned (and administered) economic system. McMillan suggests that in the mid-1980s the cumulative total of foreign direct investments in Eastern Europe could be assessed at about $1 billion.[4] This figure refers to stock and includes estimates on Yugoslavia (with a share of some 75 percent), which indicates that the foreign direct investment (FDI) for the CMEA region was much below the level of $1 billion.

After 1989 and the opening up of the former centrally planned economies, foreign direct investments obviously became an important issue in the transformation and restructuring process in post-communist Europe. As a region with a

Table 1.2
Estimated Flows of FDI to Central and Eastern Europe (US$ millions)

Country	1990	1991	1992
Bulgaria	70	250	220
Czechoslovakia	300	690	1500
Hungary	420	1900	2300
Poland	270	400	680
Romania	112	156	331
USSR	480/955	240/n.a.	–
Russia	n.a.	120	200

Notes: In-kind as well as cash transfers included wherever possible. Range for USSR as in Table 1.1.
Sources: Estimates based on McMillan (1993) and various reports of United Nations.

relatively low level of economic development, it is natural for Eastern Europe to attract foreign investments from the West and to become again (as in the prewar period) a net capital importer.

Foreign direct investments, and potentially foreign portfolio investments, can have a positive effect on the stabilization policies and affect the urgently needed economic recovery at present, first of all through their contribution to the possible improvement in the balance of payments. As is well known, most of the countries in Eastern Europe (the only exception being the Czech Republic) have balance of payments and external debt difficulties.[5] Foreign investment can also affect positively the transformation process in the region through its impact on government policies and the adoption of liberal regulations regarding banking, accounting, currency convertibility (and the enlargement of its scope), and business services. On the microeconomic level, it can positively affect the introduction of new business standards, the creation of a new business ethic, and the urgently needed education of the Eastern European managers, who lack entrepreneurial and risk-taking skills, training, and experience in many areas (e.g., product creation and development, quality control, and marketing). Foreign investment can also be a factor in addressing the very important issue in the economic transformation of post-communist Europe of destroying the monopolistic power of the domestic enterprises (the so-called centrally planned dinosaurs) and thus potentially increasing the efficiency of the economy. It can contribute to the much needed competition on the domestic market and expose the enterprises to the rivalry of national and international firms.

The plans for privatization of the small, medium, and large state-owned enterprises in Eastern Europe also increase the importance of foreign investment because they can abate the tension of the savings-investment gap of the region. Foreign financing in the form of Western portfolio investment can facilitate the privatization process. Several such investment funds were established in the last years in western Europe, the United States, and Japan—the First Hungary Fund, the Austro-Hungary Fund, the Hungarian Investment Company, the Central European Development Corporation, and others. The activities of these funds, however, have still been relatively modest in acquiring assets in Eastern Europe.

The nature of privatization in the individual Eastern European countries will obviously affect the scope and the impact of the foreign investments in the process of transformation. The voucher schemes for privatization (in the Czech Republic and Russia) tend to restrict the inflow of foreign investments, while the schemes involving direct sale of assets by the state, as in the case of Hungary, seem to have a more stimulating effect on these flows. The so-called spontaneous privatization in Poland, Hungary, and the Czech Republic also provided favorable conditions for foreign investors in the last two or three years.

It is obvious that the direct role of FDIs in the restructuring process in post-communist Europe is demonstrated and will be demonstrated in first place through their impact on a pragmatic approach to economic projects. As is well known, in the pre-1989 period in Eastern Europe, many (primarily) industrial giants were built not on the ground of sound economic calculations (for competitiveness, comparative advantage, profit and loss), using Kornai's description of "hard budget constraint," but on political-ideological considerations.[6] Foreign investments can provide directly and indirectly alternatives for the adjustment of the domestic economy to the new realities and can create sectors of growth and employment. One of the areas could be, for example, the modernization of the Eastern European telecommunications industry. Since the general political climate between East and West dramatically changed and the Western COCOM restrictions were reduced in scope, there are good possibilities for technology-based foreign investments in the region. The other obvious impact of FDIs on the restructuring and transformation process will be demonstrated through their stimulating effect on intraindustry, intrafirm trade. As is well known, the trade expansion among the Western industrialized countries is based primarily on intraindustry flows. This can have a stimulating effect on economic relations, both within the former CMEA region and in the relations between Eastern Europe and the Western countries. The expansion of trade with the industrialized West creates the basis for reestablishing the links between Eastern Europe and the world economy. Such links are obviously very important in our world of economic, political, and regional interdependence.

STRUCTURE AND GOAL OF THE STUDY

This book discusses the issues of economic transformation, privatization, and foreign investments in post-communist Europe with a focus on the period after 1989. Undoubtedly, it raises as many questions as it answers. Our goal is to establish a basis for better understanding of the scope, problems, potentials, and expected directions of economic changes, and particularly the privatization process, and foreign investments in the region.

As was stated earlier, one of the major channels for the impact of foreign investments on the domestic economies in post-communist Europe is provided through the schemes for privatization. Although the privatization strategies differ in the individual countries in the region in their scope and detail, there are five main privatization methods that can be identified:

- Commercialization followed by privatization
- Privatization through liquidation (dissolution of state enterprises as legal entities and sale of their assets)
- Foreign investments through joint ventures
- Reprivatization (restitution)
- Small-scale privatization (e.g., trades and services)

This indicates the important role foreign direct investment can potentially have in the restructuring process. The papers presented by the Acapulco panel in 1993 and the invited contributions to this book attempt to analyze the scope, potential, and problems of foreign investments in post-communist Europe and their relation to the ongoing economic and political transformation, particularly the privatization process. They focus on five Central and Eastern European countries—Bulgaria, the Czech Republic, Hungary, Poland, and Russia.[7] The study also discusses major problems of the economic transformation, emerging market structures and institutions, and regional economic developments.

The main questions addressed in this book are as follows: First, what are the trends in the privatization in Eastern Europe and developments in foreign inflows to the region in the early 1990s? Second, what are the main problems facing the Eastern European economies and foreign investors? Third, what can be done and what should be done to increase foreign direct and equity investments to the region, from the perspective of the Eastern European countries and from the perspective of the Western investors? Fourth, what is the political risk in the process of economic transformation, privatization, and increased flows of foreign capital in post-communist Europe?

In preparing the volume, we wanted to involve economists who represent a fair mixture of views and nationalities and reflect their different perspectives. The study is organized in three parts. After the introduction addressing the issue of the role of foreign direct investments in the transition, the first part turns specifically to a discussion of the economic transformation, privatization, and foreign investments from the perspective of the Eastern European countries. It includes contributions from the Russian economist Alexander Barski, of the Central Economico-Mathematical Institute of the Russian Academy of Sciences, who analyzes the problems and the perspectives of foreign investment in Russia and the former Soviet republics, and another Russian economist, Stefan Zhurek, of the Institute for the Studies of External Economic Relations in Moscow, who addresses an issue important for attracting foreign investment in the future, namely the development of commodity markets in Russia. These are followed by a chapter by the Czech economist Michal Mejstrik, which in part discusses the situation in the Slovak republic until 1992. The chapter by Władysław W. Jermakowicz, an economist who was an advisor to L. Balcerowicz, discusses in detail the potential, problems, perspectives, and lessons from the early 1990s for both the Polish government and entrepreneurs and Western investors. Gabor Bakos presents a new approach to the analysis of the privatization in Hungary, and another Hungarian economist, György Csáki, of the Academy of Sciences in Budapest, addresses the issues of foreign direct investments in his country, which is considered to be the biggest recipient of such investments among the Eastern European countries in the years since 1989. Investment policy is in the focus of the chapter by the Bulgarian economist Georgi Smatrakalev, and this is followed by a detailed overview and assessment of possibilities for foreign investments by two other Bulgarian analysts—Daniela Bobeva and Alexander Bozhkov. The Hungarian economist Gabor Bakos completes the first part with an analysis of new regional developments in post-communist Europe, mainly addressing the question of whether there is and should be a free trade zone in Central Europe. Part 2 includes contributions on the economic transformation, privatization, and foreign investment from the perspective of the West. The chapter by the Japanese economist Ken Morita discusses some problems in the economic relations between Japan and East European countries. Gabor Bakos, who has been working with the Hitotsubashi University in Tokyo since the early 1990s, assesses the scope and potential of Japanese capital in Central Europe in a case study on Magyar Suzuki. Part 3 addresses the important methodological issue of assessing political risk in doing business and investing in post-communist Europe. It is based on my work focusing on economic transformation, external imbalances, and the assessment of risk and possibilities. The main findings of the study are summarized in the conclusion.

While I write these lines, the consequences of the failed so-called second October revolution in Russia and of the Polish, Hungarian and Bulgarian parliamentary elections, which brought back to power former communists (or those stemming from the old communist network), are evident. The articles in this volume do not discuss issues regarding where future economic and political developments may go in Eastern Europe and Russia in the light of these and other events. I hope that the reader will be better served by a study comprising the analyses of Eastern European and Western experts on the first years of transformation than by works speculating on future developments. Despite the optimistic approach of the present book to the future of the economic and political transformation in post-communist Europe, it is clear that the political risk remains the major one in doing business and investing in this region.

NOTES

1. The terms "Eastern Europe," "post-communist Europe," and "former CMEA countries" are used as synonyms. Eastern Europe includes Bulgaria, the Czech Republic,

Hungary, Poland, Romania, the Slovak Republic, and the former Soviet Union (Commonwealth of Independent States and the other Soviet successor states). The terms "West" and "Western countries" are used to designate the developed economies that comprise the membership of the OECD. Please refer also to the individual authors' descriptions of the countries involved in their analyses.

2. Carl H. McMillan, "The Role of Foreign Direct Investment in the Transition from Planned to Market Economy," paper presented at the ISA Annual Convention, Acapulco, Mexico, March 1993.

3. Other Western analyses suggest, however, that the bigger recipient of foreign investment in Eastern Europe is Russia, with a share of more than 25 percent of the total (some $42 billion). Of these, more than $10 billion involve over 402 investment deals (mainly energy related), e.g., 106 greenfield projects and 285 joint ventures. Among the other Soviet successor states, Kazakhstan and Azerbaijan were also able to attract foreign direct investment, although at modest levels (*Financial Times,* 28 September 1993, p. 2). Some deals in Kazakhstan, for example, are those with the British Gas Co. and with the Italian Agip Co., which have the exclusive negotiating rights to develop the huge Karachaganak oil and gas field (one of the biggest in the world, containing an estimated 20 trillion cubic feet of gas—four times the size, e.g., of the United Kingdom's biggest gas field), and the deal involving the U.S. oil company Chevron, which will develop the giant Tengiz oil field. These deals can bring potentially some $6 billion foreign investment over the next ten years (*Financial Times,* 2 July 1992, p. 26).

As was discussed earlier in the introduction, there are considerable differences among Western assessments of FDIs in Eastern Europe. Our analyses suggest that the total figures are much below the data given here, published in *Financial Times.*

4. McMillan, p. 7.

5. For a discussion of the balance of payments and external debt difficulties of the Eastern European countries, see, e.g., Zloch-Christy (1988, 1991, 1994).

6. For an excellent analysis, see J. Kornai (1980), *Economics of Shortage,* Amsterdam, North Holland.

7. The volume does not include an analysis on Romania. Some observations on Romania are presented in Ovidiu Nicolescu, "Entrepreneurship in Romania," *Radio Free Europe/Radio Liberty Research Report,* Vol. 1, No. 38, September 1992, pp. 45–50.

PART I

ECONOMIC TRANSFORMATION, PRIVATIZATION, AND FOREIGN CAPITAL: EASTERN EUROPEAN PERSPECTIVES

2

Problems of Foreign Investments in Russia and in the Former Soviet Union

Alexander Barski

The history of foreign investments in Russia started anew in 1985–1987 and was determined by the start of Gorbachev's perestroika. As is known, the development of the perestroika process has led to renunciation of the communist concept both in the Soviet Union and in the majority of socialist countries of Europe and Asia. The development of this process put an end to the lengthy isolation of the former socialist countries from the world economic system, destroying the "iron curtain" between the economies of these countries and the rest of the world. As a result, the Soviet Union's lag behind the world level of economic and technological development, which revealed itself in certain characteristics and phenomena, has become an apparent fact. Most important, the opening of economic borders put the Soviet, and Russian among them, manufacturers in a position where a real comparison could be made between the levels of manufacturing effectiveness in Russia and that in other developed and developing countries. This comparison the Russian manufacturers have lost. Without looking into the reasons, one should only state the fact that what was happening in the rest of the developed world indicated the impossibility of further development of Russia under conditions of economic and technical isolation. On the other hand, the opening of economic borders for the flow of goods also objectively opened the way to capital flow. Earlier, Western capital used to penetrate Russia drop by drop and only under strict state control, but the new economic ideology and real requirements of the country's development forced Russia to lift the main obstacles to the inflow of foreign capital. This was reflected in the resolutions of the leaders of the state and of the party in 1987–1988 concerning the development of joint entrepreneurship and in further decisions by the Soviet and subsequently the Russian government and the Parliament on liberalization of investment activities by foreigners.

SOME HISTORICAL OBSERVATIONS

Up to now foreign entrepreneurship has not become seriously widespread in Russia and has not exerted any important influence on the development of the Russian economy. The reasons for this are historical, that is, stemming from Russian nationalism, as well as systemic, that is, of economic and legal character. Historically Russia for a long time developed under a certain isolation from Europe. Thus, a nineteenth-century Russian historian, Klyuchevski, referred to a foreign traveler of the fifteenth century who noted, on the one hand, the suspiciousness of the Muscovites toward foreigners, and on the other hand, the efforts of authorities to isolate foreigners from communication with the local inhabitants.

The attempts by Peter I to Europeanize Russia in the eighteenth century led to the start of an inflow of foreign capital. Such inflow became especially active after the abolition of serfdom in 1861. As a result, already in 1909–1914 the share of foreign investments in all investments was as high as 55 percent. That capital was concentrated mainly in heavy industries. After the October Revolution, the attitude toward foreign investments changed depending on the political and economic situation in the country. Thus, in the twenties, with the declaration of the New Economic Policy (NEP) attempts to use foreign capital in the form of concessions were made. An appropriate organizational and legal basis was elaborated and a number of Western companies received rights for exploitation of timber resources in the North of Russia, ore resources in the Urals and in the Ukraine, and so forth. However, from the end of the 1920s, with the start of the Stalinist economic system, attitudes toward foreign capital changed and became sharply negative. Under the conditions of the confrontation of the Soviet Union with practically the whole world, an isolationist doctrine of relying only on the Soviet's own strength became the basis of development. The industrial giants of the first five-year plans, in which modern Western machinery and technology were widely used, were constructed mainly at the expense of selling treasures that had been amassed by Russia: bread, timber, and coal. One of the results of such ruinous exportation was the famine of 1932–1933. Later, until the 1960s the technical potential of the country was maintained mainly by restraining inner consumption. At the same time, manufacturing machinery was being reproduced mainly at the technical level achieved in the 1930s and 1940s.

This tendency continued until the beginning of the sixties. From the sixties, after the discovery of new oil deposits, and especially after the world energy crisis of 1973, the Soviet Union obtained a powerful source of foreign currency from oil exports. This circumstance prompted the development of foreign economic relations, including the import of Western technologies and equipment and the construction of factories financed by foreign investments. The financial basis for such operations was selling raw materials, first of all oil and gas, and compensational deals such as payment for the equipment delivered by products to be manufactured in the future. Compensational deals have opened doors for the development of international cooperation in manufacturing such products as cars, complicated household utensils, and new chemical products and the expansion of extraction and export of oil and gas. Thus, first steps to overcome economic and technical isolationism were taken.

However, under fluctuating conditions of the global market and the decrease of prices for primary material resources, the country's ineffective structure of exports has revealed itself. Thus, in 1981 the share of machines, equipment, and means of transport in the aggregate exports of the USSR to all regions of the world constituted only 13.6 percent. Their share in exports to the developed countries was only 5 percent, while the share of raw materials was 80 percent. Under such an export structure, the decrease in oil prices hit the strongest blow to the Soviet economy. As a result, at the start of the 1980s, parameters of economic growth in the USSR fell abruptly, and the lag in the technological base that had accumulated began to reveal itself.

FOREIGN INVESTMENTS IN THE FORMER SOVIET UNION AND RUSSIA AFTER 1985: POTENTIALS AND PROBLEMS

The new situation evolving after 1985 accelerated radical changes in the approach to foreign investments. Naturally, a transition to market methods in the economy required the opening of economic borders not only to flows of goods but also to capital.

In January 1987, the government decree "On the Order of Founding and Operation of Joint Ventures" was issued. At the same time, a number of intergovernmental agreements on the mutual protection of investments were concluded. Toward the end of 1987, there were 27 joint ventures (JVs) in the country; in 1988, 188; in 1989, up to 90 ventures were registered monthly; and by the end of 1989 their number reached 1,086. JV fixed assets at that time amounted to 3.3 billion roubles with 1.4 billion roubles of foreign investments among them (for your comparison: fixed assets of the USSR at the end of 1984 in 1973 prices were 1.49 trillion roubles) ("USSR in figures in 1984," *Financi i statistika,* 1985, p. 51). By October 1990, in the territory of the former Soviet Union 2,051 joint ventures had been registered. Some of them remained only on paper; others broke up. For example, among 3,400 JVs registered by the middle of 1991, only 948, or 28 percent, actually functioned and were releasing products or rendering services. Among them, industrial enterprises accounted for 42 percent; services (hotels, tourist agencies, transport service agencies, advertising agencies, and so forth), 27 percent; shops and public catering businesses, 9 percent; cooperatives (in different spheres), 9 percent; and scientific and construction services, 5 percent. All these ventures employed 117 thousand people, 115 thousand Soviet citizens among them.

It is also worth mentioning that the structure of foreign investments in Russia and the distribution of joint ventures among industries do not yet meet the real requirements of the economy. Most national and foreign entrepreneurs lack the determination to abandon trading industries and other similar industries with high levels of liquidity. Investments in service and hotel industries are quite popular.

A further push forward in the growth of foreign investments in Russia was attained by decisive steps by the Russian government toward liberalization of foreign trading activities and the lifting of restrictions on the share of foreign capital in joint ventures. One did not have to wait long for the results. Already in May 1992, among 45 joint ventures that were registered, 14 JVs were companies with 100 percent foreign participation. It is also true that most foreign investors tend to invest their capital in either close-to-border, developed regions with traditions of across-the-border trade, or capital cities: Moscow, St. Petersburg, Novosibirsk, or newly formed free economic zones in Nakhodka, Kaliningrad, and others. Thus, among the 20 largest foreign investments according to the data for September 1992 (*The Delovye Lyudi Magazine,* no. 10, October 1992), 13 were registered in Moscow; 5 were related to the construction industry, 5 to the manufacturing of consumption goods, and 5 to electric equipment. Shares of the foreign partners in these ventures varied from 11 percent (Russian-Hungarian venture "Escalator") to 85 percent (Russian-German footwear manufacturing venture "Lenvest"). The scale of these ventures varied between 14 million roubles (Russian-American Crovtekh, building materials) to 1 billion roubles (Russian-American Eletrosila, power plant machinery) and 6 million dollars (a new Russian-American hotel in Moscow, Slavyanskaya).

German businessmen are the most active (in terms of invested capital) in the Russian market, with Finnish, U.S., Austrian, UK, and Italian investors following. In the last months, growing activity is being displayed by the representatives of China, South Korea, Israel, and South Africa, that is, countries with which there were practically no economic relations during the last decades. In total, representatives of 60 countries are among foreign investors registered in Russia.

However, even now, after official renunciation of the socialist concept of development, there still are those who hold views that an inflow of foreign capital will bring enslavement of the country, that selling the raw material resources so abundant in Russia is none other than selling the country, and that as a result of the development of international trade the country is turning into a raw material appendage of international monopolies. The reformist government led by E. Gaidar was on many occasions accused of close contacts with international economic and financial institutions, and he himself was accused of striving to place Russia under the command of these institutions.

Thus, sufficiently strong isolationist traditions have historical roots in Russia, and the existence of an apprehensive attitude toward foreign capital is a reality that cannot be ignored.

On the other hand, the vast territory and uniquely versatile collection of natural and mining resources indeed make it possible to satisfy requirements in raw materials for almost any kind of production. This creates an illusion of the possibility of isolated development of the country, independent from the world community. This illusion, together with the dominating practice of planning and management of the people's economy as a single technological complex, led to the actual ignoring of the commonly adopted criterion of effectiveness, which more that anything else determines the redistribution of capital. The system of centralized planned management was based on principles of direct control of the material flow of goods and services. Attempts to supplement it with the criterion of effectiveness came into conflict with the main objective of an economic manager—filling the material flow. Therefore, the search for ways to raise effectiveness has not become a natural characteristic of the economy in the planned system of management.

The actual rejection of the search for effective ways to invest capital with regard to international effectiveness was a natural consequence of the ideology and policy of isolationism, the strategy of "relying on our own strength" in the former Soviet Union.

In the USSR, the inflow of foreign capital was regulated from the center. The main criterion of decision making, together with criteria related to defense and ideology, was the criterion of supplementing technologies and production systems that did not exist in the country or were undeveloped. Therefore, quite frequently narrow decisions lacking an overall approach were made; the volume of accompanying costs for organization and modernization of related production was not considered, incomplete technologies were purchased, and so forth. Contrary to the decision makers' aspirations, this aggravated the dependence of the country on suppliers of imported raw materials and parts. The recognition of this dependence produced an even more apprehensive attitude toward attracting foreign investment.

At the same time, both statesmen and researchers note the obviously insufficient participation of foreign capital in the development of the Russian economy when compared with the other former socialist countries of Eastern Europe. Thus, in the middle of 1992 the declared contribution of foreign investors in Russia amounted to only $3.8 billion, less than in the case of Hungary. In the situation of acute crisis in the Russian economy, one of the signs of which was abrupt lowering of investment activities, the requirement for foreign investments changed from technical supplements to national investments into the necessary components in support of production. According to an estimate by the experts in the Russian Economic Ministry, the annual requirement in foreign investments for the Russian economy from 1992, until 1995 amounted to $5 billion. If we take the October 1992 exchange rate, this would come to 18 percent of all capital investments. Difficulties in attracting such a volume of investments are aggravated by the fact that during the last two to three years a principal change in the model for attracting foreign investments was taking place.

On the side of the former USSR, representatives of the state acted as the receivers of the investments. As for their partners, as a rule, they were major Western companies for whom the Soviet side was a desirable and reliable partner. Investments by small and medium-size companies did not take place. The situation changed drastically during recent years, when the state began to reduce its role in regulating the economy. The abolition of ministries managing separate industries and turning state enterprises into commercial and joint-stock companies resulted in a situation in which foreign investors had to deal with new partners—less reliable and lacking sufficient experience. On the other hand, foreign investors never faced a task of marketing research in the territory of the former USSR. In most cases investments were carried out on the Soviet side's initiative, and the Soviet side took all the risk associated with the estimation of investment effectiveness. Actually, foreign investors acted as contractors. The Soviet side also guaranteed a return on invested capital and profit on investments. At present, with the disappearance of state customers, foreign investors find themselves in a complicated position.

The vast Russian market has preserved its former size in the physical sense. But under the conditions of restructuring economic relations, the evaluation of the capacity of this market has become a rather complicated task: the prices that used to be stable are now determined as a result of supply and demand under market conditions. The structure of demand, which used to be stable, started to change abruptly both in the production and in the consumption spheres, and the pressure and monopolism of producers, which were formerly constrained by state regulation, have assumed a character resembling that of the Mafia. If one adds to this set of uncertainties accelerating inflation, it becomes clear how complicated a task it is to attempt to estimate the results of investing into the Russian economy. Under such conditions, one would expect from the economic and political managing bodies of the country great activity and interest in attracting foreign investments. Judging from hearsay, they are displaying such interest. However, this is not sufficiently confirmed legislatively.

A poll conducted among foreign businessmen living and working in Moscow has shown interesting results. Among the factors holding back the development of foreign investments in Russia, the following were mentioned: confused economic legislation, 55 percent; instability of the political situation, 39 percent; inconvertibility of the rouble, 39 percent; high taxes, 17 percent; bureaucracy and corruption among government officials, 16 percent.

It is interesting that Russian entrepreneurs give similar estimates of the situation. According to their opinion, active participation by Western businessmen in the Russian economy is handicapped by: lack of legal guarantees for entrepreneurship, 71 percent; political and economic instability, 48 percent; expectation of real reforms, 35 percent; fear of red tape and arbitrary rule of authorities, 17 percent (The ''Delovoi Mir'' Newspaper, No. 38, 1992).

Thus, both Western and Russian entrepreneurs put the confusion in Russian legislation and lack of state guarantees in the first place as a factor deterring foreign investment. Under such conditions, a crucial role is played by the laws determining the rights and privileges of foreign investors in the Russian market and by the regulations governing the circulation of foreign currencies, procedures, and forms of transfer of entrepreneurial profits—all the factors affecting decisions of potential foreign investors. As already mentioned, attempts to regulate and attract foreign investors were included in the first documents dating to 1987, which in principle opened the possibility of foreign investments in the USSR. Further steps in the sphere of regulation of foreign investments were a looking-glass reflection of the stages of political struggle related to the break from socialist concepts. Finally, on 5 July 1991, four months before the breakup of the Soviet Union, the Foundations of Legislation on Foreign Investments in the USSR were adopted. They failed to become real law, but served as a basis for the elaboration of laws on foreign investments adopted in the course of 1991 in most Soviet republics, which to a considerable extent reflected the logic of the Union law.

In Russia the Law on Foreign Investments was adopted on 4 July 1991, that is, before the final collapse of the USSR and before the start of the active reform of the economy associated with E. Gaidar's name. This law largely reflects inconsistency of the political and economic strategy of the Russian leaders caused by the struggle of political forces. Certainly, this law cannot solve all the problems that may emerge in the way of a foreign businessman who decides to invest capital in the Russian economy. Many regulations governing fundamental conditions for doing business in the country are not included. They could be included in the laws on land property, bankruptcy, and other issues. Many stipulations of the laws on entrepreneurship and on joint-stock companies, banks, and other organizations have to be corrected. This would create a necessary regulative parametric basis not only for foreign but for national businessmen as well, as many foreign investors' problems are caused by systemic drawbacks in the legislative and infrastructural protection of entrepreneurship in Russia.

When one describes the Law on Foreign Investments adopted in Russia, one has to mention that it bears many features in common with similar laws existing in the republics of the former Union as well as in the republics within the Russian Federation.

In particular, all these laws on foreign investments are based on the priority of international treaties in case of the emergence of contradictions between stipulations of these laws and international treaties.

The objective of the Russian law as stated in the preamble is to attract and to use effectively in the Russian Federation foreign material and financial resources, modern foreign machinery and technologies, and management experience. In the similar Kazakh law there is an addition that the law is aimed at forming in the Republic an open-type economy and is to serve for the purpose of fast transition of the Republic to economic principles commonly used in world practice. Thus, the exceptional significance of foreign investments for transformation of the country's economy is recognized in the law.

However, even in the first article of the Russian law (and a majority of similar laws in other republics), legislators' inconsistency is apparent. This article determines those who can become foreign investors—foreign juridical persons, foreign states, international institutions, foreign citizens, persons without citizenship, and Soviet citizens residing permanently abroad. However, next comes a restriction: the citizens have to be registered for conducting economic activities in the country of their permanent residence. Thus, a foreign citizen not only cannot start his own business in Russia if he has not established a business in his country, but, obviously, cannot without references purchase shares, which according to the law are freely traded in Russia. And the latter, as is well known, is the simplest and most common way of investing.

A 1987 stipulation limiting the share of foreign investors in joint ventures to 49 percent has been lifted. For the first time, foreign investors are granted the right to own 100 percent of their own enterprises. Investors can create a new enterprise; purchase an existing enterprise, building, or facility; or purchase a share or shares of an enterprise.

In the case of land, the situation is more difficult. According to the Law on Foreign Investments, foreign investors can purchase only the right to use land and other natural resources. This regulation of the law contradicts the constitutional amendment made in December 1992, which permits private property in regard to land.

The law also provides for certain benefits to foreign investors and joint ventures in which the share of foreign investment exceeds 30 percent. Thus, stock brought into Russia as a foreign investor's contribution to the statutory fund of the venture is not liable to customs duties. Such ventures are entitled without any license to export their own products. Currency proceeds from export of their own products are exempted from obligatory sale to the Central Bank of Russia. One should mention that according to estimates by many experts, benefits provided in the law are insufficient to neutralize the risk created by the instability not only of the situation in the country but, first of all, by the instability of legislation. In principle, in the Russian law as in the laws of other former republics of the Union and autonomous republics, guarantees from nationalization and appropriation are formulated. But lawmakers face a dilemma: should compensation be provided for in the case of a change in legislation? On the one hand, there should be evidence of the determination to protect foreign investors from arbitrary decisions at any expense. For example, the law adopted in the Azerbaijan Republic stipulates that if future modifications are to worsen an investor's position, then for the investments that have already been made, the legislation that functioned at the time when they were made shall be applied over a period of 10 years. On the other hand, such measures might make foreign investors apprehensive, by implying that the lawmaker himself is not sure of the stability and obligatory nature of his decisions.

It is clear that foreign investors frequently view such guarantees as insufficient under current conditions in the country. Therefore, the intergovernmental Russian-American Agreement signed in March 1992—the agreement on state insurance of American private investments in Russia in case of nationalization,

civil riots, or worsening of currency exchange conditions—is of great importance. In cases in which the insurance would be paid, the American investor
would receive compensation from the U.S. government, and the latter, in turn,
would demand satisfaction from the government of Russia. It is known that over
300 American companies have applied to the U.S. insurance agency with re-
quests to insure their investments in Russia. Since at present foreign investors
value guarantees they receive at the level of international law more highly than
those they obtain from Russian legislators, international cooperation in this
sphere is very important in attracting foreign investments to Russia. Such cooperation develops most successfully with the American administration. American corporations for private foreign investments and the American
Export-Import Bank are expanding their activities in Russia, and the latter offers
insurance of American exports at the rate of 85 percent of the amount of a
transaction.

Among measures taken by the Russian side in order to stabilize legislation
and provide legal guarantees, one should mention the adoption on 29 May 1992
of the Law on Pledge and, on 9 October 1992, the Law on Currency Regulation.

CONCLUSION

Institutions encouraging foreign investments in Russia are being developed.
Thus, in 1991 the State Committee on Foreign Investments was founded; its
duty is to register foreign investments and control their activity. At the end of
1992, on the basis of that committee and of the organizations of the former
Union of Friendship Societies with Peoples of Foreign Countries, the Russian
Agency for International Cooperation and Development was founded and given
much larger functions, among which are, of particular importance, providing
information for foreign businessmen and attracting them to investing in Russia.

Thus, one can state that within the country as well as internationally, the
activities aimed at the inclusion of Russia into the international division of labor
are becoming more active. Clearly, among those who make decisions as well
as among common people, the psychological consequences of the long isolation
of the country are being overcome and the recognition of the importance of
foreign investments for the rise of the Russian economy is becoming stronger.

3

Emerging Market Structures in Russia: Developments in Commodity Markets

Stefan Y. Zhurek

The development of commodity markets, privatization, and foreign investment are tightly interconnected in any economy in transition, particularly in the Russian economy. An economy that is undergoing transformation from a centrally planned to a market-regulated system requires almost simultaneous introduction of a number of policies aiming at liberalization of production, distribution, and foreign trade; macrostabilization; demonopolization and implementation of the competition policy; privatization of state enterprises; and finally opening up of the economy to foreign investment. Each of these policies depends upon the success of the other ones. None of them could prove effective if conducted in isolation.

But the crucial point is that any system has feasible limits on the extent to which it can be transformed within a given period of time, especially such a complex and large-scale system as the Russian economy. Therefore, for the reforms to be successful, the government ought to outline the priority areas for reform in the economic system; this would then boost the transformation of all other areas. This is an extremely difficult task for an inexperienced and divided state administration, given that creating the economic and commercial institutions of a market economy almost from scratch is in itself an immense task. Adding to the difficulty is the fact that each sector of the economy claims its priority over the others, but the system is simply incapable of changing all of its elements at the same time with optimal results. The neglect in the past, and hence the great inefficiencies in the economy, suggested that a fundamental and painful transition was inevitable.

In this respect, one can argue that the development of commodity exchanges, which form alternative, nonstate distribution channels and act as the price-setting mechanism for equilibrium markets, is very important in terms of the general success of economic reforms in Russia and also in terms of success in specific areas, such as privatization and foreign investment. The better the performance of commodity exchanges, the easier for the newly privatized enterprises, joint ventures and foreign companies to function in the present semimarket conditions in Russia. With the administrative regulators abolished but market regulators not in place yet, the Russian economy remains a highly monopolized economy, where lack of financial discipline and incentives for enterprises, accompanied by a lack of political stability that results in backtracking and ad hoc regulations, creates an uncertain business environment for both domestic and foreign investors.

The problems in the Russian economy have traditionally been related to inadequacies associated with central planning, centralized resource distribution and wholesale trade, irrational pricing and the lack of significant private property rights. The fundamental mistake was the overcentralization of production into large state enterprises (often monopolies or inefficient giants), with the center making too many of the microlevel decisions. The financial system allocated extra resources to loss-making enterprises, ensuring a low level of efficiency, as enterprises knew that the better the results achieved this year, the fewer the resources that would be allocated to them in the next year, the so-called ratchet effect. Unlike the case in market economies, where prices guide resource allocation, in the Soviet economy prices assumed little meaning but simply acted as accounting tools to ensure some notion of financial balance was achieved. As a result, input prices and product prices were highly distorted, which produced conditions of disequilibrium in the market. And finally, the social ownership of productive assets and the levelling of salaries produced very low material incentives for workers and managers to work efficiently.

During the first phase of perestroika, very few reforms were actually introduced, as Gorbachev's reforms aimed to improve the efficiency of the economic system while maintaining socialist ownership of the means of production. There was little overall desire to fundamentally transform the system and introduce a truly market-based economy. Some decentralization of economic decision making was introduced, but it proved to be ineffectual, given the underlying opposition on the part of the majority of the central and local authorities to the introduction of private property rights and market relations and institutions.

The crucial point was the disintegration of the Soviet Union in the winter of 1991–92, which itself was characterized by acute food shortages and real hardship for Soviet consumers. At this point, the first Gaidar government began the process of so-called shock therapy economic reform. The reform envisaged abolishing central planning almost overnight, introducing price liberalization, and introducing a far-reaching program of privatization. The Russian government followed the Polish shock therapy approach and liberalized most prices on 2 January 1992. Immediately prices leapt by a factor of 3.5 and since then have continued to increase by 2,000 percent in 1992 and approximately 1,000 percent in 1993.[1]

Unlike the case in developed market economies, where inflation is traditionally viewed as an inflation of demand, in the transforming Russian economy
inflation has three dimensions—inflation of demand (rising consumer prices),
inflation of costs (rising costs of production), and so-called monopolistic inflation (rising monopoly prices). All three add to the overall rate of inflation; at
the same time, they develop independently of each other.

Part of the blame for the continued rate of price inflation has been placed
upon the failure of the Russian government to introduce a demonopolization
program prior to price liberalization. The argument is thus that hyperinflation
has been the result of a too rapid price liberalization, which has allowed large
state monopolies to reap abnormal monopoly profits at the expense of the Russian consumer. To a certain extent, this argument is true. From the extremely
distorted set of prices in December 1991, price liberalization was required to
reduce the level of subsidies both to consumers and to state enterprises so as to
reduce the spiralling state budget deficit, which was itself putting extreme up-
ward pressure on inflation. It could be argued that it was the lack of financial
discipline of state enterprises and hence their constant demands for state budget
subsidies that forced the increase in the largely monetized state budget deficit
and hence inflation, rather than the failure of the Russian government to break
up state monopolies prior to price liberalization.

Such general observations set the broad context within which the development
of commodity exchanges in Russia will be considered. The analysis covers the
development and functioning of the existing commodity exchanges, with particular emphasis on their problems and future prospects.

HOW THE DEVELOPMENT OF COMMODITY EXCHANGES
STARTED

The Russian economic reforms have brought about an interesting phenomenon—rapid growth in the number of commodity exchanges, of which there are
already over 800. But what is behind such growth, and how significant is their
impact on the economy overall?

The first commodity exchanges in Russia appeared in 1990,[2] when a group
of businessmen decided to revive the Moscow Exchange, which originated back
in the eighteenth century. Among the first exchanges to develop were the Russian Commodity and Raw Material Exchange and the Moscow Commodity
Exchange. It took a year or so before the exchanges really began to flourish. At
that time, however, it was clear that it would be impossible to establish a classical, Western-style exchange overnight. Russian exchanges aimed more at creating "civilized," nonstate wholesale markets, providing convenient meeting
places for sellers and buyers. In other words, right from the start, most exchanges
assumed the role of wholesale, intermediary agencies. This was particularly important because until 1990 almost all industrial resources were distributed

through the centralized state agency, Gossnab, and, given its later collapse, the exchanges were supposed to form an alternative channel of distribution.

By 1992 the number of exchanges exceeded 500, and their total turnover reached as high as 50 billion rubles, compared to 500 billion rubles of resources distributed in 1990 through the state network of centralized supplies. Although inflation in 1991 amounted to almost 200 percent and in 1992 to 2,000 percent, the scale of commodity exchange trade in real terms was still rather low.[3]

In February 1992 the Russian Government adopted the Law on Commodity Exchanges and Exchange Trade, which provided a legal framework for the functioning of the commodity markets. The law defines the scope for the exchanges' activities, specifying that their primary purpose is to conduct exchange trade and not to act as individual investors and be involved in other outside, intermediary activities. It also sets up the rules and regulations for the trading auctions, and identifies some forms of trading operations, such as forward, futures, and options. Of particular importance, the law emphasizes the necessity for ethical business practices on the commodity markets.

In 1992, the development of exchanges continued, and by the summer of 1993 their number topped 800. However, only 230 of them were officially registered and only 46 were actually conducting operations. Despite the enormous number of exchanges, they are still not the main channel of wholesale trade, accounting for only 1.5 percent of the domestic trade. Today exchanges register very few transactions and in most cases have been unable to perform their classical functions of price finding and the insurance of transactions, that is, of determining the "correct" value of commodities and providing the ability to hedge buying and selling operations. In fact, having been set up as intermediary structures, most exchanges do not differ from other market mediators, which do their business only by trying to bring a potential buyer and a seller together. In Russia, where nine out of ten businesses are intermediaries, it only makes the chain of seller-mediator-buyer longer (on average it includes four to five mediators). This often postpones the final signing of a contract, or in some cases even makes it impossible.

Moreover, after the Law on Exchanges banned their intermediary outside activities, the number of actively functioning exchanges decreased drastically. One would expect that those active exchanges would provide a real market alternative to the state wholesale network, and yet even in these exchanges auctions are extremely ineffective, that is, sales account for only a very small percent of the total volume of the offerings. Not only do so-called unmarketable goods not sell well due to low demand, but even trade in raw materials, energy products, and consumer goods, for which there is much unsatisfied demand, is not very brisk.

TYPES OF COMMODITY EXCHANGES

Today there are three major types of exchanges. First, there are the formally specialized exchanges, such as the International Food Exchange (IFE), which concentrates mainly on trade in agricultural raw materials, foodstuffs, and relevant equipment. One in 20 exchanges in Russia is a specialized agricultural exchange. Second, there are so-called general, or universal, commodity exchanges, which comprise in their structure several specialized sections and trade a vast range of commodities—from raw materials and foodstuffs to consumer goods and hi-tech products; an example is the Russian Commodity and Raw Materials Exchange (RE). And third, there are regional commodity exchanges, which generally are of a universal character, for example, Moldova Republican Commodity Exchange or Kursk Commodity Exchange.

As to the scale of operations, all commodity exchanges can be defined as national and regional. National ones would typically have a so-called mother-exchange in Moscow and a number of daughter-exchanges throughout Russia; their share is equally distributed between specialized and general exchanges. The above-mentioned IFE and RE present typical examples of national exchanges. Regional exchanges would normally operate in one particular region and trade in a variety of commodities, so they would normally be general exchanges. Sometimes, however, if the region where the exchange operates is specialized in one particular area of production, then the exchange could also be specialized in that area; for example, Saratov Food Exchange specializes in grain trade, for Saratov is one of the main grain-producing regions. Another case when regional exchanges can be specialized exchanges is when they are set up in a region with access demand for certain commodities, for example, Siberian Food Exchange in Novosibirsk.

In order to better understand what these exchanges are and how they function let us examine the IFE and the RE more closely, as they are the most classical examples of contemporary commodity exchanges in Russia.

The International Food Exchange

The International Food Exchange was set up in September 1991 as a joint-stock company owned by 104 state, commercial, and private institutions (collective and state farms, big industrial conversion enterprises, transport and storage companies, and 38 foreign commercial and financial institutions) and 101 businessmen. As of 1 August 1993, the number of shareholders accounted for was 539 companies and individuals, and the number of brokerage firms registered on the IFE was 526.

The main objective of the IFE was to organize free trade in foodstuffs as well as in processing, storage, transport, and packing equipment and in securities. The IFE saw as its major tasks creating fair conditions for business, introducing realistic prices for foodstuffs (very important in conditions of overall shortage and growing inflation), and promoting an improved legal and financial framework for conducting business. The latter was to include a clearing system to guarantee execution of transactions, arbitration for the rapid settlement of trade disputes, and the creation of a unified information processing system, including research on the state of the food market both in Russia and abroad.

To fulfill its objectives, the IFE conducts all sorts of business activities, including holding regular auctions, organizing production and delivery of foodstuffs and relevant equipment, providing marketing services, and insuring all transactions. It also sells, leases, and lends its fixed and working capital to any Russian or foreign company or businessman; buys, rents, and borrows their fixed and working capital; sets up branches and subsidiaries all over the country and abroad; invests into foreign stock-holding companies; operates modern communication systems; provides training for exchange brokers and dealers; publishes regular bulletins; and conducts advertising business.

The registered capital of the IFE initially was set at 10 million rubles, and was divided into 1000 shares with a face value 10,000 rubles each. As of August 1993, the registered capital of the IFE amounted to 90 million rubles. The real market value of shares was somewhat higher, 20 times their face value. No shareholder can own more than 5 percent of the registered capital. The IFE is open to all types of businesses interested in developing food trade in Russia. Companies and businessmen can buy into the stock, which will allow them to run a brokerage agency on the exchange and to trade foodstuffs, equipment, and securities.

However, just as on other exchanges, trade is not very brisk at present. On average, the daily offerings of foodstuffs and agricultural and food processing equipment on the IFE amount to R150–200 billion and USD200–300 million.[4] Monthly turnover, however, is only about R1 billion, which suggests that only a tiny fraction of the offerings turn into real business. The most frequently traded commodities are grain, sugar, coffee, tea, meat, butter, and vegetable oil. Moreover, almost all business comes from domestic (ruble) trade, with almost no dollar trade, despite the enormous demand for imported foodstuffs.

Moreover, in the present conditions of high inflation, trade in dollars would be an extremely important reflector of real prices. In today's commodity markets brokers, in order to determine the real price of a commodity, have to assess not only the expected availability of that commodity (production and supply), but also the expected rate of inflation, which makes it ever more difficult for them to be precise in their calculations, and therefore increases risks. However, at the present stage of economic reform in Russia, it is unrealistic to expect large-scale dollar wholesale trade. Such trade is unlikely until the government stabilizes the ruble and introduces full convertibility, paving the way for the development of a nationwide network of commercial banks that conduct operations and run accounts in dollars.

Since February 1992, the IFE's brokers have been using standardized contracts. These contracts were prepared according to Western standards, but were adjusted to suit the operating conditions of commodity markets in Russia. The IFE was among the first exchanges to start using forward contracts for grain. Futures contracts are not popular yet due to the underdeveloped market conditions in Russia, in particular the common occurrence of traders renegading on contractual agreements.

Given the IFE's initial objective to bring the producer and consumer together, and in order to expand food exchange markets, the IFE recently set up twelve subsidiaries throughout Russia and abroad, namely, in Barnaul, Kostroma, Petersburg, Smolensk, Anapa, Vladivostok, Armenia, Estonia, Latvia, Bulgaria, Slovakia, and Mongolia. These subsidiaries collect and provide to the IFE information on the development of their local food markets (via modems); in return they receive processed information from the IFE on the development of food markets in Russia (exchange bulletins).

The Russian Commodity and Raw Material Exchange

The Russian Commodity and Raw Materials Exchange was set up at the beginning of 1990, but conducted its first auction only in November 1990. Today it is one of the leading structures of the Russian market economy. It has established its own network of commercial and financial institutions (banks, trading houses, insurance and investment companies, etc.), has an advanced computing system, and has started restructuring itself toward a classic, Western-type commodity exchange. The RE comprises six specialized sections: agricultural commodities, metals, fuel and energy, constructing materials, transportation and freight, and consumer goods. Until recently, each of these sections was an independent and self-managed unit, and worked, in fact, as a separate exchange.

In June 1992, in order to prevent the disintegration of the RE and to revive trade, significant restructuring was undertaken, resulting in two developments. First, sections lost their independent status and were reunited under the RE central management. Second, shares were rerated by decreasing their face value from 100,000 to 40,000 rubles, and the new principle of the registration of brokerage firms was introduced. Previously each share gave its shareholder the right to run a brokerage firm in the section in which the share was registered. Now each shareholder has the right to run a brokerage firm that can operate on: (1) one of the six sections, at the shareholder's choice, if he owns one share; (2) any three sections, if he owns two shares; and (3) all six sections, if he owns three shares. Such a policy resulted in the diversification of brokerage activities of the more than 1,000 brokerage firms registered on the RE. More than half of them are owned by companies based on private forms of ownership, while only 16 percent of brokerage firms belong to state enterprises; 2.4 percent, to joint-stock companies; 1.2 percent, to joint ventures; 1.0 percent, to banks; and under 1 percent, to individuals.[5]

However, even such powerful exchanges face the same problem of dying turnover and slack trade. While in November 1992 the RE actually handled 500 billion rubles of transactions a month, only 3 billion rubles of transactions were registered. The best-selling commodities were oil products, domestic electronics, grain, and some imported foodstuffs, namely, canned meat, beer, and other cheap, durable goods in small batches.

RECENT DEVELOPMENTS IN THE COMMODITY
MARKETS

Recently there have been two major shifts in exchange activities—the first one toward the diversification of trade on many so-called universal exchanges (such as Moscow Commodity Exchange, Russian Commodity and Raw Materials Exchange, etc.), and the second one toward the consolidation or amalgamation of exchanges with similar profiles.

The first tendency can be seen primarily in big cities, where many exchanges function as small wholesale or sometimes even retail outlets, selling whatever is available at that particular moment for sale. These exchanges do not have a particularly good future, and as soon as a proper wholesale and retail network is established in Russia, they will gradually go out of business.

The second tendency is much more optimistic. One good example of such consolidation is the creation of the Union of Food Exchanges. Given the necessity to combine forces in developing more effective and more orderly food markets, in March 1992 the IFE initiated the creation of the Union of Food Exchanges (UFE), which today consists of the 11 leading specialized food exchanges in Russia.[6] The UFE was set up in order to create a united exchange entity; to elaborate and introduce a modern concept of civilized exchange trade; to introduce joint policy in the field of applied research and technology, investment, credit, finances, and standardization; and to exchange trade information and data banks. Among the tasks of the Union is also the creation of favorable public opinion about exchanges.

The UFE's basic objective is to conduct various joint projects by means of uniting all available financial, intellectual, and informational resources of its members. The major joint projects have been identified as follows:

- To conduct synchronized trade auctions, based on the principle of "one trade theater" in order to expand trade space
- To create the infrastructure necessary for exchange operations (transportation and storage networks, banks, insurance companies, wholesale and retail outlets, etc.)
- To introduce uniform quality certificates for food products in order to bring the quality of traded foodstuffs up to world standards
- To run joint training courses for brokers
- To conducts joint research projects and to exchange research results
- To develop a joint communication network
- To develop uniform informational systems and to create on their basis a joint information network consisting of exchanges and regional information bureaus
- To introduce a multilateral clearing system and to open an interregional clearing center

In the early stages of its functioning, the UFE concentrated on exchanging information between members, using a special communications network, Iskra-

2, and on conducting joint simultaneous trading auctions. In April 1992 the UFE prepared the unified Rules of Exchange Trade, introduced standardized contracts and software, and started conducting joint auctions on a regular basis, twice a week—on Tuesdays and Thursdays.

In April and May 1992 the UFE organized an Interregional Exchange Fair, Urozhai-92 (Harvest-92), and as a result, for the first time ever grain and sugar were sold on a forward contract basis. The final turnover of the fair was R3 billion.

Given the rapid development of Russian stock markets, the UFE has opened a joint-stock department (on the basis of the stock department of the IFE). This department trades in shares of agricultural enterprises, privatization vouchers, and credit resources.

PROBLEMS OF THE RUSSIAN COMMODITY MARKETS

Commodity markets, in order to function efficiently, should meet the following criteria:[7]

- There should be a large number of sellers and buyers. The market for the commodity must be as close to perfect competition as possible.
- A stable institutional relationship should exist between the current and futures markets. This relationship is most stable when goods are traded in their rawest form on both markets, that is, futures markets can effectively exist only for raw materials, where the protection against future price instability can be guaranteed by hedging.[8]
- Traded commodities should not be in excess demand; otherwise producers would be able to sell all their goods easily, thereby eliminating the need to trade on the exchange.
- Commodities should be classified into various quality groups in order to establish standardized classification systems for quality control.
- The commodities traded should not be highly perishable. The best trading commodities are those with more stable and predictable yields, and therefore with more stable prices, such as wheat and corn.

Given the difficult economic conditions in which commodity markets have been developing in Russia, it is unlikely that these criteria can be met quickly. However, the question is whether there is a potential for the existing commodity exchanges in Russia to become a viable mechanism for the proper functioning of the commodity and futures markets.

One of the most serious problems facing Russian commodity markets, as already mentioned, is low trading volumes. The immediate reason for such lagging trade derives from more general economic problems in Russia. A malfunctioning monetary system, and as a result an unstable and weak ruble, that is, a ruble that is steadily losing its value both in terms of domestic purchasing power and the foreign exchange rate; the disruption of production and technological links between producers; and the increasingly likely danger of hyperinflation have resulted in the depression of commodity markets. The situation has been aggravated by a continuing political crisis and the lack of an adequate legal framework for effective commodity markets.

First, a critical problem withholding trading volumes on the exchanges is to great extent price inflexibility, which derives from narrow markets. While the sellers demand unrealistically high prices, the buyers apparently lack spare rubles, both in cash and bank credits. In most cases sellers do not drop the price even if goods are not selling well. In conditions of overall shortage and big demand for so-called deficit commodities, exchange dealers hope to sell them anyway, sooner or later, on or outside the exchange. In many instances the commodity markets are controlled by the Russian mafia which aims at (artificially) imposed high prices and not at market clearing prices.

Second, often transactions are not registered on the exchange, and occur outside the confines of the exchange. Such deals often originate from contacts developed between seller and buyer on the exchange at an earlier date, and according to some estimates, they exceed the exchange turnover by a factor of 5 to 10 for certain commodities. According to Konstantin Borovoi, a chairman of the Russian Commodity and Raw Material Exchange, brokers register only about 1 percent of their trades, to avoid taxes.[9] Another reason for the failure to register is that once the contact between seller and buyer has been made, the exchange is not needed any longer, as it does not provide any additional functions.

The fact that only a tiny fraction of all deals is being registered undermines the exchanges' price-setting function and distorts the actual prices, for the registered deals might not represent average price levels for all deals for that commodity, and therefore the actual price of the day might be somewhat different from that on the exchange. So unlike the case in the West, where the information on prices is the bottom line for brokers, in Russia one can see clear preferences for personal contacts.

Third, recently there has been a tendency to the switch away from money trade to primitive trading techniques such as barter deals, caused by the fact that high inflation has undermined the ability of the ruble to function as a means of exchange. And although barter is a highly inefficient method of trading, since it narrows the market significantly, in today's Russia, barter accounts for the bulk of all market transactions. Even state enterprises have switched to barter deals, with almost half of their output being sold via barter.

Fourth, competition on the commodity markets is far from perfect. Brokers offer the same commodity for sale on several exchanges simultaneously, that is, they create artificial competition among themselves. Then they choose the best deal, and simply pay fines on the other exchanges. These fines are minor (under 1 percent of the sum of the contract) in comparison with the brokerage profits. Furthermore, there is no effective mechanism for ensuring brokers' responsibility toward their customers, first of all, toward the actual owners of goods. In the case of brokers being unable to sell goods, they pay only a small fine.

Fifth, exchanges tend to trade in finished products and consumer goods rather than in commodities, which are easier to deal with and at the same time bring higher profits for brokers. This problem arises from the underdevelopment of the wholesale and retail trade networks in Russia. Trading in finished products reduces the effectiveness of commodity markets, for it does not provide an adequate mechanism for speculation and futures trading.

And finally, trade on commodity exchanges is affected by the collapsed inter-republican economic relations. The trade transactions are allowed only in Russian rubles as means of exchange; no U.S. dollars or, for example, Ukrainian Karbovanets, are accepted.

These are the problems that arise out of the country's general economic difficulties, and once the latter are resolved, these problems will be resolved automatically. However, the main problem in the development of commodity markets is the inadequacy in the organization of these markets, which requires additional effort.

1. *Commodity markets are narrowed by government licensing policy.*

    Only products for internal consumption are sold freely, while raw materials and energy products to be sold outside Russia require not only a license, granted by the Committee for External Economic Ties of the Russian Federation, but also a so-called quota—permission granted by the government to each export-oriented enterprise to sell as exports a certain percentage of its output (on average, 10–15 percent of an enterprise's output).

2. *An adequate information processing system does not exist.*

    Information was and still is the key deficit product in Russia, and this contributed to produce the conditions of shortages and is currently helping to fertilise the black economy. The majority of producers and consumers still lack essential information on supply and demand and average prices, and they have to rely on information available only within their local administrative region.

    To overcome this problem, it is necessary to develop a network of information centres at the regional and local levels, which will provide access to information for producers and consumers regardless of their location. Given the vast territories in Russia and the fact that this information should be brought to the most remote producers and consumers, such a network should include regional information centres in the capitals of autonomous republics, krais (regions) and oblasts (districts) (77 altogether), and local information centres connected to regional centres (about 350). Later on, this network can significantly expand due to the direct connection of individual businesses to local information centres. Ideally the establishment of information centres should start in places where the commodity exchanges are already present.

3. *Commodity markets are "buyer beware" markets, where the buyer does not have any guaranteed rights.*

    The lack of uniform standards for quality and quantity of traded commodities increases the risk of purchase for the buyers. The potential volume of transactions, and therefore efficiency, is reduced.

4. *There is a lack of specialization and an overdiversification in trade operations.*

Even brokers of formally specialized exchanges tend to work with whatever happens to be on offer, selling "grain one day, crude oil the next."[10] This results in less efficient decision making by brokers, as they do not learn the ins and outs of trading in one particular commodity or group of commodities. Their potential for futures deals and other forms of "civilized" commodity markets operations is thus limited.

5. *At present in Russia the commodity and financial markets are separated.*

Commodities have their own channels of distribution (commodity exchanges, direct barter contracts, etc.), and scarce financial resources have their own (state credits, central bank credits, and credits and cash of commercial banks and other commercial institutions). Often these channels do not overlap.

The problem is that banks and other credit-issuing institutions are increasingly unwilling to offer credits to unknown customers. But the majority of companies that are actively involved in economic activity have been established only recently, and therefore are unknown to the banks.

In this respect, commodity exchanges could become (and partially already are) a so-called filter for companies—members of the exchange. The most respectable and reliable of them could be filtered into the payment chamber, which is the exact place where commodity and financial markets merge. However, even a number of separate payment chambers created on various commodity exchanges cannot solve the problem; the unification of commodity and financial markets should be interregional.

6. *Another serious problem, which at the same time is a necessary condition for the development of commodity exchanges, is regional production and technological specialization of the producers.*

In some regions production of certain commodities is either underdeveloped or is not developed at all, while in the others there is overproduction. For example, often producers of agricultural equipment and fertilizers as well as processing enterprises are located in regions that are not major agricultural producers due to climatic conditions. As a result, many economic regions have overproduction of certain commodities and deficits of other commodities. This creates favourable conditions for interregional trade, which could be conducted in the civilized form of commodity exchange trade. Regions have enough commodities but are lacking information about consumers.

7. *The next condition for the development of commodity markets is the consolidation of regional markets.*

Most problems of the commodity markets reflect the fact that these markets are not sufficiently universal. At present even exchanges in Moscow do not possess adequate information on goods and prices on other exchanges. No exchange in Russia has full and reliable information on what is on offer and at what prices on the regional exchanges. This is due to lack of commercial interest in consolidation, the poor quality of communications, and the lack of financial resources to improve the situation.

8. *One of the paradoxes is that the customer lacks money, while the banks have financial resources to lend.*

The situation in today's Russia suggests that there is sufficient supply and demand for many commodities, but one of the reasons why commodity markets do not work properly are the liquidity problems of the buyers. The problem is that the three subjects of the market (producer, creditor, and customer) are separated, and in order to revive money circulation, and respectively trade, they have to be united. This is a general problem that derives from the malfunctioning banking system, and it has to be solved not only for the sake of commodity markets, but for the economy overall. However, one possible solution could be in the form of commodity stock exchanges with specialization in certain commodities or groups of commodities.

The scheme could be the following. In the hall for commodity trade the customer finds what he wants to buy. Then he goes to the hall for stock trade, that is, where share and credit resources are traded, and gets the credit he needs to buy a particular commodity (using the exchange information, network banks regularly provide information on financial resources). If the banking system in Russia worked properly, that is, as it works in the West, there would be no need for such an arrangement. But today in Russia banks do not provide credit lines, and to get credit on reasonable terms one has to specify the exact contract for which this credit would be used, which is almost impossible in the case of exchange trade.

Combining commodity trade with credit resource distribution might prove highly efficient in terms of boosting trade volumes, but it also could have its disadvantages in terms of increasing risks. One argument against such an arrangement is that it is based on the assumption that market works, commodity markets are in equilibrium, and the equilibrium price is known. But there are many reasons why the market does not work in Russia today; therefore, if banks provided direct credits for the deals in which the price level is unknown, they would take higher risks, which otherwise would have been taken by brokers.

9. *The final problem is associated with underdeveloped stock markets.*

Privatization of state enterprises often means cutting budget subsidies, and thus it raises the question of finding funds to finance privatized enterprises. Additional financial sources can be found on the stock market. For example, the best way for agricultural enterprises (provided they have been transformed into joint-stock companies) to attract additional resources is to sell their shares, for instance, to big industrial enterprises that need a regular supply of agricultural and food products. The key requirement for such joint-stock companies would be access to reliable information about potential investors, the state of the stock market, prices for similar shares, and other relevant facts. Moreover, this access should be permanent and quick, that is, it should provide updated information on any changes in correlation between demand and supply on the stock market on a regular basis.

The solution could be to connect agricultural and industrial enterprises to an information network, as described. Such a network would provide managers and businessmen with updated, reliable, and processed information about stock markets. This would improve decision making and would stimulate the development of stock markets; enterprises would quickly respond to the changes on the market, and trade in shares would be revitalized.

Thus, the successful future of commodity markets in Russia lies in the consolidation of exchanges, the creation of a unified information network that would provide access to information for producers and consumers, and the creation of an interregional payment chamber for commodity exchanges with similar profiles.

ROLE OF COMMODITY EXCHANGES IN THE ECONOMY

In terms of a free market economy, the exchanges do not make a major contribution yet. The number of exchanges itself does not indicate that the market mechanism is functioning efficiently. Overall, the share of exchange turnover in total domestic trade, in terms of value, is no more than 10 percent (and in terms of volume, even less—under 1 percent of wholesale trade), and most materials, technical resources, and consumer goods are still sold through state-run wholesale agencies.

However, in spite of all the problems, the role of commodity exchanges in the economy is becoming more and more significant. First of all, the development of commodity exchanges indicates the beginning of the creation of new supply chains and lays the groundwork for the development of a new wholesale distribution network. This might have a direct impact not only on the functioning of domestic enterprises, including newly privatized enterprises, but also on attracting foreign investment, particularly small and medium investment into production. Second, even the existing commodity exchanges, however underdeveloped they might be, have started acquiring the very important function of price setting, which in itself is an essential step toward market equilibrium. The exchanges are becoming a major reflector of domestic wholesale prices, and what is more, of intra-CIS (Commonwealth of Independent States) prices. For example, recently Kazakhstan sold grain to Russia at the exchange prices, which indicates that governments of the USSR successor states have started using the exchange prices for intergovernmental trade. Third, commodity exchanges along with stock exchanges are becoming more and more involved in trade in stocks and other securities, for example, privatization vouchers, and in this respect, they have direct impact on the price of vouchers and volume of their sales. This might also, though indirectly, have impact on foreign investment, for foreigners are allowed to participate in the privatization of state enterprises through voucher auctions. The lack of restrictions on how many vouchers investors, including foreigners, can possess and the currently low price for vouchers make it exceptionally favorable for foreigners to invest in privatization (the current investment exchange rate is only some R30 per dollar).

One example that illustrates the growing importance of exchanges is a recent dispute over the role of exchanges in the distribution of the 1992 grain harvest. Given the growing potential of commodity exchanges, there was concern among some government officials that exchanges could buy and withhold grain from the market (in effect "corner the market"), and by artificially increasing the demand for grain, could either provoke a new round of price rises or use this grain as a so-called food weapon to impose political pressure on the government. The amount of grain distributed through exchange dealers in 1992/1993, for example, was expected to exceed half of the "free market" grain.[11] And second, Russian commodity exchanges recently started organizing various unions (the Russian Exchange Union, Congress of Exchanges, etc.) with the objective of increasing their impact on the governmental economic policy to make it more radical and market oriented.

In reality, it did not happen. The immediate reason for grain not being used as a political weapon in 1992 was that trade in grain on the commodity exchanges was not very brisk at all, as many farmers were withholding grain as a hedge against inflation. Furthermore, exchanges did not have an adequate infrastructure (storage, transportation network, etc.) to accumulate large quantities of grain. And, even if the above mentioned exchanges did accumulate grain, they were not yet powerful enough to impose any pressure on the government. The insufficiently universal character of commodity markets and the fact that there are many different markets in Russia suggest reasons for the lack of monopoly and lack of any kind of unified strategy on the part of the exchanges.

GOVERNMENT'S RESPONSE

The principal involvement of the state within the field of economic life, as it is within that of individual enterprise and within the nation in general, should be the creation, support, and development of a healthy environment for business on both the national and individual levels.

In this respect, as far as the government's policy toward grain trade is concerned, the appropriate response from government should be the one that would assure adequate delivery of grain to the state reserves without hurting the free trade on the exchanges. This could be achieved by giving additional incentives to grain producers to sell to the state by raising wholesale purchasing prices for grain and introducing other forms of state support to agricultural (e.g. additional discounts for agricultural inputs).

Since August 1992, the government has been conducting a policy of raising wholesale purchasing prices for major cereals, but given the severe budget constraints and overall disequilibrium in the market, it has been unable to keep them on a par with world prices. Even the price for above-plan sales of bread-quality wheat (R80,000 in July 1993)[12] and reaching R105,000 in September 1993, lags behind world prices, and since the inflation rate remains high and the weakening of the ruble continues, in terms of both its domestic purchasing power and its further depreciation against the dollar, the disequilibrium problem will continue to exist.

There is also an external reason to further increase wholesale prices and to bring them in line with world prices, and that is to prevent the outflow of grain for exports, mainly to East European countries, while Russia itself faces huge grain shortages. However, this increase has to be followed by adequate compensation in personal income. Otherwise, it will lead to a further fall in living standards, since higher grain prices will inevitably lead to increasing costs of livestock production and hence of meat, which might affect consumption patterns.

As to the commodity markets in general, the government should change its "ignorant" attitude toward the commodity exchanges, and stop seeing their activities as purely speculative. So far it has not only been the question of the budget deficit and the lack of adequate resources for the government to support the development of commodity markets; it has also been the question of a generally negative attitude toward exchanges on the part of the government and the public. The government should relax its tight administrative control over exchange activities and even help create a more civilized market environment, to reinforce the current reforms in Russia.

CONCLUSION

Today commodity markets in Russia are in a deep crisis. The number of actively functioning exchanges is small: only 5 out of 89 exchanges in Moscow, and less than 30 of the total of 800 exchanges in Russia. Given the low efficiency of the exchange operations, the small percentage of sales conducted through exchanges, and their too diversified character (lack of real specialization), the prospects for the exchanges can be summed up as follows.

1. The problem for Russian commodity markets is that, like other sectors of the Russian economy, they will remain in deep recession for the next few years. Most problems that affect commodity markets in Russia derive from the country's general economic difficulties, particularly from the high inflation rate; malfunctioning monetary and banking systems; and the disruption of production and technological links between enterprises. These problems can be resolved only in the context of overall economic reforms in Russia.

2. However, problems deriving from the inadequate organization of commodity markets can and should be resolved in the near future. The process should begin with the government loosening its administrative control over exchanges and putting more effort into the development of a favourable business environment for commodity exchanges.

3. Further successful development of commodity markets in Russia is impossible without the consolidation of exchanges with similar profiles. This consolidation is so far very slow, due to the lack of a clear conceptual basis and practical mechanisms for cooperation and unification.

4. To promote the development of commodity markets, a unified information network has to be created. This network would unite regional commodity markets and promote the universalization of commodity markets, which are the essential steps toward overall market equilibrium.

5. A well-functioning information network for commodity exchanges would create the necessary preconditions for the unification of commodity and financial markets on the basis of an interregional payment chamber of commodity exchanges with similar profiles.

6. In the long run, the number of exchanges will have to drop significantly—to 2 or 3

dozen. This will occur partly due to the liquidation of inefficient exchanges that do not have real industrial or agricultural backup—some of which will go bankrupt, and some of which will be transformed into intermediary firms or trading houses—and partly due to the consolidation of exchanges with similar profiles, converting them into classical exchanges and providing a well-organized marketplace.

Trying to sensibly comment on economic prospects for Russia, one must bear in mind that simply creating the visible institutions of a market economy, such as commodity exchanges, is not enough, as the successful operation of these institutions depends upon a subculture of invisible institutions that cannot be created overnight but must be cultivated and developed. Prime amongst these are the concepts of new business ethic and market culture that are proving so difficult to create in Russia.

It is difficult to predict how long it will take for Russia to complete the building of the visible institutions for a market economy, and it is much more difficult to put a sensible time frame on the creation of the equally important invisible market institutions. Yet only when these invisible market institutions have been allowed to develop will Russia have completed a successful economic transformation. Again, putting a time frame on the reform process, creating the visible institutions of the market will probably take several years, but the invisible institutions of the market may well take generations to develop.

NOTES

1. The Economist Intelligence Unit, Global Forecasting Unit, Russian Federation, *Main Report,* Quarter 1, 1993.

2. In reality the first commodity exchanges in Soviet Russia appeared during the period of the New Economic Policy in the 1920s (there were 109 commodity exchanges by 1926), but they ceased to exist shortly thereafter. See Perry Patterson, "Prospects for Commodity and Financial Exchanges," in *Socialism, Perestroika and the Dilemmas of Soviet Economic Reform,* ed. John E. Tedstrom (Boulder, Co. and London: Westview Press, 1990).

3. See S. Zhurek, "Commodity Exchanges in Russia: Success or Failure?" *RFE/RL Research Report,* no. 6, February 1993.

4. The IFE was one of the first exchanges granted a license to conduct trade in dollars. Given the relative stability of the dollar and steady depreciation of the ruble, most exchange dealers offered commodities for sale for dollars.

5. Data provided by the Institute for Research into Organized Markets, Moscow. A. Yakovlev, "Exchanges and Exchange Trade in 1991–92," *Rossiiskii ekonomicheskii zhurnal,* no. 4, April 1992.

6. Members of the Union of Food Exchanges include:

• International and Food Exchange (Moscow)
• Food Exchange Urozhai (Belgorod)
• Euro-Asian Food–Raw Material Exchange (Ekaterinburg)
• Siberian Food Exchange (Novosibirsk)
• South-Russian Food Exchange (Krasnodar)

- Khudzhent Food–Raw Material Exchange (Tadzhikistan)
- Moldova Republican Commodity Exchange (Saransk)
- Chuvashnija Republican Commodity Exchange (Cheboksary)
- Moriyskaya Republican Commodity Exchange (Ioshkar-Ola)
- Viatka Commodity and Stock Exchange (Viatka)
- Kursk Commodity Exchange (Kursk)

7. This is the updated version from Stanley Kroll and Irwin Shisko, *The Commodity Futures Market Guide* (New York: Harper and Row, 1973), also published by Dana Dratch in "Russian Commodity Markets Still in Their Infancy," *RFE/RL Research Report,* no. 29, July 1993, pp. 10–17.

8. Hedging is buying or selling commodity futures contracts to protect against price changes in the current market for a certain commodity, i.e., it is a form of insurance against risks.

9. Interview with the author, July 1993.

10. Magda Sowinska, "Trading Places in the CIS: Going to the Market," *The Warsaw Voice,* 1 March 1992.

11. Estimates by a UN-FAO mission to the former Soviet Union in August 1992 to assess food balance, of which the author was a member. Data published in "Assessment of the Food Situation in the Former Soviet Union in 1992/93," Rome, September 1992.

12. *East Europe Agriculture and Food Monthly,* July 1993.

REFERENCES

Dratch, Dana. "Russian Commodity Markets Still in Their Infancy." *RFE/RL Research Report,* no. 29, July 1993.

Kroll, Stanley, and Irwin, Shisko. *The Commodity Futures Market Guide.* New York: Harper and Row, 1973.

Patterson, Perry. "Prospects for Commodity and Financial Exchanges." In *Socialism, Perestroika and the Dilemmas of Soviet Economic Reform,* ed. John E. Tedstrom. Boulder, Colorado and London: Westview Press, 1990.

Sowinska, Magda. "Trading Places in the CIS: Going to the Market." *The Warsaw Voice,* 1 March 1992.

Wegren, Stephen. "Building Market Institutions: Agricultural Commodity Exchanges in Post-Communist Russia," unpublished manuscript, 1994.

Yakovlev, Alexandr. "Exchanges and Exchange Trade in 1991–92." *Rossiiskii ekonomicheskii zhurnal,* no. 4, April 1992.

Zhurek, Stefan. "Commodity Exchanges in Russia: Success or Failure?" *RFE/RL Research Report,* no. 6, February 1993.

4

Economic Transformation, Privatization, and Foreign Investments in the Czech Republic

Michal Mejstrik

The most important observation to make about the privatization process in Cze-choslovakia is that it is well under way. Privatization is seen as an extremely important part of reform package together with stabilization and liberalization and is supported both by the public and by Parliament, an important consideration in assuring that the process maintains its momentum. One of the most important goals to keep in mind is to make sure that the whole process does not get mired down in details or in controversies about its problems. The Czech Republic has embarked on an unprecedented path that should lead not only to the stabilization and liberalization, but also to very rapid privatization, of its sector of large enterprises. The process of large-scale privatization in the Czech and Slovak Republics is so unique that it deserves special attention, for if it succeeds in achieving its goals, it may well serve as a source of experience for large-scale privatization throughout both Central and Eastern Europe, including Russia.

Czechoslovakia's privatization program, now divided into separate programs for the Czech and Slovak Republics, has been the most unique part of its reform strategy. In addition to more than 100,000 restitution claims settled, over 30,000 small firms were auctioned in small-scale privatization and 4,000 out of 6,000 large firms are being privatized in the first and second waves of large-scale privatization, which should be completed by the end of 1994. In the privatization process, foreign participation is also encouraged, and total FDI amounted to $600 million in 1991 and $1200 million in 1992.

As far as the problems of privatization can be judged, it is clear that there have been many. But no process of such large-scale economic change can be problem free. Several problems and loopholes were addressed by the amendment to the Law on Large Privatization, as well. The most important policy pursued

Table 4.1
Size of the State Sector

Country	% of output
Czechoslovakia (1986)	97.0
East Germany (1982)	96.5
Soviet Union (1985)	96.0
Poland (1985)	81.7
China (1984)	73.6
Hungary (1984)	65.2
Austria (1978–9)	14.5
West Germany (1982)	10.7

Source: Author's estimates.

within the large-scale privatization was the promotion of competitive privatization bids, allowing various offers, including the voucher system, and also direct sales, public auctions and tenders, and other means of property transfer. This policy, however, altered the process from its originally conceived voucher form, adding traditional case-by-case sales privatization, and caused many unforeseen problems that required immediate attention.

BUILDING POLITICAL SUPPORT FOR THE CZECH DESIGN OF LARGE-SCALE PRIVATIZATION

As described in the paper Mejstrik (1993), in the mid-1980s, Czechoslovakia, like the other Eastern European countries, found itself with 96.7 percent of its net material product (NMP) dominated by the state sector and only 0.7 percent of NMP contributed by the non-farming private sector (see Table 4.1).

The main controversy in Czechoslovakia over the speed, depth, and tools of the transition process was between gradualists and radicals. The reappraisal of the long-standing tradition of the prevailing state sector and the means of transformation to private ownership was a focus point of the controversy about economic policy. The gradualist reformers rooted in the 1960s wanted to postpone privatization to the future and saw it as a very gradual process, because the reform process of 1968 had not recognized the importance of privatization at all. Gradualist arguments against speedy privatization pointed to the large-scale layoffs and unemployment which might result as well as the need to have more functional markets before businesses were forced to operate self-sufficiently. A further argument was that to minimize the problems associated with privatization and to receive maximal returns on the sale of these enterprises, it would be better to restructure firms' operations before privatization.

The radicals proposed speeding the procedure up and minimizing the privatization period for at least some state-owned enterprises (SOEs). Their main argument was that one cannot renew the functioning of a market economy without renewing private ownership. The main purpose of privatization is to create inviolable fields for sovereign rule by the owner (and exclusion of interference by the government, except for generally recognized duties like taxes). Radicals also point to the fact that in the interim period preceding privatization, ambiguity about ownership and accountability has generated economic and ecological irresponsibility and nontransparent financial relations.

Various means of privatization were considered. The desire for rapid transformation meant that the use of standard methods alone (i.e., public sales, auctions) was not possible in Czechoslovakia, given that the level of public savings was not enough to buy all of the state property. This problem was especially acute because most citizens with a significant amount of savings were either ex-party members or ex-black-marketeers, neither of them very popular. The inadequacy of relying only on selected standard methods of privatization is one of the reasons why privatization seems to be stalling in Hungary and Poland.

Efforts to sell off to the first coming foreign company were seen as a politically unacceptable form of "spontaneous" privatization that could provide existing managers, often Communist party functionaries, or nomenclatura, "golden chances" after selling out to foreigners (at low prices). The experience of Hungary shows that the effort to reverse the prepared agreements with foreign investors could mean loss of government credibility abroad.

The final resulting blueprint has involved a combination of standard methods with other processes designed to compensate for factors peculiar to Czechoslovakia. Basically, those proposing to privatize an enterprise may choose from a variety of means of privatization, with government organs responsible for deciding which proposed method is the most applicable. The general idea which prevailed finally was the privatization initiated bottom-up and supported by the booming group of small and medium-sized entrepreneurs.

In adopting their large privatization policy, the Czechoslovak government and Parliament decided, by Act 92/1991 (passed in February 1991), to speed up the course of large-scale privatization of state-owned enterprises (SOEs), including state farms (one-third of all agricultural land). Overall, large-scale privatization has been divided into two waves. The government made rough lists of enterprises to be privatized in each wave, and final proposals for each wave are made by the branch ministries. Some enterprises—roughly 15 percent—are not to be privatized at all or are to be privatized later, in addition to 5–10 percent of property to be privatized through restitution, 10 percent through transformation of cooperatives, and 15 percent through transfer to municipalities. Thus large-scale privatization covers 55–60 percent of the property of large enterprises. The original conception was to privatize enterprises quickly and to allow new owners (and not the government) to restructure. There have been only a few exceptions to this policy so far. For example, the government has overseen the creation of restructuring strategies for the steel industry, the mining industry, and the telecommunications sector, which will include organizational changes prior to privatization.

RESTITUTION AS ONE OF THE POINTS OF DEPARTURE

One part in the large-scale privatization was played by restitution, the return of property to original owners or their heirs. The large-scale restitution law passed in February 1990 covers assets expropriated through the nationalization effort that started February 28, 1948, and also covers forced gifts and out-of-law restitutions and rehabilitations. This law gives full rights to return the property or to provide other forms of reimbursement to the original owners whose property was expropriated or who were forced by tax and rental policy to provide their property to the state as a gift in 1950s and 1960s. Under this law, more than 20,000 demands for restitution have been met. Many involve financial reimbursement or ownership of shares rather than actual return of property. All privatization projects that are submitted (see below) must provide confirmation that restitution claims have been met or must provide a means of meeting restitution claims. In order to compensate for restitution demands, 3 percent of the value of every firm undergoing privatization will be set aside in a National Restitution Fund. The original property owners (physical persons only, not former shareholders) are also given priority in buying back the parts of companies that are not subject to restitution (i.e., parts that were newly erected after the firm was expropriated).

Restitution has also had specific effects on agriculture. Two-thirds of all agricultural land has never been nationalized, but owners were not able to act as property owners because they were forced into cooperatives. Currently, cooperatives are being transformed into several kinds of new legal entities in accordance with Federal Law 42/1992 Coll., on Regulation of Property Relations in Cooperatives. This law mandates that the title to net asset value in cooperatives will be distributed in the following way: after calculation of net asset value, 25 percent of assets will be sold for money (for book value) to eligible persons (see later section). The goal of this measure was to provide some capitalization for transformed cooperatives. The remaining 75 percent of property will be distributed to the three production factors (land, capital, and labour). Landowners will be given 50 percent of remaining titles to cooperative property, those who contributed capital will get 30 percent, and those who contributed labour participation will receive 20 percent. The Transformation Law also created transformation councils that will decide the future of the transformed cooperatives. The council may create a genuine cooperative, a cooperative of the owners, a joint-stock company, or a limited liability company, or the co-op can be liquidated.[1]

THE PROCEDURE OF LARGE-SCALE PRIVATIZATION

For each of two waves of privatization, each enterprise selected on a list had to present its own basic privatization project before a set deadline. The structure of the privatization project is obligatory (see Figure 4.1). There have been no

Figure 4.1
Privatization Project Requirements

a.   the enterprise's name, and property for privatization;

b.   information on how the state acquired the property to be privatized;

c.   identification of the property unusable for business purposes (i.e. debts, unusable fixed assets and stocks);

d.   valuation of the property to be privatized (usually book value, except in the case of Foreign Direct Investment, in which case an official assessment of "market value" is required);

e.   manner of transferring the property to be privatized, including the settlement of claims of entitled persons;

f.   when establishing a commercial company, the definition of its legal form;

g.   when establishing a joint-stock company, the distribution of stock shares and their value or type, as well as information on whether and how investment coupons will be used;

h.   if local property is to be sold, the location and method of sales, pricing, and the conditions and terms of payment;

i.   in some cases, the proportion of the privatization process proceeds to be handed over to the National Property Funds of the republics;

j.   the manner of transfer of intellectual property rights, which must be discussed in advance with the Federal Bureau of Inventions;

k.   the privatization project implementation schedule.

In cases of direct sale, unpaid transfer, or commercialization, the privatization project should also contain a business plan and recommendations concerning the object of business activities, information on potential buyers or investors, information on the existing and anticipated market position of the enterprise, and information on the number and qualification structure of the enterprise's workforce.

workers' councils since April 1990 (which makes a great difference in comparison with Poland and Hungary), and thus company management has the main input on the formulation of the firm's basic privatization project. There were clear rules and clear deadlines for the submission of projects, an attribute which has been lacking in privatization programs in most reforming post-socialist nations.

Following the submission of basic projects, any other person or enterprise is allowed to submit a competing privatization project, again until a certain deadline. In order to promote the supply of technology, organization, and management through foreign direct investment, potential foreign buyers are permitted to collaborate with Czech firms on the elaboration of basic or competing privatization proposals or to submit their own competitive proposals. Decisions about project approval are made by the relevant (Czech or Slovak) Ministry of Privatization, which also receives advice from the founding ministries (i.e., the

Czech or Slovak Ministries of Industry, Agriculture, or Trade), and if the project involves direct sale, until mid-1992 the Economic Council of the republican government had to approve it. In such cases, the government had two weeks to review and alter the Economic Council's decision. Now, the former role of the Economic Council is played by an Interministerial Committee on Privatization (see later section).

Actual implementation of privatization projects approved by the Ministries of Privatization is left to the Funds of National Property of both republics. This role is extremely important when organizing public tenders and auctions and preparing contracts for transfer of enterprises. The Funds of National Property also act as temporary owners of firms until they are transferred to private ownership.

There are already many state-owned joint-stock companies (JSCs) that have been created in the past two years through commercialization of SOEs. Other enterprises have proposed commercialization as part of their privatization project. Through their proposed projects, enterprises suggest what portion of their shares will be privatized through various means, including standard means such as direct sale, public auction, or public tender, and more unique methods such as distribution of shares to the public through vouchers.

The original conception was that most projects would be basic projects and would concentrate on the voucher method, and that the Ministry of Privatization would play a passive role in approving these proposals. Circumstances changed this conception, however. A larger number of competing proposals than had been expected led to a greater degree of flexibility in employing various means of privatization, but also concentrated a large degree of power in the Ministries of Privatization through the process of evaluation and approval of privatization projects. On average, three competing projects were added to each basic project suggested by the enterprise management and were submitted by the deadline of the privatization first wave.

A great strength of the Czech privatization process is its flexibility, in that it allows privatization through a wide variety of methods. There is an inaccurate conception that privatizing nations must choose between the "Hungarian approach" (case-by-case privatization using standard methods of privatization) and the "Czech approach" (mass privatization through the use of vouchers). In fact, the nontraditional voucher method is only one of various possible means of privatization in the Czech Republic, privatization projects are reviewed on a case-by-case basis, and all standard methods are used as well.

THE PRIVATIZATIONS TO DATE

As mentioned, there have been two waves of privatization scheduled. Both waves are now under way—all privatization projects have been submitted for the first wave, and the Ministries of Privatization have completed the approval process for all projects that are included in the first wave of voucher privati-

Figure 4.2
Timetable for One Wave of Privatization (including actual dates of Czechoslovak first wave)

SUPPLY

DEMAND

Privatization Projects Prepared
(first wave: basic projects prepared first
[by Oct.31, 1991], then competing projects
[by Jan. 20, 1992])
(second wave: all projects prepared at the
same time [from April-June 16, 1992])

Vouchers Sold and Registered

Standard methods used to express
demand for enterprises and
constantly updated (bidding,
proposals of direct sale)

Review of Projects by Branch Ministries
(first wave: undefined, sometimes coinciding
with review by the Privatization Ministries)
(second wave: branch ministries will have
two months after projects are submitted)

IPFs founded (Oct. 1991-Feb.28,
1992), list of IPFs publicized,
IPF advertising campaigns begin

Review of Projects by Privatization
Ministries, primarily review of projects
involving vouchers (Jan-Apr 1992 – in
the second wave, the Privatization
Ministries will review projects only after
branch ministries have completed their reviewing process)

"Zero Round" -- citizens allocate
investment points to IPFs
(Mar 1-Apr 26, 1992)

Registration of Firms by Commercial Courts
(Apr-May 11, 1992)

PUBLICATION OF LIST OF ENTERPRISES IN VOUCHER
PRIVATIZATION
(May 18, 1992)
VOUCHER PRIVATIZATION
(First wave: Round 1:May 18-July 7, 1992, Round 2:July 8-Aug. 25,
Round 3:Aug.26-Oct.6, Round 4:Oct.7-Nov. 17)
FURTHER PROJECT EVALUATION BY PRIVATIZATION MINISTRIES,
PRIVATIZATION THROUGH STANDARD METHODS

Note: remaining projects that involve vouchers will be included in the
following voucher wave.

zation. For the second wave, all projects were submitted by July 16, 1992, except
for those in selected branches of the economy (e.g., health care). Figure 4.2
illustrates the timetable of privatization in 1992.

As of mid-January 1993, the Czech Republic Ministry of Privatization reported having evaluated nearly 8,600 of the roughly 11,300 projects submitted
in the first wave, of which almost 2,000 had been approved, creating nearly

Table 4.2
Project Submission and Approval, by Jurisdiction, Czech Republic

	Firms under jurisdiction of Ministry of:				Firms under local government/municipality	Other**	Total
	Economy	Trade	Industry	Agriculture			
Total projects, wave 1	759	1116	4553	2967	1605	491	11291
Total projects, wave 2	982	716	1640	1019	4	104	4465
Total firms, wave I	199	237	1067	644	524	105	2776
Total firms, wave 2	95	83	461	285	3	13	938
Wave I projects reviewed	575	809	3210	2249	908	525	8074
Wave 2 projects reviewed	185	152	172	100	2	6	617
Total projects approved	136	141	736	433	233	64	1745
Property approved (billion KCS)	57.1	22.2	241.0	106.6	20.1	21.0	448.0

** The category "Other" includes the Ministry of Health Care, for which only a small number of projects have been submitted so far, but for which many projects will be submitted in the near future due to a later deadline.

Source: Karel Cermak, Czech Republic Ministry for Privatization. Author's Estimates.

4,000 new business units (see Tables 4.2 and 4.3). This still left about 2,700 first-wave privatization projects in front of the Ministry. The Ministry was also just getting under way the evaluation of second-round projects, of which it had received almost 4,500. Further projects from the health care sector were expected to be received in the near future.

The Slovak Republic had received about 1,500 projects on 736 firms in the first wave, of which 430 were approved for the first wave of voucher privatization. By late November, projects had been approved for 874 economic subjects of total value 165.3 billion Kcs. Of those, 188 were approved for direct sale, 20 for public auction, 10 for public tenders, 7 for restitution, 95 for unpaid transfer, and the remaining 544 were directed to voucher privatization. First-wave projects that involve voucher privatization but are approved too late for the first wave of vouchers will be included in the second wave of voucher privatization.

At first, most of the projects that were approved involved vouchers, simply because both republics hurried to evaluate voucher projects earlier than other projects in order to fulfill their quotas for voucher privatization. More recently, however, the shares of other means of privatization, especially direct sale, have been increasing (see Table 4.3).

THE ROLE OF FOREIGN CAPITAL

After discussing some main issues concerning privatization in my country, let me turn now to another important aspect of privatization, namely, the role of foreign capital in this process.

As we saw, the most important document in the large-scale privatization process is the privatization project, written by the management of the firm or by any other potential investor who might have interest in gaining part control of the firm. Foreign entities are welcome to write their own proposals for the privatization of any given firm or to collaborate with Czech partners on the elaboration of projects.[2] These projects are reviewed, as we saw, by the republic branch ministries (i.e., Ministry of Industry, Agriculture, etc.) and finally approved or rejected by the republic Ministry of Privatization.

Projects involving direct sale or foreign involvement also had to receive the approval of the government's Economic Council until recently, when it was decided that the council's role would be assumed instead by an interministerial commission of evaluators.

The rules for foreigners who wish to invest through large-scale privatization are not very different from the rules applying to other investors (except for the extra approval that they require). Nonetheless, the procedures involved are quite complex. Elaboration of a privatization plan often involves interaction with management; then project submitters must negotiate with branch ministries, with the Ministry of Privatization, and finally with the government's Economic Council. These four steps (often prolonged by the fact that a team of American experts

Table 4.3
Approved Privatization Projects in the Czech Republic, First Wave (January 19, 1993)

Approved method of privatization	Number of bus. units	Share of units	Total value of property (million KCS, 28 KCS=US$ 1)
A: Public auction	336	8.60	3,902.1
B: Public tender	308	7.88	10,924.2
C: Direct sale	1005	25.72	25,955.3
D: Commercialization into joint stock structure	1028	26.31	289,523.7
E: Privatization of an already existing state-owned joint stock company	191	4.89	130,670.1
F: Unpaid transfer to municipalities, pension funds, banks, or savings banks	1040	26.61	9,688.7
Voucher privatization (out of D and E)			238,041.4
Property to be returned to original owners			765.8
Property partially written off as unusable			10,621.8
Remaining value of assets partially written off			1,621.7
Property to small privatization			1,325.5
Expected earnings on auction of stocks			343.9
Total (Total number of projects = 1,968)	3908	100.00	485,342.8

Source: Karel Cermak, Czech Republic Ministry for the Administration of State Property and Its Privatization. Author's estimates.

at the Czech Ministry of Privatization also must review all projects with foreign involvement) mean that potential foreign investors must undergo a long, torturous process before their privatization plan is fully evaluated—and there is still no guarantee that the plan will be accepted. From the other side in the course of the approvals the companies' market situation can change and lead to the resignation of the foreign investor.

As a result, foreign investment through the large privatization, although significant, has not been as great as could have been hoped for. It seems quite possible that many foreign investors are waiting until shares are in the hands of new owners, in which case foreign investors may be able to acquire ownership by negotiating with the owners only, and not with management, two ministries, and the government.

One further policy that is notable is the so-called "family silver" policy, which requires that certain traditionally strong and viable enterprises be kept in domestic ownership. There is no list of exactly which firms fall under this rule, but such traditionally strong industries as beer production, porcelain, Becherovkà (a special liqueur), and other significant firms may be protected from foreign investment. Nonetheless, the enterprises falling under the "family silver" rule make up only a very small part of the Czech economy, and do not considerably exclude foreigners from a role in privatization.

As for foreign participation, in the first wave of privatization, there have been negotiations with 220 potential foreign investors in the Czech Republic. The total book value of assets involved in these negotiations is almost 50 billion Kcs ($1.7 billion). By mid-1992, 50 deals had been closed with 15 billion Kcs ($.5 bil.) of investment. Considering that book value of these properties was only 8 billion Kcs, the potential for inflow of foreign capital in the remaining 170 properties—that employ 100,000 workers and encompass about 40 billion Kcs ($1.4 bil.) in book value—is quite likely to exceed the estimated book value. A special group of American advisors has been assisting the Czech government in negotiations with potential foreign investors. Foreign participation was significantly smaller in the Slovak Republic.

Total foreign investment realized in the CSFR in 1992 totalled 30.7 bil. Kcs ($1.1 bil.) Through the end of 1991, the amount was 19.0 bil. Kcs ($640 mil.) (see Table 4.4). Total foreign direct investment since the onset of economic reform has thus totalled 49.7 bil. Kcs (over $1.7 billion). Of this amount, the vast majority was invested in to the Czech Republic. Foreign investment in the Czech Republic was 28.4 bil. Kcs ($1 bil.) in 1992, and since the beginning of the reform investment in the Czech Republic through the end of 1992 totalled 45.0 bil. Kcs (over $1.5 bil.). Thus, the Czech Republic accounted for over 92 percent of foreign investment in 1992 and over 90 percent of overall foreign investment in the CSFR. In 1993 FDI accounted for $450 million, foreign loans to enterprises for some $750 million and portfolio foreign investment for some $200 million.

The total amount of investment appears quite large at first glance. However,

Table 4.4
FDI in the CSFR through 12/31/92 (billion KCS)

	Through the end of 1991	1992	Total
CSFR	19.0	30.7	49.7
Czech Republic	16.6	28.4	45.0
Slovak Republic	2.4	2.3	4.7

Source: Hana Piskova, Czech National Bank. Author's estimates.

it is important to note that, first of all, much of the total investment is accounted for by a few large deals. Second, compared to Hungary, which has a smaller economy but has attracted roughly $4 billion in the period 1990–92, Czechoslovakia has not actually attracted as much as it might consider necessary to smooth its economic restructuring.

On the other hand, 1992 can be considered a successful year as far as attracting foreign capital (at least in the Czech Republic), because the nation was able to attract almost twice as much FDI in 1992 as it did in the preceding years. In addition, FDI in Czechoslovakia in 1992 exceeded investment in Hungary for the first time, thus showing that even though the CSFR was behind in the early years, its commitment to reform has made it increasingly attractive to foreign investors. Given the nation's relatively slow start in attracting foreign investment (see Table 4.4), the positive development in 1992 can be taken as a sign that future prospects for foreign participation in the Czech economy are strong, although Slovakia's prospects are not so clear, as will be shown.

A significant portion of foreign investment in 1992 came through the privatization process (before 1992, this was not the case). The Czech Republic Fund of National Property—the executor of privatization projects and therefore the organization that receives payment in cases where foreign entities purchase participation in Czech companies—received almost 14 bil. Kcs ($500 mil.) from foreign investors in privatization, almost all of it coming through the sale of shares in Czech enterprises.

Although the share of investment by foreigners in privatization has been large (in fact, larger than that received from domestic buyers in large-scale privatization in 1992), it is still quite likely that some investors are waiting until after the privatization process to try to enter the Czech and Slovak economies. Once the process is completed, ownership rights will be clearer and prospective foreign investors will not have to face the challenge of negotiations on various levels with different authorities. In addition, it is likely that some Investment Privatization Funds (IPFs) will need liquid assets and be willing to sell shares in enterprises to foreign investors at relatively cheap levels—with no government intermediation required to complete the deals. Even though the Czechoslovak privatization process has moved quickly and foreign participation has not been insignificant, it is possible that the structure of the process has discouraged some foreign investment and that there will be an increase once the process nears completion.

The Sectoral Structure of Foreign Investment Through 1992

The two sectors that have received the largest amount of foreign investment are "transportation equipment" and "miscellaneous manufacturing" (see Table 4.5). It is worth pointing out that the large amount invested in each of these sectors is mainly due to one large investment—in the first case, the investment of Volkswagen into the Skoda Automobile Plant; in the second case that of Philip Morris into the Czech Tabak (tobacco) company. Other sectors where foreign interest has been strong are construction (13.7 percent of all FDI, 21.5 percent of FDI in 1992), food processing (10.9 percent of total FDI, 17.6 percent in 1992), and banking (9.9 percent overall, 10.1 percent of FDI in 1992).

The largest deals that have been made in the Czech Republic so far are Volkswagen's investment in the Skoda Automobile Plant (Germany), Philip Morris's acquisition of a share of the cigarette manufacturer Tabak Kutna Hora (United States), Linde's investment in the firm Technoplyn (Germany), Glaverbel's acquisition of the glass manufacturer Sklo Union, and investment into the chocolate factory Cokoladovny Modrany, which was realized by the French firm BSN in cooperation with the Swiss firm Nestle and the European Bank for Reconstruction and Development. The largest investors in Slovakia include K-Mart, Volkswagen, Henkel-Palma, and Molnlycke (see Table 4.6). It is interesting that the largest investor in Slovakia, K-Mart, is a retail and distribution chain, and in fact its investment in Slovakia is part of an investment in the Czechoslovak market as a whole. The largest investors in the Czech Republic have been mainly in manufacturing.

Foreign Investment by Country of Origin

It was generally assumed that Germany would be the largest investor in the Czechoslovak economy, given its proximity and historical links to Czechoslovakia. In 1991 Germany was by far the largest investor in terms of total money invested, although this measure is skewed by the huge amount of money that went into the Skoda-Volkswagen deal. In 1992, however, the largest investor was the United States (27.2 percent of investment), again based mainly on the one large investment made by Philip Morris. The second largest investor for 1992 was France (20.7 percent), third was Germany (16.9 percent), fourth was Switzerland (8.5 percent), followed by Belgium (8.2 percent) (see Table 4.7).

A surprisingly small share, under 6 percent of total investment, came from neighboring Austria in 1992. A large proportion of investment from Austria was directed to the Slovak Republic (see Table 4.8), probably because of the proximity between Vienna and Bratislava, which are separated by less than 50 kil-

Table 4.5
Foreign Direct Investment in CSFR and Czech Republic, by Sector, 1992 and Total (million KCS)

Sector	Total to CSFR by 12/31/92	Total to CR by 12/31/1992	Sector	To CSFR in 1992	To CR in 1992
Transportation equipment	15,059.7	12,195.5	Misc. manufacturing	7,943.4	7,787.9
Misc. manufacturing	9,112.4	8,860.6	Construction	6,582.8	5,959.7
Construction	6,800.7	5,995.8	Food processing	5,399.9	4,994.5
Food processing	5,399.9	4,994.5	Banking	5,084.6	2,862.5
Banking	4,938.2	4,626.1	Chemicals	2,042.4	1,959.0
Other	10,392.4	8,287.1	Other	5,631.5	4,826.7
Total	49,685.3	44,957.6	Total	30,684.6	28,390.5

Source: Hana Piskova, Czech National Bank. Author's estimates.

Table 4.6
The Largest Investors in the Slovak Republic and Their Countries of Origin (as of 12/31/1992)

1. K-Mart	USA	7. Hoechst-Biotika	Germany
2. Volkswagen	Germany	8. Prva Stavebna Sporitelna	Austria, Germany
3. Henkel-Palma	Austria	9. Naftoprojekt-CP	Canada
4. Molnlycke	Sweden	10. Whirlpool-Tatramat	Italy
5. Samsung-Calex	Korea	11. MG Tatragas	Germany
6. Ludova Banka	Austria	12. Probugas	Germany

Source: Slovak Republic Ministry of Privatization. Author's estimates.

Table 4.7
Foreign Direct Investment into the CSFR and Czech Republic, 1992 and Total (million KCS)

Country	Total to CSFR by 12/31/1992	Total to CR by 12/31/92	Country	To CSFR in Year 1992	To CR in Year 1992
Germany	19,117.4	16,818.0	USA	8,358.3	8,183.5
United States	10,181.4	9,702.0	France	6,381.9	5,895.9
France	6,864.8	6,774.2	Germany	5,174.0	4,476.3
Austria	3,428.7	2,188.1	Switzerland	2,619.2	2,093.6
Belgium	3,411.4	3,411.4	Belgium	2,487.6	2,487.6
Other	6,679.7	6,063.9	Other	5,663.7	5,253.6
Total	49,683.4	44,957.6	Total	30,684.7	28,390.3

Source: Hana Piskova, Czech National Bank.

Table 4.8
Foreign Direct Investment in Slovakia (through 12/31/92)

Country	Total investment (billion KCS)	% of Total investment	Number of companies
Total	6.6	100.0	2,825
Austria	1.8	27.3	908
Germany	1.6	24.0	489
USA	1.3	19.2	110

Source: Slovak Republic Ministry of Privatization.

ometers. In total through the end of 1992, Germany still is the largest investor, although its share has dropped from near 50 percent at the end of 1991 to only 38.5 percent of total investment.

FDI in the Czech Republic in the First Quarter of 1993

The first quarter of 1993 has provided some encouraging signs that FDI in the Czech Republic is picking up as the effects of the nation's breakup are subsiding and as privatization continues at full steam. In the first quarter of 1993, foreign investment in the Czech Republic totalled 8.8 bil. Kcs (US$302 million), an increase of almost 31 percent over foreign investment in the first quarter of 1992, bringing overall foreign investment to 53.7 billion Kc (US$1.86 billion).

PROBLEMS OF LARGE-SCALE PRIVATIZATION

There are many problems that have been associated with the large-scale privatization process. On the supply side, they are often related to the quantity and quality of submitted privatization projects and the difficulty involved in writing them. On the demand side of voucher privatization, they are mostly related to the lack of regulation on IPFs and the inadequacy of currently existing institutional structures. In general, voucher privatization has suffered from a lack of foresight in regulation, which of course is to some degree inevitable when developing a completely new technique in a changing economic environment. For the second wave a more secure system should be in place.

It is important to note that despite problems encountered, the Czechoslovak voucher privatization process has been run in a highly sophisticated and well-organized technical manner, especially considering its huge scope of activity. The whole process has been supported by the general public's confidence in the enterprises being privatized, an important factor that has not been so prominent in many other reforming nations. The sophisticated computer network, used by the Center for Voucher Privatization and the registration places, has played a pivotal role in the whole procedure. In fact, after the end of voucher privatization, existing databases and networks will be used for the Center for Securities, which will maintain share accounts for the new shareholders from voucher privatization on the new stock exchange.

It is also worth noting that voucher privatization has been completely self-financing. Initial costs of setting up computer networks and the registration places were covered by loans, which were repaid using proceeds from sales of voucher booklets and stamps. The unexpectedly high rate of registration even led to a slight surplus.

Problems in Privatization Projects and Evaluation

The case-by-case privatization process requires the evaluation of firms' market value, which is not easily established, given past pricing systems, inadequate benchmarks of value, and poor accounting systems. The process of evaluating market value is also costly. The market value of the firm seen as initial fixed price offer might, of course, be equal to zero for a poor asset (with low expected cash flows etc.) or be many times greater than the book value for a good asset (for example, for internationally competitive firms). Anyway, to assess the market value of the firm from expected cash flows on the basis of distorted product and input prices (based on domestic individual costs and markup combined with nontransparent subsidies) is somewhat naive. Hence modifications of common evaluation procedures are required case by case to indicate potential (international) competitiveness or bankruptcy of the firm. Nevertheless under existing conditions of trade expressed in book value, citizens are often wary of foreign buyouts, as there are accusations that the national heritage is being sold off too cheaply. Even with the help of the voucher process, with its unique method for establishing a market price for stocks, a real price equilibrium will probably not be attained for some time.

Many competing projects propose the breakup of existing large enterprises. For the most part, this is a positive development, because of the overconcentration of Czechoslovak SOEs. It would allow the creation of a currently missing sector of small and medium-sized firms. Unfortunately, in many cases competing projects are trying to divide something that is technologically indivisible. On average, each approved privatization project has led to the creation of about two new business units.

Many projects presented weak or poorly elaborated business plans. In addition, due to time constraints and lack of qualified staff, the Ministries of Privatization have had great difficulty in comparing and evaluating these business plans as a part of the decision-making process in evaluating privatization projects.

Management's Role in Privatization

It is beyond doubt that firm management had a great degree of control over the whole privatization process. Given the facts that management had an information monopoly on the elaboration of privatization projects and that managers are naturally the most familiar with the condition and productive capacities of their firms, it can be argued that firm management has more or less controlled the privatization process. These advantages were compounded by the fact that supervision of firms by branch ministries was very weak and the state planning agency was completely dismantled, so that there were no owners (i.e., government institutions) able to influence management. Following are some of the

Table 4.9
Elaborators of Approved Privatization Projects (1/19/93)

Author	Number of projects	Percent of pro- jects approved
Total projects approved	1,968	100.0
Enterprise management	1,267	64.4
Management of individual plants (subordinate management)	109	5.5
Interested buyer	386	19.6
Original owner	53	2.7
Ministry	10	0.5
Consulting firm	36	1.8
Local privatization council	37	1.9
Other	45	2.3
Local founding institution	16	0.8
Trade union	1	0.1
Not listed	8	0.4

Source: Karel Cermak, Czech Republic Ministry for the Administration of State Property and its Privatization. Author's estimates.

ways in which management was able to use its position to gain advantages in the process of project compilation and evaluation.

Often, management of enterprises refused to deliver (or delivered very slowly) information necessary for other parties interested in developing competing projects. This conduct was made legally punishable by the amendment to the Law on Large Privatization, which was passed in February 1992. In fact, this strategy was quite successful for company managers, considering that almost two-thirds of projects approved so far have been those submitted by enterprise management (see Table 4.9). This number was much higher than the 25 percent of all projects originally submitted by enterprise management. Many of these projects proposed management buyouts of the enterprise.

Management of state-owned firms often took advantage of its position to strip assets to cover operating losses and provide themselves with increased income. Also, managers were able to set up parallel companies and use transfer prices to sell products almost at a loss to the private companies they owned, thus transferring large profits to themselves. These practices could even in some cases lead to bankruptcy of the state-owned company, which could then be cheaply acquired by the new, liquid private company.

A loophole in privatization legislation allowed existing management to sign long-term rental agreements, which de facto predetermined the fate of the property before privatization. This loophole was addressed by the amendment to the law on privatization. Many firms entering privatization have inherited heavy debts from the past (e.g., due to distorted price structures), creating a bad precondition for privatization and an obstacle to the formation of feasible business plans. In fact, since the process of privatization has taken a whole year, management "waiting for new owners" has acted with little restraint, and these debts have increased further over the recent past.

One can suggest a very close relationship between the method of privatization, its capital costs, and new managerial priorities. Here I disregard founding many parallel private companies used to transfer the profits of SOEs into private hands. The original anticipation of SOEs' managers, as already mentioned, was that money-neutral voucher privatization interconnected with widely spread ownership could be regarded as the safe way of their survival. But then the rapidly growing investment privatization funds with more than 70 percent of vouchers shares appeared and fired many companies' directors (although they have not often had replacements ready). It had called for a further wave of privatization proposals suggested by the company's directors, costly proposals.

All of these factors put together meant that in many cases managers of state-owned enterprises were able to elaborate proposals that allowed them to take over ownership of their firms through management buyouts and buy-ins. In many cases, these were managers who had been appointed after the changes of 1989, and often very capable individuals. Although in some cases managers were able to exploit their position in the privatization process, in the end the large number of management buyouts and buy-ins may turn out to be a positive development, since these may well be the people most qualified to be governing the privatized firms under local conditions, especially given the limited number of qualified managers in the nation.

Problems in Privatization Procedures and Rules

The privatization process in Czechoslovakia is an unprecedented process, and thus many rules and procedures were not thoroughly defined beforehand. Although the procedure has run somewhat smoothly, it is important to acknowledge that the procedure of learning-by-doing required some changes in midcourse, which have resulted in certain costs. In addition, sometimes it has been unclear under which jurisdiction certain activities have belonged, leading to problems for evaluators and potential investors. Following are some problems caused by unclear or changing regulations.

- Constant changes in legislation during the transition period (e.g., the new commercial code) were not reflected in privatization projects, which therefore needed time for adjustment.
- The "mother," supervising branch ministries also had to review the projects, and their conclusions were sometimes at odds with those of the Privatization Ministries, often supporting existing management. In fact, the inherited hierarchy and coalitions were still largely in place, although this situation is gradually changing.
- Selection procedures and rules were not prepared in time, so there is not a consistent, transparent means of evaluating projects. Some rules do exist; for example, in cases where there are two or more competing projects, competitive forms of privatization

(e.g., public auction, public tender) are preferred over direct sales to predetermined buyers. Decision makers are under permanent time pressure as well as lobbying pressure from various groups with vested interests. The new conception formed for the second wave should help to make the process of project evaluation and approval more objective.

• Foreign capital participation is seen as an important contribution to the development of Czechoslovakia's industry. Nonetheless, foreigners were often discouraged by the tangled web of negotiations that had to be undertaken in order to participate in privatization. Given the standard process, it was quite likely that foreigners would have to negotiate with enterprise management, then with branch ministries, then with the Privatization Ministry and its advisers, and perhaps then with the government's Economic Council. In such a case, it would have been easier to wait until the enterprise was privatized and then try to buy in. This problem has been addressed, at least to some degree, by the new conception of privatization brought in after the June 1992 elections (see later section).

• As mentioned, the Czech side has not received any compensation from Slovakia in spite of the fact that Slovak shareholders have obtained a large amount of Czech property through vouchers, whereas Czechs have gained ownership of only a small amount of Slovak property.

Problems of the Funds of National Property, IPFs, and Ownership

As part of the privatization process, a new institutional framework was introduced. The creation of Investment Privatization Funds (IPFs) and Funds of National Property (FNPs) has had several consequences within the framework of privatization. Some of these problems are due to the inability of the new organizations to start functioning optimally, some due to the lack of regulatory framework for their activities. One of the major problems is the transfer of ownership away from the FNPs, interim holders of the shares of all firms being privatized.

• The newly created Funds of National Property (FNP) of the Czech and Slovak Republics serve as temporary owners of privatized property. These funds implement decisions made at the ministries, including decisions on enterprise contracts and the composition of enterprise boards of directors, as well as organizing privatization activities such as auctions and tenders. By the end of 1992, the Czech FNP had implemented only about 40 percent of the approved privatization projects forwarded to it by the Ministry of Privatization, an indication that it is operating at less than optimal speed, and a large amount of property is remaining in the hands of the FNPs. It is worth noting that the FNPs cannot operate smoothly as owners of such a vast portfolio.

• The transfer of ownership for almost all firms in the voucher process could not take place until the end of the wave. Thus, even though some firms were completely privatized in the first round, they still had to wait four to five months to actually be put under new ownership. In addition, since the law on securities has been passed only recently and for other reasons, it was difficult to transfer ownership of firms from voucher privatization to the new owners quickly. IPFs have actively tried to circumvent this problem with some mild success, but for the most part the Funds of National Property remained the owners of huge amounts of property for quite a while.

At any rate, a significant number of shares will remain in the FNPs' hands after the voucher privatization. It is not yet clear how the FNPs will privatize this property and whether they will be able to participate actively as owners of the firms in which they hold shares.

- Laws concerning the establishment and regulation of stock markets in Prague and Bratislava were passed only in April 1992. These markets were able to function from May 1993, but how efficiently they might commence operation is still quite questionable.[3] There is also trading through the so-called RM system, based on computer networks and databases inherited from voucher privatization, which can provide some opportunities for trading to begin smoothly.[4]

- The law regulating the behavior of IPFs was not passed until April 28, 1992, after IPFs had completed gathering investment points from citizens (some problems with the IPFs were elaborated above). This law does provide needed guidelines on diversification of risk and on general disclosure, but it was passed very late in the process, and the continual changing of rules can only have a negative effect upon performance of the IPFs.

- Given the (possibly excessive) option offers that were made by the IPFs, it is possible that some will face bankruptcy or mergers when these options mature. The number of funds seems not to exceed 100 in the medium run. This is especially true because the average book value of assets per coupon book was almost 70,000 Kcs ($2,300) when the IPFs began making their offers, but because more than twice as many coupon books were registered before the registration deadline, this figure has fallen to around 35,000 Kcs ($1,100) per coupon book. The application of law on investment funds may alleviate this problem by recognizing open and closed funds, the latter of which are not obliged to fulfill their promises. At least part of the concern about this issue was alleviated by a recent poll that revealed that there is in fact an increasing demand for the shares of some funds, which could compensate for those who choose to cash in their shares. In fact, Harvard Capital and Consulting, for example, has offered to begin to redeem its options for cash even now at a rate discounted from its original offer by the actual nominal interest rate, but response has been quite limited.

- It is still unclear how active a role shareholders will have in the corporate governance of the IPFs, which have been controlled by their founders until now. Currently, the only way that shareholders can act is to sell off their holdings. For IPFs which are owned by a large, fragmented group of voucher holders, it seems unlikely that the new shareholders will be able to group together to influence fund management.

Problems of Financing of Divestitures through the Leveraged Buyout Process

Overall, there have been 277.8 million auctions, public tenders, or direct sales. In current conditions of limited financial savings, a large share of such sales have involved large loans from leading banks (or FNPs paid by installment) to support leveraged buyouts. In fact, financial restructuring problems have been

Table 4.10
Rates of Growth of Monetary Aggregates, January–September 1992, CSFR

M1	M2	Total credits	Loans to enter-prises*	Loans for privatization
6.8%	12.7%	14.3%	12.6%	96.7%

added by the further increase of leverage of companies caused by very costly privatization sales through the leverage buy-outs organized often by managers.

The huge growth of loan activity for privatization can be seen in Table 4.10. Loan growth was expected to be even larger for the fourth quarter of 1992. In fact, the largest share of privatization loans so far has been for small-scale privatization (see Table 4.11), which suggests that loan activity for large-scale privatization will increase greatly during 1993. Small-scale privatization is nearly over, so lending for this program should be minimal in 1993. On the other hand, available domestic funding is limited, given the government's program of tight monetary policy and the limited available domestic savings. These factors have caused interest rates to grow, based on the high demand for loans.

Less than 5 percent of privatization loans were short-term, nearly two-thirds were medium-term, and the percentage of long-term loans has been growing only slowly. With the burden of inherited debt (see earlier section) and privatization bank loans, the situation for many companies privatized through loans is difficult, due to their unfavorable capital structure. Under the newly introduced tax system, with very long-term depreciation and 45 percent taxes on profits, government regulation has increased the financial strain on businesses in the short term. Perhaps changes of tax and depreciation regulations could mitigate the financially tight situation facing many privatized firms in the near future, in order to help them survive this difficult period.

Unfortunately, the availability of foreign loans to enterprises is limited by the condition that interest rates on loans more than four times a firm's capital stock should be paid out of after-tax profits, rather than being included as costs.

Given the short-term dangers facing many firms privatized through loans, it seems that the government should reach a compromise between macroeconomic stability (i.e., balanced budget, tight money) and microeconomic-based development. This type of policy should not be confused with expansionary promotion of state-owned firms (as was done in the past), nor should it be considered a long-term policy.

Fine Tuning of the Conception of Privatization: The New Privatization Ministers and the Second Wave of Privatization

In both the Czech and Slovak Republics, new ministers of privatization were appointed as part of the formation of new governments that took place after the

Table 4.11
Loans Financing Privatization, CSFR (billion KCS)

	31.12.1991	30.6.1992	30.9.1992
Small-scale privatization	18.2	28.3	28.8
Large-scale privatization	–	1.3	7.0
Total	18.2	29.6	35.8

Source: Monetary Survey, SBCS, Praha; Ales Bulir, Privatization Newsletter No. 11, 1992.

June 1992 elections. Both new ministers promised to address the "lack of definition" that had generally plagued the privatization process. In each republic, this involved a clearer definition of which privatization methods would be given priority, more transparent methods of choosing between projects, less bureaucratic entanglements, and less room for use of personal contacts in getting proposals approved.

One of the major questions to be resolved was the manner in which the resolution of the nation's future would influence the course of privatization. With regard to this question, the two ministers arrived at two important conclusions: the first wave will be completed and its results will be respected; and the second wave should be carried out separately by the individual republics.

The first decision, that the results of the first wave will be respected, resulted from several factors. Perhaps most important was that to alter the first wave in any way would further delay the transfer of enterprise ownership into private hands, a result that was seen as unacceptable. A further factor in determining that the first wave would continue unchanged was the respect for the rights of shareholders who have already obtained shares. According to this original agreement, any legal measures that may have to be enacted (i.e., governing foreign ownership of shares after the federation separates and Czechs and Slovaks each own significant numbers of shares in the other nation) would have to be taken in such a manner that they would not infringe upon the rights of those who are already shareholders of firms. However, as mentioned above, the Czech Ministry of Privatization has already gone back on this agreement, pointing to the fact that Slovaks would benefit disproportionately if no compensation is provided for the Czech property that they obtained in the first wave.

The second decision, that the second wave of voucher privatization should be conducted separately by the two republics, resulted from the conclusion that a united privatization process could eventually be held up by legal obstacles when the federation breaks up. Under the existing privatization mechanism, it should not be difficult to undertake the second wave on a republican, rather than a federal, level. A process run in this matter will be much easier to adapt to the new circumstances now that Czechoslovakia has divided into two states. Furthermore, it is felt that the voucher privatization is a transfer of something of significant value to the population. Therefore, in the case of national separation, there should be no reason why either republic's government should want to make such a transfer to foreign citizens.

The two republican privatization ministries worked independently on the formation of their "new conceptions" of privatization. Each republic's Ministry of Privatization has specified several changes that will be manifested in the actual process. In the Czech Republic, the main emphasis is on a more precise definition of the steps involved in the privatization process. First of all, steps in the approval process were taken to resolve differences between the Ministry of Privatization and other ministries involved in the evaluation of privatization proposals. Disagreements, which formerly were resolved by the Economic Council of the Government, will now be addressed by a special interministerial Government Privatization Commission. This policy change will clarify the overall process, while also simplifying procedures for foreign investors, who will deal with representatives of several ministries through the commission rather than having to scramble between the various ministries.

A second important change in the Czech Ministry's conception of privatization has been the approach to standard privatization methods. For smaller firms (book value under 50 million Kcs, $1.7 mil.), standard methods will have priority. The use of direct sale as a means of privatization has been criticized because much of the population does not see it as a fair means for the transfer of property. Thus, the ministry has decided upon several conditions. In cases where only one proposal is submitted and it proposes direct sale, it can be approved only if the price offered is greater than the book value of the assets. Where several proposals are made, those suggesting competitive methods (i.e., auction, tender) will have priority. When several proposals are made, all of which propose direct sale, then a nonpublic competition will take place in which all project submitters may bid, and the deciding criteria will be price. In the past, the ministry had tried to rely on several criteria, but practice revealed this method to be nontransparent and difficult to administer.

Then-minister Dolgos suggested the Slovak new conception of privatization as a "step toward transparency." The main developments that it was meant to involve were an increased reliance on standard methods—mainly public tender and competitive methods—and a decrease in the overall significance of the voucher privatization scheme. Unfortunately, there were not firm grounds for such a concept because of weak demand for Slovak firms.

THE FIRST EFFECTS OF PRIVATIZATION ON RESTRUCTURING

These were already discussed in my previous paper (Mejstrik 1993). As mentioned, one of the major problems facing firms is the lack of liquid assets. In order to mitigate their limited liquidity, many firms, especially privatized firms, are restructuring their financial flows on the basis of production restructuring in favor of their permanently liquid customers. This practice was made easier by the liberalization of trade, which made it possible for all producers either to export directly or to export through private trading companies, many of which have recently been established. This emphasis on exports has dramatically increased the share of CSFR trade with developed market economies, notably with the European Union (EU), since 1989, indicating that a desirable reorientation of trade toward mostly liquid firms in the West is taking place and that the pendulum driven by the transition to private enterprise is switching the trade pattern of 1980s back to the pattern enjoyed by prosperous, capitalist Czechoslovakia in the 1920s. In trade it led to an overall positive balance of payments in 1991 and 1992. Given the shocks to CSFR trade caused by disruptions in trade within the Council for Mutual Economic Assistance (CMEA) and increases in the price of oil from the USSR, even the slight deficit is better than had been expected. The ability of Czechoslovak firms to succeed in Western markets reflects positively on their prospects for future prosperity and on the ability of the new private sector to adjust to the requirements of global markets.

Industrial production declined and companies started to cut the inherited overemployment. The extremely low level of unemployment in the Czech Republic (2.6 percent) in these economic conditions has been mainly a result of the newly established Czech private sector. There are many active entrepreneurs in the Czech Republic, especially in the service and construction businesses. Developments in the service sector reflect a supply response to a long-term excess demand for services. In construction, many small construction start-ups were established to satisfy demand created by the restructuring needs of new owners (single proprietors or partners) who gained property through restitutions and privatization buyouts or tenders.

The major issue for the near future as regards privatization and foreign investment is the problem of the exercising of new property rights. This problem is coming to the forefront in those cases where privatization of certain firms has already been approved or achieved through vouchers, but legal obstacles have prevented the new owners from taking control quickly. Some IPFs are already starting to act as owners, and it has been determined that all participants of voucher privatization will be given their shares. However, the corporate governance issue still has not been solved.

CONCLUSION

Perhaps the greatest problem of large-scale privatization and for the inflow of foreign investment has been the lack of a firm legal framework. The effects of changes in regulations have been to make the rules of this process unclear for potential investors and other project submitters and for the organizers of the IPFs. In spite of this problem, however, the first wave of vouchers has been completed and the majority of first-wave projects have been evaluated (although not yet implemented). The second wave learned from the lessons of the first, and thus had a much sounder foundation for operation from its beginning, not suffering as much from the government's frequent changes in policy. The second wave started in the summer of 1993 in the Czech Republic, slightly later in the Slovak Republic. The Czech Republic offered over 100 billion Kcs worth of (book value) property in its second wave of voucher privatization. The second wave was run separately in the individual republics, and the Slovak Republic does not plan to give priority to the voucher scheme as a means of privatization.

The Czech and Slovak privatizations, even with all of their controversies and criticisms, are happening, and still are supported by the public, especially in the Czech lands. What will be important in the near future is to concentrate on the restructuring and reorganization of newly privatized enterprises in order to create a properly functioning market economy. Some important progress has already been made in the dramatic reorientation of foreign trade toward Western markets. Given that the original conception was to privatize enterprises quickly and allow new owners (and not government) to restructure, there clearly still remains much restructuring work to be done.

NOTES

1. See Jan Mladeck, "Transformation, Restitution and Privatization in Agriculture," *Privatization Newsletter,* No. 9, October 1992, for further details on the agricultural transformation.

2. First-wave privatization projects were due by late January 1992. The deadline for second-wave projects was mid-June 1992.

3. For more information about the new stock markets, see CERGE Reform Round Table Working Paper No. 6, "Stock Markets in the CSFR," 1992.

4. For more information on the functioning of the RM System, see the article by Dusan Triska in *Privatization Newsletter,* No. 9, November 1992.

REFERENCES

Bulir, Ales. (1992). "Financing Privatization and Monetary Growth." *Privatization Newsletter* No. 11, December.
Czech Fund of National Property. (1991, 1992). *Annual Reports* for 1991, 1992.
Mejstrik, M. (1993). "Enterprise Restructuring and Its Economic Precondition in the Czech Republic." Draft of paper for IIASA Workshop on Enterprise Behavior under the Conditions of Economic Reform in the Russian Federation, 6–8 July.
Mladek, Jan. (1992). "Transformation, Restitution and Privatization in Agriculture." *Privatization Newsletter,* No. 9, October.
Privatization Newsletter of Czech and Slovak Republics. (1992). Nos. 1–16. Charles University, Praha.

5

Privatization and Foreign Investment in Poland, 1990–1993: Results, Problems, and Lessons

Władysław W. Jermakowicz

The ultimate aim of privatizing the Polish economy is to create a basis that will increase the efficiency of the national economy. Only when real and responsible owners come into possession of companies can one expect that privatization will bring an increase in national economic efficiency. Foreign direct investment (FDI) as a mode of privatization can bring in strategic investors motivated by entrepreneurship and interested in profitability, efficiency, and the long-term development of a company, and with capabilities to realize these goals. By bringing in a package of machinery, equipment technology, management and marketing techniques, and expertise, foreign investors facilitate the transformation of the whole economy and its integration into a global economy (Rojec 1993).

This chapter is designed to address the role of foreign investment in the Polish privatization process. It presents the experience of three years of privatization efforts in Poland and concludes with the obstacles encountered in privatization and the lessons that can be drawn from the experience of privatization and foreign investment in Poland.

SPONTANEOUS VERSUS CENTRALLY CONTROLLED PRIVATIZATION

As other countries of Central and Eastern Europe, Poland started the process of systemic transformation when its economy was dominated by state-owned enterprises (SOEs). The nonfarm private sector in 1989 accounted for 10.3 percent of industrial production and employed less than 14.1 percent of all the nonagricultural labor force. This sector consisted mainly of unincorporated businesses in crafts, services, and retail trading.

The real turnaround for the private sector began after the first Solidarity-controlled government came to power in September 1989. From that time to mid-1993, the number of private firms more than doubled, private domestic incorporated firms increased fourfold, and the number of incorporated foreign firms increased more than thirty times (see Table 5.1). By the end of 1993, the private sector already accounted for more than 90 percent of all firms, employed more than 42.7 percent of those in work outside agriculture, and contributed more than 31 percent of total industrial output.

By far the most important practice in privatizing the Polish economy is spontaneous, uncontrolled privatization.[1] This type of privatization involves setting up green-field (new) private businesses, either incorporated or unincorporated, by both Polish and foreign investors; advancing the autonomous growth of existing private businesses; and advancing assets privatization, where the state enterprises get rid of part of their assets, which are sold off or leased out, mostly to private firms (Balcerowicz 1993). Spontaneous privatization encompasses approximately 99.9 percent of all new private businesses (all the crafts and the lion's share of incorporated firms).

Spontaneous privatization, although very vital for the Polish economy, is beyond the main area of discussion of this chapter. Focus is put on the centrally controlled privatization of state-owned enterprises (SOEs). This controlled privatization contributed, until 1993, to the privatization of only .13 percent of all firms (2265/1,784,516), which, because of their size, produced one-fifth of the private sector output and employees, approximately one-third of the whole labor force in that sector.

CENTRALLY CONTROLLED PRIVATIZATION IN POLAND—METHODS AND RESULTS

In September 1990, the Ministry of Privatization (MoP) prepared and published its Privatization Program, which assumed that in the years 1991–1995 50 percent of all enterprises would be privatized (''Program Prywatyzacji'' 1990).

At that time, great optimism prevailed that privatization and foreign investment would solve many of the country's economic problems and that the process would be accomplished relatively quickly. The illusory nature of this view became apparent when the newly established Office of the Plenipotentiary for Transformation Changes together with Western experts began preparing the legal, regulatory, and institutional framework for privatization. These foreign experts initially focused almost exclusively on a firm-by-firm sale strategy, not unlike the programs in which they participated in other parts of the world. ''This customized approach is,'' as Lipton and Sachs (1991, p. 12) wrote, ''likely to bog down for political, economic and financial reasons well before a significant portion of state firms are actually privatized.''

Subsequently, a more realistic view developed that recognized privatization would not only take time but would also require a multitrack approach com-

Table 5.1
Growth of Private Sector in Poland, 1989–1993

Periods	All firms #	Private firms #	Incorporated firms domestic #	foreign #	Polonia firms	Share of private sector (without agriculture) industrial (%)	employment (%)
12/31/89	872,881	858,430	15,681	429	841	10.3	14.1
12/31/90	1,217,839	1,201,915	33,239	1,645	862	11.6	20.9
12/31/91	1,542,525	1,493,701	47,690	4,769	787	18.4	40.3
12/31/92	1,878,956	1,719,304	59,077	10,131	716	31.0	42.7
06/30/93	1,966,384	1,784,516	63,489	12,804	714	.	
TOTAL*	100%	90.7%	5.6%	0.7%			

Computations based on the *Statistical Yearbooks*, GUS, (1991 and 1992), and *Prywatyzacja*, No. 7, July 1993.

*As of June 1993.

prising separate privatization paths for the various categories of enterprises, often with a simultaneous use of different methods of privatization within a category. This new strategy assumed an implementation of five main roads of privatization:

1. Commercialization followed by privatization
2. Privatization through liquidation, in other words, by the dissolution of enterprises as legal entities and the sale of their assets
3. Foreign investment through joint ventures
4. Reprivatization (restitution)
5. Small-scale privatization ("Program Prywatyzacji" 1990)

Exempting small-scale privatization and restitution, three paths—commercialization, liquidation, and joint ventures—are practically the only methods contributing to the numbers of state-owned firms that are privatized.

Table 5.2 provides statistics on the progress of the Polish economy's privatization using all three paths. The time span is divided into five half-year periods starting July 1990, when the Law on Privatization was declared, and ending June 30, 1993.

The official statistics displayed by the Polish Ministry of Privatization (MoP) show that in the middle of 1993, from a total of 6,838 SOEs, 2,265 firms, or about 33.1 percent of all SOEs, were taking part in the privatization process, which is undoubtedly an impressive achievement. The reality, however, is more dreary.

First of all, the selection of figures for computation seems to be inaccurate. The MoP intentionally uses the remaining number of nonprivatized firms from the last period as a basis for comparison, in this case the number of 6,838 firms from 1993. A methodologically correct calculation would consider the number of SOEs existing when privatization started in 1990, a larger number of firms, 8,347. Then this percent would be 27.1 percent (2,265/8,347) rather than 33.1 percent.

Next, the data on commercialization and liquidation represent only firms that were either commercialized, that is, were being transformed into single-person State Treasury corporations with 100 percent state ownership, or were in the liquidation process and were still in the State Treasury's possession. The real number of completely sold firms was much smaller, amounting to 783. Taking into account these reservations, the real share of privatized firms in the middle of 1993 amounted to 9.3 percent (783/8,347), much lower than the officially published data.

Table 5.2 also shows that the momentum of Polish privatization had already slowed by mid-1993. The process started with 107 SOEs in the second half of 1990 and hit its peak in the second half of 1991, when 754 enterprises were designated for privatization. Later, from period to period, the number of firms

Table 5.2
Commercialized, Liquidated, and Joint Venture Firms (in units)

Periods	All SOEs #	Designated for privatiz. #	%	Commercialized #	%	Designated for liquidation #	%	Joint Ventures all #	with SOEs #	%
12/31/89	7,357	0	0.0%	0	0.0%	0	0.0%	429	325	75.8%
12/31/90	8,347	107	1.3%	10	0.1%	97	1.2%	1,216	264	21.7%
06/30/91	8,591	398	6.1%	155	1.9%	347	4.0%	1,195	101	8.5%
12/31/91	8,346	754	9.0%	147	1.8%	607	7.3%	1,956	75	3.8%
06/30/92	8,180	502	6.1%	155	1.9%	347	4.2%	2,852	74	2.6%
12/31/92	7,344	291	4.0%	20	0.3%	271	3.7%	2,483	69	2.7%
06/30/93	6,838	213	3.1%	17	0.3%	196	2.9%	2,673	33	1.2%
TOTAL*	6,838	2,265	33.1%	504	7.5%	1,865	27.2%	12,375	616	4.5%

Computations based on *Dynamika Prywatyzacji* (1991–1993), information provided by the Ministry of Privatization.

*As of June 1993.

declined, and in the first half of 1993 decreased to a record low of 213 firms. Apparently, the firms most prepared for privatization had already been sold, and each new enterprise designated for sale needed more preparatory work. Also, resistance against privatization had begun to grow.

FOREIGN DIRECT INVESTMENT

Foreign direct investment (FDI) is understood here as establishing a majority or minority ownership in another country's business entity. Control over a foreign entity distinguishes FDI from foreign portfolio investment (FPI) which is made in financial instruments (e.g., government bonds or stock) without taking a controlling interest in the business entity. Although international portfolio investment is gradually becoming a very important factor on the Polish stock market, its impact on Polish privatization will not be discussed here.

The next issue in foreign direct investment is the choice between green-field (new) investment and acquisition of an existing local company. In the case of Poland, this choice is modified into green-field or privatization. In this chapter green-field foreign direct investment, although very important for the Polish economy, is left aside, and focus is put on the FDI as a part of the privatization process.[2] FDI implies privatization everywhere acquisition or partnership involves a local company in state-owned ownership.

As a part of the privatization process in Poland, FDI can take place in all three main privatization paths. Foreign entities can participate in privatization by partial or full acquisition of a state-owned company by purchasing shares of already commercialized companies offered either in the form of an initial public offering (IPO) or direct sale. Next, foreign entities can establish a new company by acquiring assets of the liquidated SOEs contributed to the new companies by the State Treasury. And lastly, the foreign entities can establish joint ventures by establishing a new company with state-owned enterprises not participating in privatization through the liquidation process. The first two methods can be called direct acquisition; the last one can be called indirect acquisition.

Foreign indirect acquisition investment has some tradition in Poland. It started in 1976 when the first Joint Venture Decree was passed by the Polish Council of Ministers (Decree 1976). This decree allowed the first foreign investment in Poland in the form of Polonia partnerships—firms owned by Polish emigrants. In 1977 the first three firms were registered; by the end of 1980 their number had increased only slightly to 45. In 1982 foreign investment possibilities were extended to all foreigners in the form of foreign small enterprises (Law 1982). The first joint venture law allowing full foreign participation, independent of origin and open for investment in a majority of the economy's fields, was passed by the Polish Sejm on April 23, 1986 (Law 1986). In 1989 the number of joint venture firms increased to 429.

The start of the official privatization program in 1990 gave the foreign indirect investment acquisition new impetus. From that moment direct investment could be made not only in the form of joint ventures but also in the form of direct acquisition, in which a foreign investor buys a share (partially or entirely) in a local company or its assets.

In the following sections, the role of foreign direct investment in the Polish privatization program through direct acquisitions (commercialization and liquidation) and indirect acquisitions (joint ventures) is presented and discussed.

COMMERCIALIZATION

The transformation of state-owned enterprises into single-person, treasury-owned joint-stock companies is known in Poland as commercialization. Commercialization is achieved through replacement of the founding body, the branch ministry or the local authority, with a corporate institution of the general meeting of shareholders (which is played temporarily by the MoP). Next it proceeds through a replacement of the workers' council with a supervisory board representing the owner, and through the replacement of the old management body with an executive board. These formal changes, it is assumed, adapt the legal structure of state-owned companies to the requirements of capital corporations. In reality, however, they usually change only the founding body, and through an elimination of the workers' council the changes lead to the strengthening of the firm's executive.

Under Polish conditions, priority for commercialization is granted to those enterprises that have a clear development strategy, have a higher profitability than an average firm for the given industry, and present the Ministry of Privatization with a specific privatization program. The SOE is also required to submit a number of supplementary analyses giving a more detailed diagnosis of the company's economic and financial condition. The information may include balance sheets, performance and cash flow audits, and the legal status of company assets. These documents are prepared by independent specialized consulting companies contracted by the Ministry of Privatization after advertised bidding. After commercialization is granted, the MoP appoints the members of a supervisory board, and the company is entered into the Trade Register.

Single person joint-stock companies can be privatized under one of three methods: initial public offering (IPO), direct sale, or mass privatization.[3] As shown in Table 5.2, in the three years from 1990 to 1993, 504 state-owned enterprises were commercialized, which constitutes some 7.3 percent of all firms or 22.2 percent of firms designated for privatization. The largest number of those incorporated were transformed into corporate forms by initial public offering or direct sale; the remaining 183 were designated to the mass privatization program (see Table 5.3).

Commercialized, fully privatized (completely sold) firms numbered 76 until the middle of 1993 (15 percent of all commercialized firms). From those sold, 60 were privatized through direct sale and 16 through the initial public offering method. No one firm was privatized in the framework of the mass privatization

Table 5.3
Companies Privatized through Commercialization (in units)

Periods	IPO #	Privatized through direct sale #	total #	%	Mass privatization #	%
12/31/1990	5	1	6		0	0.0%
06/30/1991	2	5	7		0	0.0%
12/31/1991	3	14	17		64	8.4%
06/30/1992	1	5	6		114	24.5%
12/31/1992	2	15	17		5	1.5%
06/30/1993	3	20	23		0	0.0%
TOTAL	16	60	76	3.4%	183	8.1%

Computations based on *Dynamika Prywatyzacji* (1991–1993).

program (MPP). Although 183 State Treasury companies are stored and ready to enter National Investment Funds, due to the lack of state legislation, they are idle, awaiting proper decisions. Therefore, the MPP is not discussed here.

Direct sale of commercialized companies to mainly institutional (foreign and domestic) buyers is the most efficient method used so far by the Ministry of Privatization. In direct sale, buyers take a majority holding (sometimes up to 80 percent) in the firms at a price negotiated with the Ministry of Privatization.

Companies privatized by this method fall into various groups: ball bearings, breweries, cables and wires, cement and lime, confectionery, construction, electronics and telecommunications, furniture, glass, machine tools, mechanical and electrical automotive components, paints and lacquers, power engineering, pulp and paper, rubber and tire manufacturing, and shoes—all in the most attractive sectors of Poland's economy.

The most effective period of direct sale was the second half of 1992 (see Table 5.4). If in 1990 roughly one million shares were sold for $5.7 million, then in the second half of 1992 some thirty-one times more share value was distributed among strategic investors. In the first half of 1993, some 53 percent decline in the value of directly sold shares is noticeable.

The direct sale method is ideally suited for foreign investors. Thus, of the 60 firms directly sold, 31 were sold to domicile persons and 29 were sold to foreign investors. Those companies sold to foreign persons brought $329.7 million to the State Treasury, twenty-one times more than the companies sold exclusively to strategic Polish investors. The average firm sold to foreign investors in the framework of direct sale was seven times as large as the average firm sold through the direct sale method to a Polish person. Of these 29 foreign investors, 14 were from Germany, 8 from the United States, and 3 from Austria. Foreign investors also committed themselves to invest an additional $614.9 million as a future contribution to the equity. These future investment commitments, paradoxically, exceed all revenues from direct sale.

Table 5.4
Shares Distributed in the Framework of Direct Sale (in thousands of U.S. dollars)

Periods	Total price $	Strategic investors $	%	Employees $	%	Managers $	%	Foreign investors $	%	Foreign commitment #	%
12/31/90	7,188	5,752	80.0%	1,435	(20.0%)			5,750	0.0%		
06/30/91	56,983	40,691	71.4%	7,764	13.6%	5,520	9.7%	38,000	79.9%	29,100	55.9%
12/31/91	52,028	36,556	63.7%	9,520	17.9%	893	1.7%	28,850	55.5%	34,575	80.4%
06/30/92	42,742	27,228	76.5%	8,028	18.8%			24,132	56.4%	375,621	160.0%
12/31/92	234,741	179,658	62.6%	48,469	20.6%	280	2.4%	59,400	73.9%	87,921	80.5%
06/30/93	109,229	68,354	62.6%	37,415	34.2%	980	2.4%	173,592	54.4%	87,921	80.5%
TOTAL	502,912	358,199	71.2%	112,431	19.4%	7,673	1.5%	329,724	65.6%	614,938	104.8%

Computations based on *Dynamika Prywatyzacji* (1991–1993).

Furthermore, during the signing of agreements, foreign firms contractually agreed to fulfill a few additional conditions. As shown in Table 5.5, the most popular was the preservation of the labor force in the company for a period of between 12 and 18 months. This condition was mentioned 18 times out of 29 agreements. In second place was the commitment to continue investment spending according to an approved investment plan (12 out of 29), followed by the promise to reinvest profits during the next five years and the promise to provide more advanced technology, licenses, or know-how. Lastly were the commitments to preserve existing social service facilities such as day-care centers, health centers, vacation facilities, and so forth, the promise to invest in environmental protection facilities, and the promise to preserve the existing product mix.

The most financially viable firms were sold in the direct sales framework for a total value of a little less than half a billion U.S. dollars, which at the same time was less than one percent of the state equity value.

Initial public offering (IPO) is another method used by the Ministry of Privatization for the sale of commercialized companies. This method, sometimes known as the British-style case-by-case method, plays an essential role in the development of Poland's capital market and is the second main source (after direct sale) of budget revenues from privatization.

In December 1990 the first five enterprises, all relatively successful medium-sized firms, were offered for sale along the line of the British model. Foreign firms of financial consultants were involved in the valuation process and the preparation of detailed prospectuses for each company. Television advertising was used to publicize the flotation of shares and to generate interest among the public. The cost of privatization of these five companies was relatively high, estimated by some observers to be about $6.7 million, or some 8.2 percent of the value of the companies privatized. In April 1991 the Warsaw Stock Exchange started its operation with the shares of these five companies. During

Table 5.5
Value of Shares of Firms with Foreign Participation Sold in the Framework of Direct Sale (in thousands of U.S. dollars)

Company	Total price	Strategic investors	Employees	Others	Foreign investors	Invest. Commit.	Conditions to be fulfilled
1. CELULOZA	150,000	120,000	30,000		120,000	175,000	LT
2. TELFA	37,500	30,000	7,500		30,000	48,500	TLW
3. TELETRA	25,000	20,000	5,000		20,000	55,500	LTW
4. POLLENA BY.	24,211	23,000	1,211		23,000	15,000	
5. ELTA	22,807	12,454	4,595	5,760	11,632	15,000	PT
6. POLAM	22,523	15,012	4,507	3,004	15,000		
7. PZT-TELKO	21,625	1,750	19,895		17,300	24,500	LTW
8. ALIMA	16,667	10,000	3,197	3,469	10,000	11,100	LE
9. POLLENA RA.	15,822	10,000	2,762	1,060	10,000	15,000	RI
10. AMINO	12,500	10,000	2,500		10,000	17,000	LER
11. SZKLO BIA.	10,000	8,000	2,000		5,200	1,600	LR
12. OLMEX	7,857	5,500	1,574	783	5,500	14,000	LWT
13. POLLENA ND	7,500	6,000	1,500		6,000	5,000	REI
14. MIESO	7,273	5,816	259	1,198	4,000	13,000	RI

15. FAMPA	7,188	5,752	1,455		5,750	11,286	LW
16. OLZA	6,875	5,500	1,375		5,500	4,500	LT
17. SANITARIATY	6,250	5,000	1,250		5,000	14,000	LI
18. BYDGOSKIE	5,333	1,600	1,068		1,600	10,500	LP
19. POLLENA WRO.	5,250	4,200	1,050	2,665	4,200		LRI
20. ROMEO	4,865	3,892	973		3,892	700	LWI
21. MEFTA	3,922	2,352	903	667	2,000	4,000	LTRI
22. CHIFA	3,750	3,000	750		5,000	4,000	E
23. POL-FAB	3,125	2,500	625		2,500		LTRI
24. POMORSKIE	3,125	2,500	625		2,500	2,500	TI
25. FAKOP	2,750	2,200	550		2,200	35	LTWI
26. WIZAMET	1,875	1,500	575		1,500	3,500	LREI
27. MALTA	1,625	1,300	325		1,300	10,000	LRI
28. PORCELANA	1,143	800	543		800	1,000	
29. TECHMA	583	348	119	116	350		
Total with foreign	436,944	519,956	98,264	18,722	329,724	457,221	
percent in all	86.9%	89.5%	87.4%	60.6%	100.0%	104.0%	

Computations based on *Dynamika Prywatyzacji* (1991–1992) and "Zobowiazania" (1993).

Explanations:
L – promise to preserve employment during the next 12 to 36 months
E – commitment to spend funds on environmental protection
R – promise to reinvest profits during first 3 to 5 years
I – promise to spend funds in accordance with Investment Plan
P – promise to preserve existing product mix,
T – promise to provide new technology, licenses, and know-how
W – promise to preserve existing social facilities

1991, 1992, and the first six months of 1993, twelve other companies followed the same procedures and were floated on the stock exchange.

The shares sale in the framework of IPO (as shown in Table 5.6) undergoes strong fluctuations due to the long time period needed to prepare firms for sale (approximately one year) and the high rotation of persons at the post of the Minister of Privatization. As history shows, the sale regularly slowed during the first six months of a new minister's tenure and intensified during the next six months. The first six months was like a warm-up period for public offer; the next six months entailed the completion of the work. The high price of shares sold in December 1990 came at a time when Krzysztof Lis finished his one-year appointment as Chairman of the Committee for Ownership Changes (and later as Vice-Minister). The second peak in December 1991 came when Minister Janusz Lewandowski was finishing his one-year appointment. And the third peak came in June 1993, when the same person, after a half-year of forced break, was finishing his service in Prime Minister Hanna Suchocka's government. Minister Tomasz Gruszecki's half-year appointment in the spring of 1992 did not bring the expected results.

Altogether, a total value of $213.2 million shares was distributed among different types of shareholders. The general public was offered from about 30 to 83 percent of the shares in a public offer and received an average of 53.4 percent of the shares. Active private investors, some institutional and some foreign, were sought, and 5–40 percent of shares were privately placed. The employees were offered up to 20 percent of the shares at a 50 percent discount. The remaining 10–20 percent of shares were usually kept initially by the State Treasury. Initial public offering, although the most publicized method, transferred less than 0.2 percent of state equity (in 1989 prices) into private hands.

In light of the dispersion of share ownership, the involvement of active strategic investors is particularly important, as it ensures that some of the firms' owners are directly involved in their own firm's management and that problems arising from the separation of ownership and control are minimized.

As shown in Table 5.7, four foreign investors purchased a minority ownership in privatized companies. PepsiCo purchased 40 percent of the controlling stock interest in Wedel for 1,664 billion zlotys, with 65 percent of the voting power. In Exbud, a German construction company purchased 17.4 percent of the shares (the same amount was acquired by the president of the company, Mr. J. Zaraska.) In Swarzedz, Paged Westphalen GmbH, with six British investment funds, purchased 517,000 shares, which gave them a 20.7 percent control of the stock. In Koszalin, one of the German breweries purchased a stake of 30 percent of the shares in the local brewery. Foreign investment constitutes only 8.9 percent of all equity and plays more than a marginal role in this method. The lion's share of stock went to small Polish private investors. At this moment, it is practically impossible to assess how many shares in public offering were purchased by foreign investment funds or foreign natural persons in the framework of foreign portfolio investment.

Table 5.6
Shares Distributed in the Framework of Initial Public Offering (in thousands of U.S. dollars)

Periods	Total price $	Public offering		Strategic investors		Employees		Managers		Foreign investment	
		$	%	$	%	$	%	$	%	$	%
12/31/90	54,757	31,578	57.7%	2,063	3.8%	10,726	19.6%	2,063	3.8%	2,063	3.8
06/30/91	15,217	10,261	67.4%	500	3.3%	3,045	20.0%	978	6.4%	1,800	11.8
12/31/91	58,261	22,504	36.6%	15,878	27.3%	19,261	17.6%	9,445	16.2%	14,700	25.3
06/30/92	21,913	13,797	63.0%			2,974	13.6%	657	3.0%	460	2.1
12/31/92	12,783	5,050	39.5%	4,960	38.8%	625	4.8%	2,128	16.6%		
06/30/93	50,287	30,689	61.6%	5,596	11.1%	10,057	20.0%				
TOTAL	215,198	115,880	53.4%	28,997	13.6%	46,684	21.9%	15,269	7.2%	19,025	8.9

Computations based on *Dynamika Prywatyzacji* (1991–1993).

Table 5.7

Ownership Structure of Firms with Foreign Participation Sold in the Framework of Initial Public Offering (in thousands of U.S. dollars)

Company	Total price	Public offering	Strategic investors	Employees	Managers	Foreign investors
1. WEDEL	36,174	7,235	14,470	7,325	7,235	14,470
2. EXBUD	11,789	5,305	2,063	2,358	2,063	2,063
3. SWARZEDZ	8,696	6,087	435	1,759		1,800
4. KOSZALIN	1,553	445	460	307	307	460
Total with foreign percent in all	58,192 27.3	19,072 16.7	17,428 60.0	11,729 31.1	9,605 62.9	18,793 100.0

Computations based on *Dynamika Prywatyzacji* 1991–1993.

Table 5.8

Firms Liquidated through Bankruptcy and Privatization

Periods	All to be privatized #	Designated for liquidation #	Designated for liquidation %	Via bankruptcy design. #	Via bankruptcy closed #	Via privatization designat. #	Via privatization sold #	Total closed or sold #	Total closed or sold %
12/31/90	130	72	55.4%	49	0	48	0	0	0.0%
06/30/91	375	271	72.3%	124	21	122	79	100	26.7
12/31/91	753	607	80.6%	361	23	246	35	58	7.7%
06/30/92	466	310	66.5%	189	54	158	157	191	41.0%
12/31/92	528	308	93.9%	130	40	141	242	282	86.0%
06/30/93	213	196	92.0%	114	8	82	68	76	53.8%
TOTAL	2265	1764	77.8%	967	126	797	581	707	51.1%

Computations based on *Dynamika Prywatyzacji* (1991–93) and Biuro Analiz (1993).

PRIVATIZATION THROUGH LIQUIDATION

The very name "privatization through liquidation," as Gomułka and Jasiński (1993, p. 4) write, "is misleading insofar as the SOEs privatized in this way are, in fact, usually in a relatively secure financial position." Under this procedure, a given enterprise is dissolved or finally becomes an SOE because, from the legal point of view, privatization of SOEs as SOEs is impossible. An SOE could neither sell itself nor be sold as a whole, and any revenue from selling its assets had to stay in the given enterprise, preserving its value in this way. That is why, as Gruszecki writes (1990a), to be privatized, the SOE had to be either transformed into a company (commercialized) or liquidated.

When a state-owned enterprise is put into liquidation, the liquidator assumes the capacities of general manager and takes over running the enterprise. If the enterprise being liquidated is in financial straits, then the liquidation institutes bankruptcy proceedings, and this is an example of *liquidation through bankruptcy*. Should the decision be made with regard to a financially sound enterprise, the founding body then acts on the assumption that, following privatization, the assets of the enterprise in question will be better managed and put to more effective use than would the assets of a state-owned enterprise. This is an example of *liquidation through privatization*.

During three years, the Minister of Privatization authorized privatization through liquidation of 1,764 SOEs (see Table 5.8). The larger part of them, some 967, were designated for liquidation through bankruptcy; the smaller part, some 797 SOEs, for liquidation through privatization. The proportion of both methods is generally the same for all analyzed periods and scores about 55:45. Of all firms authorized for privatization through liquidation, 707 firms (82.2 percent) were completely closed or sold. Privatization through bankruptcy, although engaging more firms, constituted a much smaller share among those completely liquidated, 17.8 percent. A few factors contributed to this fact. First, potential buyers show little interest in purchasing social premises (nurseries, daycare centers, apartments, sports centers, holiday resorts), which belong to the liquidated enterprises (Groszek and Cieśla 1993). Even an attempt to transfer these properties at no fee was inefficient.

Second, the lack of experience and the low motivation of professional liquidators also play an important role. Former directors of SOEs usually serve as liquidators, and they very often appear to be influenced by old sentiments— they attempt to preserve the enterprise as a whole, no matter whether this is practical or not. They are also not personally interested in speeding up the process, in lowering its costs, or in increasing its revenues. Legal obstacles with unclear property rights add their own momentum. Obtaining an ownership title requires lengthy, costly legal procedures, and cannot be afforded by firms in a weak financial position.

The assets of liquidated companies can be sold by auction sale, by lease, and by merger.

An *auction sale* involves the sale of assets at a price contained in the application of liquidation. The buyers are generally the management and employees (or a group of employees) of the enterprise. Recently, as a means of facilitating the sale of these companies, it has become possible to pay for the assets in installments.

The *leasing* method allows for the transfer of an enterprise's assets to the company's managers and employees with the participation of other investors upon their contribution of a minimum share of capital equivalent to at least 20 percent of the capital of the former state-owned enterprise as a preset annual fee. The fee is calculated on the basis of the discounted cash flow value of the asset plus an interest rate equivalent to 75 percent of the current refinancing rate but no higher than 30 percent per annum. Eventual purchase of the leased assets is negotiable at the end of the lease period. Only Polish citizens can participate in the leaseback option, although they can draft in foreign partners/investors later.

Contribution-in-kind (merger) is the only method that allows for foreign investment. A new company, jointly owned by the State Treasury and the private or foreign investor, is set up, and assets of the liquidated enterprise are transferred to it as the treasury's share. This method may be used to found a shareholder company of the State Treasury with domestic or foreign equity and then to make shares or State Treasury stocks available to employees of the company and other individuals as well as to corporate investors. Payment for shares or State Treasury stock contributes to the national budget.

Two methods appeared to be most effective, with 560 leasing cases and 147 auction sale cases. Auction sale appears to be most frequently used in the case of privatization through bankruptcy (86.4%); the leasing method has proved to be the most popular method of liquidation for privatization (78.3%). The popularity of leasing emerges from two causes: employees are treated preferentially in terms of access to assets and in the fact that only some may have to pay for the leasing contract. The results of implementation of the contribution-in-kind method appeared to be very disappointing. This method was applied 43 times, but in reality only five enterprises were dissolved this way. Four of them were in the agricultural sphere, and no one foreign investor was involved in the merger.

The experience of the three years from 1990 to 1993 clearly indicates that privatization by liquidation is the simpler and more practical alternative available to the authorities. While the number of firms that have proceeded through privatization by commercialization has reached barely 76, the applications for liquidation approved by the Ministry of Privatization reached nine times more in June 1993. The liquidation method also allows the avoidance of a number of serious obstacles that have beset commercial privatization since the beginning of the transition.

This does not mean that the liquidation method is free of problems. The most important is the considerable number of delays in the liquidation course. Depending on the enterprise, the proceedings last from six months to almost three years, and the share of sold properties amounts to usually 15–80 percent. According to the researchers from the Research Institute of the Market Economy in Gdansk, the average liquidation process takes over two years, an average of four times longer than was planned (Dąbrowski et al. 1992).

JOINT VENTURES—INDIRECT ACQUISITION

Establishing a joint venture with a foreign firm has long been a popular mode for Polish firms. The first joint ventures (JVs) in Poland started in the late 1980s as Polonia firms owned by Polish emigrants. In 1982 JV possibilities were extended to all foreigners in the form of foreign small-scale enterprises (Law 1982). In 1986 another law allowing creation of joint venture companies was adopted (Law 1986). Both legal acts were written into the foreign investment law accepted in December 1988 (Law 1988) and revised in December 1989 (Law 1989). The Privatization Law of July 1990 opened the possibility of participation in the privatization process to foreign investors (Law 1990). Finally, a new liberal Foreign Investment Law was adopted by the Polish Parliament on June 14, 1991.

All legislation prior to June 14, 1991, was based on administrative licensing as well as on control of profit repatriation by foreign owners; those restrictions, however, were gradually softened after each revision (Bochniarz and Jermakowicz 1991). At the same time, special tax treatment for foreign firms was imposed. The essence of this policy contained extensive tax vacations (three to six years) and other tax relief. As Błaszczyk and Dąbrowski (1993) write, this created many legal abuses such as the creation of fictitious joint ventures by domestic entrepreneurs to avoid taxation.

Generally, the 1991 Foreign Investment Law was constructed on the principle of equal treatment of both foreign and domestic firms, with some minor exemptions. Firms that are totally or partly foreign-owned are subject to the same tax treatment as domestic firms. The possibility of tax vacations when investment exceeds two million ECUs exists only until the end of 1993. New foreign firms can be created only in the form of a joint-stock company or a limited liability company. Most activities need registration only.[4] The new legislation allows free profit repatriation abroad.

The start of the official privatization program in 1990 gave joint ventures in Poland new momentum. From that point, two opposite tendencies are observable: until the middle of 1993 the number of all joint ventures increased thirteen times, and the number of Polonia firms declined 15 percent (see Table 5.9).

Until the end of 1989, most foreign investments concentrated on trade, service, and the small-manufacturing sector, and represented a rather small scale of activity. In 1992 manufacturing dominated (3,463 firms, total foreign investment $916.8 million) and surpassed construction (757 units, $170.4 million), services ($151 million) and the energy industry ($72 million). Trade amounted to only

Table 5.9
Joint Venture Firms (in units)

Periods	All SOEs #	Polonia Firms #	Joint Ventures		
			All #	With SOEs #	Percent %
12/31/89	7,337	841	429	325	75.8%
12/31/90	8,347	21	968	264	21.7%
06/30/91	8,591	-6	1,195	101	8.5%
12/31/91	8,346	-69	1,956	75	3.8%
06/30/92	8,180	-52	2,852	74	2.6%
12/31/92	7,344	-19	2,483	69	2.7%
06/30/93	6,838	-2	2,673	33	1.2%
Total	6,838	714	12,556	941	7.3%

Computations based on Dynamika Prywatyzacji (1991-1993), information provided by the MoP, and "Report" (1991).

$21.1 million of the foreign equity investment. The first large joint ventures came in 1990, when Asea Brown Boveri created joint ventures with the power engineering industry plant Zamech in Elbląg and Dolmel in Wrocław. The acceleration of foreign investment engagement started in 1991 as a result of the jump start of the large privatization process on one hand and the liberalization of foreign investment law on the other. At that time, Thompson established a joint venture with the Polish kinescopes producer Polkolor in Piaseczno and invested $35 million, with a future investment commitment of $100 million. The real breakthrough occurred in 1992, when Fiat, Lucchini Group, Epstein Engineering, and 66 other foreign entities established joint ventures with Polish state-owned partners (see Table 5.10).

As shown in Table 5.11, until the end of 1991 the total equity of joint ventures amounted to $301.8 million; one year later it was more that ten times larger. Foreign investment increased ninefold during the same time; joint ventures with SOEs decreased. During the same time, the average size of the firms, measured by equity, increased more than five times.

Also during the same time, the tendency of a declining number of state-owned firms establishing joint ventures with foreign firms becomes very clearly observable. In 1989 the state-owned firms constituted 76.7 percent of all joint ventures, while at the end of 1992 they constituted only 8 percent. During the same time, however, the average size of foreign participation in these joint ventures increased tenfold. This trend continued into 1993. These tendencies are understandable. If in 1989 joint ventures were the only attractive method to improve the financial situation of SOEs, then, three years later, apparently more attractive paths for privatization existed. This creates a declining share of joint ventures in all SOEs. It still must be remembered that joint ventures with the

Table 5.10
The Five Biggest Foreign Partners in Joint Ventures in Poland

No	Foreign investor	Polish firm	Area of activity	Engagement (equity + debt)	Future investment commitment
1	Fiat	FSM	Car industry	180,000	1,800,000
2	Asea Brown Boveri	Dolmel, Zamech	Power engineering	70,000	175,000
3	Epstein Eng. Golub Co.	Mostostal	Construction	36,000	100,000
4	Thompson C.E.	Polkolor	TV sets	55,000	100,000
5	Lucchini Group	Huta Warszawa	Steel industry	34,800	56,000

Source: State Foreign Investment Agency (March 9, 1993).

Table 5.11
Growth of Joint Ventures in Poland, 1989–1992 (in thousands of U.S. dollars)

Periods	All JVs #	Equity				JVs with SOEs	Equity of JVs with SOEs			
		Total	Foreign	Aver.	%		Total	Foreign	Average	%
12/31/89	429	60,100	28,000	65.3	1.6%	325	38,480	15,500	43.1	.8%
12/31/90	968	155,300	77,200	79.6	4.5%	264	82,525	40,200	146.2	2.6%
12/31/91	3,151	301,800	155,700	49.4	9.1%	176	183,973	83,850	442.3	7.6%
12/31/92	5,335	3,168,100	1,451,200	272.0	84.8%	143	1,491,890	847,600	5,074.1	88.9%
Total	9885	3,685,300	1,712,100	169.0	100.0%	908	1,797,000	987,150	5,706.0	00.0%
%	100%	100%	46.5%			8.0%	48.8%	54.9%		
Average		363.8	169.0				1049.5	628.4		

Computations based on information provided by the Ministry of Privatization and Foreign Investment Agency (from March 9, 1993).

state sector, although they constitute only 8 percent of all joint ventures, engage 48.8 percent of all financial assets and 57.7 percent of all foreign investment.

Concerning the countries of origin, U.S. investors were the first on the list in the period 1990–93 ($804.8 million), Italian the second ($214.8 million), and Austrian the third ($133.9 million). Germany, which led in numbers, occupied the seventh position with a mere $58.2 million investment in Polish joint ventures. If we take into account future investment commitments, Italian firms ranked first (due to two big projects, Fiat investment in FSM and Lucchini investment in the Warsaw Steel Processing Factory) with $1,950 million. American investors were second ($1,134 million). French investors took the third position ($204 million). The total foreign engagement amounted to $1,712,100 (U.S. dollars), and foreign future commitments amounted to close to $4 billion (U.S. dollars). In the state sector, foreign engagements amounted to close to $1 billion, and the future commitment in state-owned firms was estimated at the level of $2 billion.

SUMMARY

Contrary to popular fears (for some) and hopes (for the others), foreign direct investment did not become the major lever of the privatization process in Poland. Despite the significant acceleration of foreign investments during 1992, FDI inflows in Poland had not met the government's expectations as of 1990–93. Poland was still behind other central European countries in terms of the relative size of foreign investments and the role of foreign capital. Altogether, foreign investors brought to Poland $2.150 billion by 1993, which placed Poland in third place after Hungary and the Czech Republic. Per capita, Poland was far behind Slovenia, Hungary, the Czech and Slovak Republics, Estonia, and Croatia.

The role of foreign direct investment in the Polish privatization program is more than marginal. From $2,150,000 of foreign investment, only $1,350,000 (62.8 percent) was used as a privatization vehicle for Polish SOEs. From this number, indirect acquisitions accounted for approximately $1 billion. The rest came from direct acquisitions: $329,724,000 from direct investment and $19,023 from IPO sale. Foreign investment did not have any impact on the privatization by liquidation sale.[5] Generally speaking, this $1,350 million of foreign investment constitutes only 1.67 percent of the whole state-owned equity in prices from 1989.

Several major flaws contributed to these results. First, legislative bottlenecks and political strife surrounding the privatization program resulted in compromise solutions between two dominating positions: securing the efficiency of privatization, and speeding privatization. Efficiency was stressed from the very beginning in the Hungarian privatization program, speed in the Czech and Russian privatization programs. Poland stands at the crossroads, trying to apply both goals simultaneously. As a result, the efficiency gains in the operation and performance of most privatized companies is rather modest as yet. Moreover, the assumed speed of privatization has not been attained either. This lack of consistency is especially visible in discussions on the mass privatization program. MPP, as a basic idea, is designed to accelerate privatization in situations with a lack of purchasing power and with obstacles that result from the slow and costly business valuations. As a result of imposing mass privatization programs, Czechoslovakia succeeded in privatizing 14 percent of their state-owned assets during one year. Similarly, in the Russian Federation, thanks to voucher privatization during six months of 1993, some 15 percent of state assets were distributed to voucher holders. Poland, which pioneered the idea of free, decentralized voucher distribution, decided to introduce a centrally regulated system of mass privatization. In this system, the MoP establishes twenty National Investment Funds (NIFs) managed in part by Western management groups. It centrally assigns enterprises participating in the program to these funds and then centrally obliges citizens to have a share participation in all these funds. Free trade of funds' shares would start after two years. Trade with enterprise shares would start after ten years, when NIFs are dissolved. The main rationale behind these schemes was the expectation that foreign management groups would purposely restructure firms to increase their financial standing and their price before their final sale. The restructuring and efficiency appeared to be more important than the speed of privatization, thus both undermining the whole original idea of mass privatization and slowing the Polish privatization process.[6]

Second, applied by the Polish Ministry of Privatization, the centralized top-down privatization model appeared to be less efficient under Polish conditions than in East Germany and significantly slowed the privatization process. The conceptual and organizational capacities of the MoP administration were very limited. MoP employed less than 30 employees in 1990, 270 employees in 1991, and 400 employees in 1992 (together with regional offices), one-tenth of the Treuhandanstalt in East Germany. The bottom-up approach to privatization bore the heavy criticism that it leads to undervaluation of companies, inside trading, and a differentiated approach to privatization. The dilemma still exists as to whether privatization and FDI should be made in a centralized way at a slow pace and with governmental constructivism, or in a decentralized way at a fast pace and with many abuses of the law, as in the Russian Federation. The Polish authorities applied a centralized approach (with the exception of privatization through liquidation) and had to pay the price with a slowed privatization pace.

Third, the Polish Ministry of Privatization fulfills three different functions: that of the State Treasury, the policy formulation creator, and the department store responsible for the sale of state-owned enterprises. This allows for a fast information flow and fast decision making; however, it makes the whole process very politically sensitive. Four elections brought four ministers.[7] Each new minister started his tenure by designing a new organization structure with changes in the top civil servants, thus introducing the feeling and actuality of chaos and insecurity. As a result, the lack of effective organization in the Ministry of

Privatization is only a poorly kept secret. The lack of clear procedures and clear organization structure creates a fuzzy division of responsibility in the area of privatization decisions, especially when foreign investments are connected with the privatization of existing state-owned enterprises. The idea of separating the last function from the three named by establishing a few incorporated privatization agencies organizationally independent from the MoP was developed by a team headed by this chapter's author during Minister Gruszecki's tenure. The MoP should have a majority of equity ownership in these agencies, and they are expected to compete for the sale of companies selected for sale by the MoP. Unfortunately, this concept, known as "Gruszecki's department stores," was never pursued by his followers.

Fourth, a high level of legal instability and uncertainty created frequent, somewhat chaotic changes and delays in legislation. The first example was the delay in passing the basic privatization law, which cannot be justified by the initial macroeconomic imbalances or the need to focus on the stabilization program (Bossak, Szanyi, and Popa 1992) The second example was a delay in the passing of a legislative framework for a mass privatization program. Originally, it had been expected that this law would be passed at the end of 1991. It was rejected by the Sejm on March 18, 1993, and again passed by the Polish Diet three months later. Other examples are restrictive land legislation, very late liberalization of the foreign investment law (only in the second half of 1991), the nationalization of casinos in the spring of 1992, and the delaying of liberalization of the insurance market for foreign firms until 1999. All these decisions are based on antiforeign sentiments, especially among the peasants' and the nationalistic parties.

Fifth, Poland is still a country with a high Country Risk Rating. According to *Euromoney* (September 1991), Poland's ratings were 43.0 (1990) and 40.0 (1991), and Poland occupied respectively the 74th and 57th positions among 133 countries. Her rating improved at some point after the debt reductions in 1994, but it still remains high. During the last four years, four governments ruled the country and five prime ministers were nominated. Solidarność, one of few labor unions registered in Poland, called more than one thousand strikes in this period. From October 1991 to May 1992, 186 of the called strike or protest actions were labeled "wild" or illegal. The bureaucracy is still formidable. The foreign investor starting his enterprise has to conform to 830 norms (598 state and 232 branch) and is expected to submit, during the preliminary project analysis, opinions from 29 administrative units in 47 different areas (Zybała 1993). To encourage foreign investment, Poland should allow foreign investors to purchase land without a permit from the Polish Interior Ministry, and Poland should return to stronger tax exemptions for foreign investors.

Sixth, Poland made steps to resolve the problem of foreign debt to private banks (London Club) in 1994, but the memory of bad debts and credit worthiness risks, as Błaszczyk and Dąbrowski (1993) stress, harms new private credits and therefore delays the privatization process and direct foreign investment.

LESSONS

By 1993, three years of experience with privatization and four years of experience with joint ventures provided interesting material for an analysis and for confrontation with the assumptions, programs, expectations, and results. Such an evaluation has to be cautious because the nature of the process is very complex and can be assessed from various points of view. The following conclusions could be drawn from the Polish privatization experience.

First, at the early stage of any economic reform leading to a market economy, there is a dilemma as to whether to privatize or to liberalize and stabilize the economy first. In Poland the decision was made in favor of liberalization and stabilization. The recession that followed had a negative impact on privatization policies and their implementation. Poland's experience seems to show that both processes should be carried out simultaneously. The sale of state property to the public for inflated amounts would remove the "money overhang" (as it did in 1990–91); the liberalization and stabilization, in turn, would lead to increased confidence in foreign investors with regard to buying property. Delays in one of these processes leads to asymmetry and negative effects at both the micro and macro levels.

Next, the Polish experience shows that between two alternative options, whether to increase the efficiency of privatized enterprises or to increase the speed of privatization, the second option should be preferred. The mass privatization program after the Czech or Russian model can accelerate this process and apparently, after privatization, increase the efficiency of new firms. The opposite procedure seems to be unsuccessful. The speed of privatization is also important because privatization, after the first enthusiasm, usually gains much political attention and is used by opposition parties as an argument against the government. The high cost of privatization, long associated with the preparation for sale, undermines social and political support for the privatization program. According to CBOS, a kind of Polish Gallup Institute, between September 1990 and April 1993 the proportion of people who thought that privatization is good for the Polish economy diminished from 44 percent to 28 percent, and the share of people who opposed privatization increased from 8 percent to 28 percent ("CBOS" 1990, 1992). The delay in privatization may have additionally increased the number of opponents to privatization, and this again may have led to the slowing of the process. The process is that the Ministry of Privatization falls under more detailed observation by the legislative body and is accused more and more of unethical behavior, of antinational preferences (due to the state property sale to foreigners), and of leading the country into economic disaster. Therefore, social and political support for privatization is of crucial importance. The Ministry of Privatization must maintain an active information campaign about the progress and positive results of privatization. It should also look for political support from main political actors.

Another lesson concerns the pace of privatization. After the fast growth of privatized firms during the first year, a clearly visible process of deceleration is apparent. This process is an effect of the growing resistance from employees to any form of privatization. Such resistance results from the fear of the unknown: losing a job, working harder, facing bankruptcy, and so forth. The positive effects of privatization, like higher individual outcomes, cannot outweigh the first negative feelings. Therefore, it is very important to reduce apprehension and encourage employees to participate in the program. From this point of view, it is necessary to provide employees with higher benefits from the SOEs' sale. The benefits designed in the 1990 Privatization Law, which stipulated that employees could acquire 20 percent of shares for half price, appeared to be too low. For that reason, in the Social Pact these benefits are increased to 10 percent of shares for free and the next 10 percent for half price. For the sake of speed of privatization, however, employees should benefit in privatization in higher shares rather than minority ownership in 15 percent of the stock. Interestingly, this problem does not exist in the Czech Republic but is observed to an even higher degree in the Russian Federation.

The experience with the first privatized companies shows that privatization does not bring dramatic economic results immediately. It does not automatically create successful management; it only creates the groundwork for it. To have positive effects from privatization, as shown by the experience with the first five firms sold by IPO, a strong strategic investor is necessary. A high dispersion of shares among a very high number of investors creates "orphan corporations" without a program and without strong "corporate governance" (Hashi 1993). The sale in tranches proposed by Lipton and Sachs (1991) for small and large investors, as applied in the case of Swarzędz, Wólczanka and subsequent firms, did not solve the problem. The Polish experience shows that the highest economic effects are provided by firms in which one clear strategic investor is identifiable. This investor brings his own management philosophy, culture, and know-how. The direct sale method best fits these requirements. The initial public offering method works best when it is combined with the sale of the majority ownership to a strategic investor (observable in the case of Wedel).

The Polish privatization experience indicates expectations that privatization will create a strong source of budget revenues appear to be unfounded. In all the years privatization was carried out, budget revenues from privatization were much below expectations. In 1991 it had been expected that revenues from the privatization program would reach 15 billion Polish zlotys (PZL). In fact, the proceeds from the sale of state-owned enterprises and assets amounted to only 3 billion PZL. In 1992 the figures were a little better but still much below expectations: 12 billion versus 4 billion PZL. The experiences of other postcommunist countries including East Germany do not in any one case support expectations concerning revenues from privatization. Privatization brings positive macro effects, but higher expenses than revenues is the price that has to be paid for macroeconomic restructuring.

One positive lesson from the Polish privatization program is confirmation of the usefulness of different privatization methods. For very large firms, mass privatization is the program most suitable. For large and medium-size enterprises, the program of commercialization combined with public or private sale is most suitable. For medium-size and small SOEs, the most promising and best suited for a country with limited capital seems to be the method of privatization through liquidation. This method seems not only the most popular but also the most effective. The method is simpler, less costly, and quicker than commercialization. It clearly stimulates savings, involves management and employees, and receives the highest social acceptance. This method leads to the rational restructuring of enterprises without causing tension between management and employees.[8]

Another positive lesson from Polish privatization is that the integration of two earlier-mentioned functions, the State Treasury function and the policy-making function in the Ministry of Privatization, appears to be very effective. The minister operates simultaneously as an owner and as a policy maker. This personal union removes the basic dilemma, observable in other post-communist countries, of whether state-owned firms should stay in the state's possession and be restructured or should be privatized. All Polish privatization ministers enjoyed fewer interinstitutional conflicts of the type observed in the Russian Federation between the Committee for Privatization (policy) and Property Funds (treasury) and between similar authorities in the Czech and Slovak Republics. This made the privatization process in Poland more efficient. Nevertheless, the Minister of Privatization still needs organizations that will carry out sale functions for him, like advertising, tenders, auctions, preparation of agreements, closing contracts, and so forth. In this respect, the necessity of establishing the incorporated privatization agencies is inevitable.

The last lesson drawn from the Polish experience is that the speed of privatization increases when the process of privatization is decentralized and carried out by local authorities.[9] This supports the bottom-up approach discussed by Gruszecki (1990b) and Blanchard and Dąbrowski (1993). This method has successfully completed privatization of small enterprises, and this method has also carried out privatization through liquidation.

NOTES

This chapter has been underwritten by Market Access Europe, The ACE Programme Management, Brussels, Belgium, in the framework of the project entitled Foreign Direct Investment and Privatization in Central and Eastern Europe. This project is carried by the Centre for International Cooperation for Development (CICD), Ljubljana, Slovenia, whose support is gratefully acknowledged. The author offers thanks to Dr. Leszek Balcerowicz (the Main School of Economics, Warsaw), Dr. Stanisław Gomułka (London School of Economics, London), Dr. Iliana Zloch-Christy (Harvard University), as well as to Dr. Munir Quddus and Dr. Marie Bussing-Burks (University of Southern Indiana, Evansville) for their comments and contributions. Special thanks go to Dr. Jane Thompson Follis for her help in the preparation of this chapter.

1. Gomułka (1993) defines spontaneous privatization as organic privatization. The two names can be used interchangeably. The spontaneous or organic type of privatization involves setting up new private businesses and the autonomous growth of existing private businesses. The latter is due to so-called asset privatization (Balcerowicz 1993), which encompasses the purchase of equipment, machinery, or transportation means from the state-owned enterprises.

2. Green-field investments made by foreign firms have started to be a big contributing factor. The largest such investments are Curtis International in electronics and construction ($100 million), Polish-American Enterprises Fund (financial engagement of $114 million), Solco Basel in pharmaceuticals ($35 million), and Procter & Gamble in sanitary products ($48.8 million plus $190 million of future investment commitment).

3. The fourth method, privatization through restructuring, started in September 1993 and is not discussed here. This method assumes that management teams—individuals and/or institutions, domestic and/or foreign—would be invited to compete with each other in terms of restructuring plans and assessments of how much a given enterprise is worth apart from salaries. The management teams would receive the share of after-tax profits that corresponded to their own contribution to the capital of the company. Additionally, the management groups would receive 70 percent of the factual growth in share prices multiplied by the number of shares sold to third parties (Stankiewicz and Jermakowicz 1991). Eleven firms have already entered into the program, and five management groups have been established exclusively by foreigners or with foreign partners (Jermakowicz, Jermakowicz, and Końska 1993).

4. The individual permission of the Minister of Privatization is given in such cases as the management of harbors, the defense industry, legal consultations, wholesale trade dealings with import of consumer goods, and the real estate market. The same rule applies to areas where domestic firms need licenses.

5. According to the State Foreign Investment Agency, the main reasons for the reluctance of foreign business entities to invest in Poland are unstable law and taxes (91 percent responses), social unrest (71 percent), high investment risk (76 percent), strong labor unions (76 percent), slow pace of Polish reforms (51 percent), excessive employees' wage claims (38 percent), and technological backwardness of the country (32 percent) (Zybała 1993).

6. The operational concept of free voucher distribution was prepared in 1988 by two Polish economists, Janusz Lewandowski and Jan Szomburg (1989). Their concept assumed that each individual would receive a voucher with a fixed face value that could tender shares at the fixed price after a quick valuation, which would be transferable and tradeable, and which could buy either shares or claims on investment funds. In December 1990 Janusz Lewandowski was nominated as Minister of Privatization, Jan Szomburg became his adviser, and both started to introduce their concept into practice. Work on the program accelerated, and many foreign experts from the World Bank, the International Financial Corporation, and some Western Banks (S. G. Warburg, J. P. Morgan) were strongly involved in this work. When I met J. Lewandowski four months later in March 1991, he shared ideas quite opposite to his original concept. He was convinced that the process should be centrally regulated with nontransferable and nontradeable vouchers, which could neither buy shares in privatized companies nor be sold on secondary markets. Even the proposal of a single central national investment fund was discussed (and fortunately this idea was strongly opposed by Professor Stanisław Welisz's statement that a similar fund had already been tried by J. Stalin). After a few years

it is still hard to evaluate what caused the change in Lewandowski's opinion. His original concept, with small modifications, was later successfully introduced in Czechoslovakia and in the Russian Federation. Poland until November 1993 was stuck with political and organization obstacles in its program introduction.

7. Apart from Krzysztof Lis, who set up the privatization bureaucracy in 1989 and 1990 but never became cabinet minister, Waldemar Kuczyński (autumn 1990), Janusz Lewandowski (1991), Tomasz Gruszecki (the first half of 1992), and Janusz Lewandowski (again in the second half of 1992 and the first nine months of 1993) were in charge of privatization.

8. According to Jacek Bukowski, Director of the Privatization through Liquidation Department in the MoP, the designers of the Polish Privatization Law, Krzysztof Lis and others, regarded privatization through liquidation as a secret weapon to accelerate the privatization process. The public's attention had to be focused on a few highly advertised public offerings, and at the same time the MoP and other founding bodies, without publicity, planned to dissolve and sell assets of hundreds of SOEs. It is now hard to evaluate if this statement is an ex post facto rationalization of what really later happened or a confirmation of the Machiavellian abilities and visionary skills of the first designers of the Polish privatization program.

9. The MoP has thirteen regional offices, but their role in the privatization process is almost exclusively subsidiary.

REFERENCES

Balcerowicz, Leszek. 1993. "The Polish Way to the Market Economy." London, un-
    published draft.
"Biuro Analiz Informuje: Proces Prywatyzacji" (Research centers informs: Privatization
    Process). 1993. *Prywatyzacja*, Warsaw, May.
Blanchard, Olivier, and Marek Dąbrowski. 1993. "The Progress of Restructuring in Po-
    land." *Post-communist Reform: Pain and Progress, WIDER 3 Report*, Helsinki.
Błaszczyk, Barbara, and Marek Dąbrowski. 1993. "The Privatization Process in Poland."
    CASE—Center for Social and Economic Research, Warsaw, March.
Bochniarz, Zbigniew, and Władysław Jermakowicz. 1991. "Direct Foreign Investments
    in Poland." *Development and International Cooperation*, vols. 7–17, June.
Bossak, Jan, Miklosz Szanyi, and Christian Popa. 1992. "Privatization in Central and
    Eastern Europe." CERGE, The Center for Economic Research and Graduate Ed-
    ucation. Faculty of Social Sciences, Charles University, Prague, December.
"CBOS: Opinie o prywatyzacji gospodarki." 1990. *Centrum Badania Opinii Społecznej*,
    Warsaw, March.
"CBOS: Opinie o prywatyzacji gospodarki." 1992. *Centrum Badania Opinii Społecznej*,
    Warsaw, December.
Dąbrowski, Janusz, Michał Federowicz, Anthony Levitas, and Jan Szomburg. 1992.
    "Przebieg procesów prywatyzacyjnych w polskiej gospodarce. I raport z badań:
    wrzesień–grudzień 1991" (Progress of privatization processes in Poland's econ-
    omy. First Research Report: September–December 1991). *Transformacja Gos-
    podarki*, No. 23, Instytut Badań nad Gospodarką Rynkową, Gdańsk.
Decree No. 123 of 1976 of the Council of Ministers. May 14.
Dynamika Prywatyzacji. 1991–1993. Department Delegatur Analiz Prywatyzacji, Min-
    isterstwo Przekształceń Własnosciowych. No. 1–16, Warsaw.

Gomułka, Stanisław. 1993. "Poland: Glass Half Full." In R. Portes, ed., *Economic Transformation in Central Europe: A Progress Report*. Brussels: Office for Official Publications of the European Community.

Gomułka, Stanisław, and Krzysztof Jasiński. 1993. "Privatization in Poland 1989–1993: Policies, Methods and Results." Unpublished manuscript. London, July.

Groszek, Mieczysław, and Stefan Cieśla. 1993. "Liquidation and Bankruptcy—Regulations, Experience, Results. The Case of Poland." Unpublished manuscript. Warsaw, April.

Gruszecki, Tomasz. 1990a. *Privatization, Initial Conditions and Analysis of the Government Programme (August 1989–mid-April 1990)*. Warsaw: Stefan Batory Foundation.

————. 1990b. "Privatization in Poland in 1990." In *Implementation of the 1990 Polish Economic Program*, Proceedings of an International Conference. Warsaw, November 15–16.

Hashi, Iraj. 1993. "The Polish Privatization Process and the Prospects for Employee-Owned Enterprises." *European Business and Economic Development*, vol. 1, part 4, January.

Jermakowicz, Władysław, Eva Jermakowicz, and Beata Końska. 1993. "The Management Contracts as a Restructuring Tool. The Polish Experience." In Marko Simoneti and Andreja Boehm, eds., *The Industrial Restructuring in Central and Eastern Europe*. Ljubljana: Central and Eastern European Privatization Network.

Law of 6th July 1982, on Conducting Small Manufacturing by Foreign Legal and Physical Persons on Polish Territory.

Law of 23rd April 1986, on Companies with Foreign Capital Participation.

Law of 23rd December 1988, on Economic Activity with the Participation of Foreign Parties—The Polish Foreign Investment Law.

Law of 28th December 1989, on the Polish Foreign Investment Law. The Law on Economic Activity with Participation of Foreign Parties.

Law of 13th July 1990, on Privatization of State Enterprises (Privatization Law).

Law of 14th June 1991, on the Companies with Foreign Participation.

Lewandowski, Janusz, and Jan Szomburg. 1989. "Property Reforms as the Basis for Social and Economic Reform. *Communists Economies*, vol. 1, no. 3.

Lipton, David, and Jeffrey Sachs. 1991. "Privatization in Eastern Europe: The Case of Poland." In *Privatization in Eastern Europe: Current Implementation Issues*. Warsaw: EDI/ICPEDC Publication.

"Program Prywatyzacji." 1990. *Ministerstwo Przekształceń Własnościowych*.

"Raport o stanie prywatyzacji w Polsce." 1992. Warsaw: Ministry of Privatization, August.

Rojec, Matija. 1993. "Foreign Direct Investment and Privatization in Central and Eastern Europe. Some Facts and Issues." Second Annual Conference of Central and Eastern European Parliaments—"Privatization and Foreign Direct Investment." July 5–6, 1993, Warsaw, Poland, CEEPN.

Stankiewicz, Tomasz, and Władysław Jermakowicz. 1991. *The Management Contract (the so-called Business Contract) as used in the Restructuring Program for Treasury-Owned Joint Stock Companies*. Warsaw: The Ministry of Privatization, the Restructuring Committee, Centrum Prywatyzacji, December.

"Zobowiazania niepieniężne kupującego wobec Skarbu Państwa" (Non-monetary obligations of the buyer against the State Treasury). 1993. *Prywatyzacja,* May and June.

Zybała, Andrzej. 1993. "Nieobecność ustprawiedliwiona" (Absence justified). *Wprost,* October 24.

6

Hungary's Road to Privatization

Gabor Bakos

In contrast to neighboring countries, Hungarian privatization has a prehistory, that is, privatization had actually begun prior to the systemic change of 1990, even in the early 1980s. Thus, for instance, beginning in the early 1980s private taxis were allowed, and restaurants, hotels, and shops were opened on a private or rental basis; further small-scale industrial activities with first up to 20 and later up to 40 employees were allowed. These small private businesses helped considerably to improve the service sector, which had a direct impact on citizens' everyday life.

Although large industrial firms remained untouched before the systemic change, nevertheless, their structure and management underwent essential changes. As for the organizational structure, from the early 1980s large industrial conglomerates and trusts were broken into smaller units; for example, the nationwide shoe industrial trust and the meat industrial trust ceased to exist, and member companies were granted an independent life. This organizational decentralization was a rather important step in creating smaller economic units for the change to a market economy. After the systemic change, these units became economic actors on the market in a real sense. This feature clearly distinguishes Hungary's case from the Czechoslovakian and the Russian case, where the systemic change meant a double challenge of not only introducing market rules but breaking up the mammoth industrial organizations, too. The continued existence of large organizations is a serious barrier to a change to a market economy, since through their monopolistic position they distort market prices as well as exert strong influence on the government, leading to the perpetuation of soft budget constraint.

The decentralization of large industrial organizations between 1980 and 1986 helped the later privatization by creating smaller units. In this period 400 new industrial enterprises were established, through splitting earlier monopolistic trusts in the food industry. Thus, 10 trusts were split into 50 medium-size units. Other enterprises formed 200 subsidiary companies; this change was promoted by tax allowances.

On the enterprise level, two novelties were introduced. One was self-management: directors could be elected by the workers, and the workers' council consisting of their representatives could make decisions in strategic and business affairs. The second was the workers' economic associations, that is, workers after their normal working hours could undertake work from other companies or even from their own. For this work they could use the company's equipment, and they could earn higher wages since these earnings were exempt from the company's progressive wage taxation. The aim of these two attempts was to use more the assets efficiently, to concentrate the activity of workers in the same profession instead of another one in the shadow economy, and to raise the workers' living standard. The results were, however, not positive. Under the new self-management, people cared more about increasing wages than production restructuring. So it could happen that a company split off one of its factories and sold it but the money was transformed into wages and not put into modernization. The workers, on the other hand, saved their energy during the normal working hours for the better paid extra work; consequently, wages rose over general productivity. This proved again that overdistribution cannot be stopped unless there is no real proprietor of the assets. The overdistribution had a dramatic consequence; it accelerated inflation.

Though the economic result of these management novelties was dubious, they nevertheless contributed to the development of managerial skills and a sense of efficient work performance on the side of workers.

Consequently, when finally the moment for privatization arrived with the systemic change in 1990, the soil was already more or less prepared for the radical move toward a market economy. An unsatisfactory feature probably was the limited number of small and medium-size companies, which in the beginning just after the 1990 change, hindered the development of flexible market relations through monopolistic positions, but soon thereafter their number began mushrooming through new private foundations.

CHARACTER

Similarly to the 1968 economic reform, the Hungarian method of privatization was conceived pragmatically, which is another distinctive feature from the privatization methods adopted in neighboring countries.

The choice of the pragmatic approach was rooted mainly in the shortage of potential domestic capital to buy up state firms on the one hand, and in the budgetary deficit on the other—or rather, the budgetary deficit-cutting pressure from the International Monetary Fund (IMF). The relationship between the budgetary deficit and privatization may at first not seem self-evident. In concrete terms, it meant the intention to use the earnings from selling state companies in a fifty-fifty proportion to cover the budgetary deficit and to upgrade loss-making state companies for later selling, respectively. Also, privatization policy makers were aware of the necessity of upgrading state companies before putting them up for sale. Therefore, the capital-raising aim became the most important point in the privatization conception. As a result, ideas about the voucher-type or cross-ownership-type privatization were discarded,[1] since there would be no new capital raised and, moreover, no new influential owners would be created. The ownership would remain shared by many; hence no change in the management could be expected. In Czechoslovakia or Russia, where the voucher type of privatization was accepted, the lengthy process of exchanging vouchers for shares and, in turn, selling the shares to real owners, or the concentration of shares in the hands of a few owners only retards privatization without resulting in any new capital.

The pragmatic approach in Hungary also solved the dilemma of privatization versus reprivatization. Namely, it was decided not to give back state firms to their earlier owners, but to give them to new ones. The only exception was land, where former owners or their descendants, according to the ownership status of the year 1947, could get back their property. Due to the method of realization, however, the original amount of land was not returned to them.[2]

The task of privatization was immense. Altogether, 2,200 state enterprises were to be privatized, of which 350 employed between five and ten thousand people. All fields of the economy were open for privatization except energy, medical care, and part of the transportation and telecommunication industries. The new government's program envisaged a three-year period for putting the 2,200 companies into private hands, which would mean the privatization of 30–35 percent of total state assets [19]. Actually, this 30–35 percent of assets to be privatized means that it was not the aim to privatize a dominant part of the economy, though the companies targeted for privatization were key ones, but rather to introduce a new, mixed ownership system in which, together with private companies, companies owned by the public sector, local governments, pension funds, and so forth, would also exist.

The 2,200 state enterprises had assets at a nominal book value of Ft 2,000 billion. The potential stock of private savings was estimated at the same time at only one-tenth of the assets' value, so it was apparent that privatization should be based on inviting foreign investors.

In order to provide a certain supervision and to operatively handle privatization, the State Property Agency was set up in 1990, which together with well-known Western auditing companies like Price Waterhouse, Barclays de Zoete Wedd, Ltd., and Baker and Mc Kenzie, selected companies for sale and prepared valuations of the companies to be sold.

Table 6.1
Transformation of State-Owned Companies

	Dec.31 1990	Dec.31 1991	Dec.31 1992	Apr.30 1993
Number of companies	27	218	602	760
Book value (bill. of Forint)	26.19	345.07	645	650.85
Value acknowledged for transformation (bill. of Forint)	41.47	465.20	1,364	1,439.18

Note: Data refer to companies belonging to the State Property Agency (SPA).
Source: [7]; for 1993: [13] vol. I, p. 100.

RESULTS

The results after three years are shown in Tables 6.1–6.3. It becomes clear that of the 2,200 companies intended for privatization, about one-third in number as well as in book value could be transformed. Although the figures may vary according to sources,[3] it can be concluded that the target could not be fulfilled; the pace was too slow. Also, the total revenue of a mere Ft 130 billion is far from the original book value of Ft 650.85 billion of the assets sold. This ratio generally reflects the real market value of the assets in sales for foreign investors; that is, the assets were sold at one-third to one-quarter of their book value. What is in accordance with the expectations is the dominant role of foreign capital, its share in the revenues being 71.4, 80.8, and 60.7 percent in the years 1990–1993.

Thanks to the free atmosphere of enterpreneurship, many new companies opened (Table 6.4). Almost 80 percent of them, however, employed less than 20 people (Table 6.5). The private sector contributed already 39 percent to the gross domestic product (GDP), with cooperatives contributing 45 percent (Table 6.6). Small private organizations are rather active in exports; in 1992 alone their deliveries rose by 126 percent.

The large number of new establishments is, however, fallacious. Many small companies are hibernating because after initial market failures they are waiting for a new opportunity, or they exist only on paper. This is supported by the evidence that their registered capital remained at Ft one million or so, which is the minimum limit required for setting up a shareholding company. In practice, the number of companies active on the market is estimated at 2,000 to 2,500, which is almost identical with that before privatization. In this sense, privatization did not contribute (or has not yet contributed) to creating a competitive market.

Table 6.2
Revenues from Privatization

	1990 bill. Forint	%	1991 bill. Forint	%	1992 bill. Forint	%	1993 bill. Forint	%
Total revenues	0.7	100.0	30.4	100.0	67.6	100.0	29.3	100.0
of which against Forints								
cash	0.2	28.6	4.3	15.9	17.5	25.9	8.8	29.5
loans	-	-	1.0	3.3	9.1	13.4	9.8	32.9
foreign exchange	0.5	71.4	24.6	30.8	40.0	60.7	11.2	37.6
compensation vouchers				2.3		3.5		

Source: [13] Vol. I, p. 101.

METHODS OF PRIVATIZATION

The law on transformation was enacted in 1989, allowing state enterprises to transform themselves into shareholding and limited companies. Transformation was stimulated by tax allowances. As a result, many enterprises transformed into smaller units, taking with them the assets and leaving behind a merely formal company office. This period of "hollowing out" continued until March 1990, and is called "spontaneous privatization" because no state authority controlled the real value of assets and the process itself. Using this opportunity, many state enterprise managers, the "nomenklatura," personalized state assets under often formal shareholding company establishment deals with foreigners, thus securing for themselves a new footing in the market economy. To provide a controlled flow of privatization, the State Property Agency (SPA) was set up in March 1990.

The SPA then launched *centrally initiated programs*. The first privatization program involved 20 companies with a total assets value of Ft 70 billion in 1990, followed by the second privatization program involving 22 companies. In addition, there was a preprivatization program aiming at retail outlets (domestic trade, restaurants, services, gasoline stations). In this latter case, accumulations of citizens helped by credits bought the assets.

Enterprise-initiated self-privatization targeted medium-size enterprises, which could find new owners through privatization consulting firms (not the SPA). In two steps, 420 and 210 enterprises were involved. The decisive majority of investors were Hungarian citizens, many of them using the opportunity of employee buyouts.

Employee partial ownership programs enabled employees to acquire the

Table 6.3
Results of Privatization

	Planned (A)	Realized as of 1993; (B)	Performance (%) (B/A)
Number of companies	2,200	760*	34
Book value (bill.Forint)	2,000	650.85	32
Revenues (bill. Forint)		128.5**	

*   30 April 1993

** July 1993

Source: Compiled from Tables 6.1 and 6.2.

shares of their enterprise. They were helped by preferential loans, installment payments, and profit tax allowances. By July 1993, 24 sales were realized.

Privatization by leasing aimed at bridging the problem of capital shortage. Here also, tax preferences were granted.

Compensation vouchers acquired by citizens as a compensation for their nationalized property or land could be exchanged for shares in state companies. The market value of compensation vouchers is only 50–60 percent of their face value, because the supply of state assets offered for exchange is limited by the SPA.[4]

The *small investor shareholder program* aimed at involving masses of citizens. According to the program, shares could be purchased by individual citizens up to a maximum of Ft 100,000 to be repaid within five years without interest. The program started in early 1994.

Privatization is being helped through special *credit facilities* to back domestic investors. One is the credit line of the National Bank of Hungary; the second is the so-called existence loan (E-loan) channelled toward small investors through the commercial banks (and refinanced by the National Bank of Hungary). To help small investors borrow through extending guarantees, the Small Enterpreneurs' Guarantee Fund and the Credit Guarantee Corporation were set up.

In 1992, as a new institution, the Hungarian State Holding Company was established. Its role is to manage the state assets to be retained in state ownership for a longer run.

A special field is *agriculture,* where *reprivatization* was allowed. Cooperative members or nonmember owners could get back their land. As for the members, the majority of them (80–85%) opted for a new cooperative form. However, the transformation, including re-forming cooperatives and privatization of land, tore up effective cooperation between the large-scale production of cooperatives and

Table 6.4
Number of Economic Entities

	1988	1989	1990	1991	1992	1993, 31 July
Incorporated economic associations	919	5,191	19,401	42,697	59,363	69,104

Source: [13] Vol. I, p. 89.

private farms. This resulted in an abrupt decline of agricultural output throughout 1991 and 1992.

EVALUATION

After three years of experience, though the overall balance when comparing results to initial targets is negative, still, there are some positive developments. The main advantage is, probably, that the pragmatic line has been followed throughout this period. This means, first, that state property was sold against effective money and created new owners. Second, it was positive that compensation claims to be satisfied by distributing state property were restricted.[5] In this context, even the manipulations of exchanging compensation vouchers for land or shares, which led to considerable loss in original property for the former owners, could be assessed positively.

In the final analysis, however, the meaning of new capital becomes dubious, since revenues from selling the state assets were sucked up by the increasing deficit of the state budget. Originally, half of the revenue was supposed to be reinvested in loss-making companies to upgrade and restructure them. There is, however, no evidence that such a recycling of revenues took place.[6]

The main deficiency in the privatization process was its slowness, according to widespread criticism. The general explanation for this is that the three-year privatization plan was too ambitious and that in fact a longer period is necessary, so that an emerging new wealthy class will be able to buy up state assets. More concrete reasonings blame the SPA for the slowness (for example, [11]), saying that its small staff was unable to handle the process or that the SPA consciously delayed it. In addition, however, it must be mentioned that negotiations concerning a given enterprise usually stumbled on two difficult problems. The first concerned the real value of the assets. Foreign investors were in a stronger position because of the oversupply of assets. But the SPA did not want to agree on a bargain sale to foreign investors. Thus the idea to invite them for an open tender did not realize. According to Table 6.3, the SPA could in the end get an average of only one-fourth to one-fifth of the book value of the assets, and even less in cases where the assets were sold to foreign investors. Second, in several cases negotiations were delayed on the side of the enterprise, where employees

Table 6.5
Concentration of Labor Force

No. of employees	Share of companies in total (%)
300 -	2.9
51-300	8.5
21-50	10.5
- 20	78.3

Source: Central Statistical Office, 1993. Author's estimates.

were averse to privatization, fearing severe restructuring and dismissal. Considering the ensuing massive unemployment, however, the slowness is hardly to be blamed; a faster process would have caused more severe problems.

During the early 1990s the world economy entered a depression together with a contracting capital supply. Western Germany, one of the most powerful potential investors, became involved in the reconstruction of Eastern Germany as a result of unification, while the start of privatization in Czechoslovakia, Poland, and Russia deflected capital flows from Hungary.

Remarkable also is the fact that foreign capital entering Hungary in competitive industries preferred establishing new facilities to buying existing assets, which is a further factor in the slowness of privatization [7]. A striking example is Magyar Suzuki, which trained unskilled labor and erected a new plant instead of using existing capacities in the automobile industry [3]. These faciltes mean a real market restructuring and help create a competitive market. Those foreign investors who bought existing assets usually conserved the market structure. They were for the most part content with buying a company and acquiring its market share in the Hungarian economy, so they just kept running production or instead sold their own products through the sales network of the purchased company. Since the Hungarian market is shared by usually two to five companies, the foreign investor at once acquired 20–30 percent of the market, securing for himself an oligopolistic position whereby the need to modernize equipment or increase the market share was not compelling. Due to this circumstance, the participation of foreign capital did not always promote competitive markets.

An interesting phenomenon is the considerable growth of private savings since the systemic change (1990). There are various reasons for this, such as the increased saving propensity due to the emergence of a new wealthy class and the higher risk in everyday living for lower-income masses. Concerning the real increase in savings, there are several estimations, one even denying any increase but attributing it to the ballooning effect of inflation.[7] For our purposes, the certainty is, however, that citizens were not willing to spend their savings for buying shares. And when buying securities, they instead bought state bonds,

Table 6.6
Composition of GDP by Sectors (percent)

	1991	1992
Economic associations in private ownership	15	18
Small entrepreneurs	18	21
Private sector (without cooperatives)	33	39
Cooperatives	8	6
Total private sector	41	45
Economic entities of central and local governments	59	55
GDP total	100	100

Source: [13] Vol. I, p. 92.

guaranteeing a safe interest rate. But due to the fact that these bonds were covering the deficit in the government's budget, this private spending was just a part of the crowding-out effect; that is, it was not put into investments to boost restructuring or production. Such spending has no connection with helping privatization.

Toward the end of 1993, we witnessed a situation where the good and attractive state enterprises had already been sold and the loss-making ones left over were unlikely to attract any interest from investors irrespective of the price. It is then that privatization arrived at a stalemate when no new methods or further liberalization could be helpful.

At this point an important question had to be raised. Was it necessary to sell the well-functioning, successful companies? In developed Western economies, privatization is usually preferred if the performance of a company is deteriorating; through privatization an upgrading is expected from private initiative. Actually, the conception of privatization was a pluralistic system with different forms of ownership, allowing for state ownership, too. Probably it would have been a better solution to put on sale at the beginning just a few good companies to attract interest, and to retain other successful ones, because in the case of selling successful companies, the new (foreign) owner laid off employees, thereby increasing unemployment.

The stalemate can be characterized by a relative surplus of free capital, mainly due to the loan facilities to help privatization, on the one hand, and a supply of loss-making companies, on the other. However, the free capital is not willing to buy these companies because of the high risk connected with them. Under such circumstances, a further pumping up of the demand side would not be useful. To solve the problem, M. Tardos suggests the "privatization of the privatization,'' that is, setting up holdings as managing umbrellas for upgrading bad companies, thus making them attractive for investors [15].[8] Another proposal suggests applying cross-ownership [11].[9] The problem with these proposals is that the holdings, in fact, would be state management bodies, probably with administrative functions performing like company management did in the old system, lacking any interest in strategic development and capital efficiency. Cross-ownership, again, would be of no benefit for acquiring capital or creating new managerial interests. Finally, leasing or a trusteeship might seem to a foreign investor a less expensive venture than investment, but he would not be able to escape from restructuring the company. In order to accomplish this, he would inevitably have to invest, if not his own money, then funds from loans. And here we come back to the problem of investments.

In this case, however, investments are not a purely monetary phenomenon, where nominal and real interest rates, level of bank reserves, and so forth, have to be taken into consideration, because the bad enterprises have not been cost, profit, or interest sensitive; in many cases they are not even interested in their own survival. Such a situation can arise because of the naive hope that market liberalization and privatization will automatically lead to effective management and restructuring. It was also a serious failure of privatization that, contrary to the principles, the revenue from selling state assets was not recycled in order to upgrade bad enterprises. This happened, actually, not by accident. Namely, to upgrade bad companies, some strategic vision is necessary, be it called industrial policy. But since the 1990 systemic change, industrial policy was considered a foe to the change to a market economy, a foe resembling the perpetuation of earlier governmental intervention. Therefore, it was impossible to work out, or at least to apply any industrial policy. Hence, at present investment decisions must be a result of an industrial policy, and for this, an industrial policy concept must be worked out.[10]

NOTES

1. Cross-ownership means that companies mutually own the decisive stake among themselves. This form is especially developed in Japan, where banks, trading houses and insurance companies are also participants. A Japanese professor, M. Iwata, suggested that post-socialist countries carry out privatization through cross-ownership. His main concern was the capital shortage and the goal of preventing inflationary money emission. Therefore, according to his plan, the bank would give targeted money in form of credit to enterprises, which could use this money only for buying shares from each other. When selling their shares, enterprises could also use their earnings for buying the shares of other enterprises. Finally, at the end of the process, the money would be withdrawn (*Business Review,* Hitotsubashi University, vol. 30, no. 1, August 1990 [in Japanese]).

2. Land was not returned at its natural size but through a value adjustment. First, original owners received a so-called compensation certificate with a face value that could be exchanged for land. This exchange was organized in the form of a licit procedure during which the land's price increased. Consequently, the certificate's unchanged face

value could only buy a parcel of land smaller in size than the original one. Thus, proprietors could recover in terms of size only about one-tenth to one-fifteenth of their original land.

3. According to another source (*Népszabadság,* 20 May 1993) only 18.69 percent of the Ft 2000 billion state assets could be privatized. It must be admitted that data in different sources vary; e.g., the National Bank estimates the total revenue from privatization for 1992 at Ft 67.6 billion (Table 6.2), while the report of the SPA puts it at Ft 72 billion ([7] p. 23).

4. A. Kurcz, "Keszpenz helyett" (Instead of cash), *Figyelö,* 30 September 1993.

5. The suggestion to grant compensation for political damages, for example, was declined.

6. As Mr. Imre V. Csuhaj, cabinet chief of the privatization minister, explained in an interview, the SPA must transfer from the revenue a considerable part to the state budget for deficit covering; further, it must pay dividends on the enterprises under the SPA (payable to the state budget) and contributions to central funds like the employment fund, the regional development fund, and the agricultural fund; help small banks and insurance companies; and make contributions to write off debts of enterprises to be privatized. In the final balance, expenditures exceeded revenue for 1993 ("Tobb a kiadas, mint a bevetel" [Expenditures exceed revenues], *Népszabadság,* 28 January 1993).

7. A. Simon calculates that in 1992 savings in real terms were on the same level as in 1989 [14].

8. In fact, this is an old idea of Tardos, suggested by him earlier during the discussion on privatization in the late 1980s.

9. Mihalyi also mentions the leasing, trusteeship agreements.

10. N. Tardos, in his lecture on Hungarian transition [17], went one step further than in his article [16], where he wrote only about holdings and other new forms of privatization by mentioning explicitly the necessity for an "industrial policy," leaving its content, however, unspecified.

REFERENCES

[1] "A magyar ipar jövöképe. A kormány középtávú iparpolitikája" (Future vision of Hungarian industry. The government's medium-range industrial policy). Budapest, Council of Ministers, January 1993.

[2] Bakos, Gabor. "Reforms versus systemic transformation in Eastern Europe." Paper for the International Studies Association's 31st Convention, Washington, D.C., April 1990.

[3] ———. "Japanese Capital in Central Europe." *Hitotsubashi Journal of Economics,* December 1992.

[4] ———. "After COMECON: A Free Trade Area in Central Europe?" *Europe-Asia Studies,* November 1993.

[5] Erdös, Tibor. "Válságelmélet és válságellenes gazdaságpolitika" (Crisis theory and anti-crisis economic policy). *Közgazdasági Szemle,* no. 9 (1993).

[6] ———. Lecture on Hungary's Transformation. Delivered at the Institute of Economic Research, Hitotsubashi University, 10 November 1993.

[7] Éves jelentés az állami vagyon privatizációjáról, Állami Vagyonügynökség, 1992 (Yearly report on the privatization of state property). Budapest: State Property Agency.

[8] Gaál, Gyula. "Lépésvesztés—államháztartás 1992–1993-ban" (Losing pace—state budget in 1992–1993). *Közgazdasági Szemle*, nos. 7–8 (1993).

[9] Hegedoüs, Miklós. "Egyensúlyvesztés—növekedés nélkül" (Disequilibrium—without growth). *Figyelő*, 21 October 1993.

[10] Kornai, János. "Transzformációs visszaesés" (Transformational recession). *Közgazdasági Szemle*, nos. 7–8 (1993).

[11] Mihályi, Péter. "Plunder—Squander—Plunder." *Hungarian Quarterly* (Summer 1993).

[12] Oblath, Gábor. "Veszélyes vizeken" (On dangerous waters). *Figyelő*, no. 19 (1993).

[13] *Recent Economic Developments in Hungary. Vol. I: Report, Vol. II: Tables.* Budapest: National Bank of Hungary, September 1993.

[14] Simon, András. "A megtakaritási csoda" (The savings miracle). *Figyelő*, 24 July 1993.

[15] Tardos, Márton. "A rendszerváltás és a közgazdaságtan" (Systemic change and economics). *Közgazdasági Szemle*, no. 9 (1993).

[16] ———. "Kiút a mélyülő gazdasági válságból" (Way out from the deepening economic crisis). *Népszabadság*, 4 October 1993.

[17] ———. Lecture on Hungarian Transition. Delivered at the Institute of Economic Research, Hitotsubashi University, 12 October 1993.

[18] "Több a kiadás, mint a bevétel" (Expenditures exceed revenues). *Népszabadság*, 28 January 1993.

[19] "Tulajdon és privatizáció" (Ownership and privatization). *Figyelő*, 23 August 1990.

7

Foreign Direct Investments in Hungary

György Csáki

The revolutionary events of 1989, the high expectations and hopes of 1990 as well as the disillusions of 1991 have placed central Europe—namely Poland, the former Czechoslovakia, and Hungary—high on the economic and political agenda of the early 1990s. The collapse of the former communist regimes and the disintegration of the former Soviet empire obviously carry with them a new map of Europe. The novelty is obvious, but the new frontiers are fairly obscure.

The new democracies are eager to join the community of the democracies and market economies: their hope is that there will be no more than a few steps on the road toward Europe. But awareness of the difficulties has rapidly increased as these countries reflect upon such worrisome signs as the massive amount of deutsche marks invested in the "eastern Landers of the Federal Republic" without immediate success, the 60 percent abstention at the Polish parliamentary election in October 1990 and the left-wing government in late 1993, and the unexpectedly slow path toward a market economy as well as the deepening tensions and later the "amicable divorce" between the Czech Republic and Slovakia and the general view that Hungary is Europe's most pessimistic people, although Hungary had by far the best odds at the starting line of the course toward the market economy. All of these factors are realistic, important signs of the difficulties to be overcome.

"The growing stress on home-grown capitalism means closer attention must be paid to solving the dilemma *how to build capitalism without capital.*"[1] Therefore, major capital inflow is a must and even a predominant condition of any kind of economic modernization. Because of the significant indebtedness of the country and the historical evidence of the advantages of foreign direct investments (the inflow of technical know-how and professional skills and abilities, the possibilities of joining global networks of research and development [R &

D], production, and marketing, etc.), a massive flow of foreign direct investments is of predominant importance for Hungary, as for all the economies of transformation in Central and Eastern Europe, in the establishment of a modern market economy. In fact, foreign direct investment is a precondition for Hungary's joining the world economy.

As far as Hungary's abilities to absorb foreign direct investment are concerned,

it occurs against a macro-economic background that is more stable than in Poland and similar to Czechoslovakia's (although more burdened with external debt). It follows the liberalisation of domestic prices and external trade. But in addition to these points, which are broadly matched in both Poland and Czechoslovakia, it has the advantage that other reforms, in particular of financial system, are at a much more advanced stage. This has to give Hungary considerable advantages. . . . implementing privatisation ahead of the development of domestic financial markets is very much a second-best option, something that Poland and Czechoslovakia are right to choose given the constraints they face, but to be avoided if possible. Hungary is in the fortunate position of being able to privatise at a time when her financial system is already the most advanced in eastern Europe.[2]

And

up to now Hungary has relied the most on foreign investment to flesh out the private sector, attracting more than $5.5 bn since 1988, over half of the total for central and eastern Europe. But foreign investment alone cannot transform the economy. Most Hungarian consumer goods companies attractive to multinationals have been sold and foreign economic penetration has come close to its political limits. Increasingly foreign investors are looking to Poland which has four times the population of Hungary or the Czech Republic—and an economy stimulated by the dynamism of home-grown Polish entrepreneurs.[3]

In light of the fairly large advantage Hungary had enjoyed in 1988–1991 over its Central European counterparts in Poland and (then) Czechoslovakia, the Hungarian transition process from the former centrally planned, command economy toward a fully and truly market economy can serve as an example for the latecomers. Hungary has been—it is more and more obvious nowadays—a test country in Central and Eastern Europe that served as an example for Western direct investments in the region. An example, however, is not necessarily seen as a model. Yet we hope that our analysis of the Hungarian transition, its success as well as its failures, can contribute to a general understanding of the transitional development and thereby can help the other Central European countries avoid the same obstacles.

THE GLOBAL ECONOMIC CLIMATE OF THE EARLY 1990s

Foreign direct investments, FDIs, for short, from countries in the Organization for Economic Cooperation and Development (OECD) amounted to as much as

USD 195,936 million in 1989, reached its highest ever amount of USD 215,132 million in 1990, and then declined to USD 172,167 million in 1991, amounting to no more than USD 137,446 million in 1992. This latter amount is less than two-thirds of the amount for 1990.[4]

The dramatic decline of Japanese FDIs and the important decline of those from unified Germany could not be balanced by the significantly increasing foreign direct investments of some less important capital exporting countries, such as Austria, Belgium, and Denmark.[5] After Japan's FDI of USD 44,130 million in 1989 and the record of USD 48,024 in 1990, no more than USD 30,726 million was realized in 1991, and this decreased to the extremely low level of USD 17,248 in 1992—a 60 percent decline in two years' time. German FDIs totaled USD 23,128 million in 1990 and only USD 18,015 million in 1992.

Irrespective of the general decline, there has been an important increase of FDIs in Central and Eastern Europe (including the former Soviet Union): six months prior to March 1993 as many as 979 transactions were executed, at a total investment value of USD 11.2 billion, compared to the 350 deals and USD 8.5 billion in total investments in the previous half-year period. The United States led the ranking, making, in the twelve months prior to September 1992, 219 deals and investing USD 8 billion.

It is fairly surprising that the second largest Western investor in Central and Eastern Europe is Italy, followed by the UK, and Germany is only in fourth place, with some USD 3.6 billion investment.[6] As far as investment methods are concerned, establishment of joint ventures is the most popular, although more and more green-field investments have taken place, and the speeding of the privatization process allows Western investors to make a growing number of takeovers too.[7]

As far as Hungary is concerned, the picture is fairly rosy; at least, foreign economic diplomats are content with the performance of their own investors. But really, prior to March 1993, Japanese investors put more than USD 300 million into Hungary, while no more than USD 231 million in Austria and USD204 million in Portugal. German firms invested DEM 467 million in Hungary in 1991 and DEM 826 million in 1992, although German foreign direct investments declined by almost 22 percent. The United States has provided 40 percent of the total foreign direct investments in Hungary so far, with especially large transactions (the GE-Tungsram takeover, the Marriott Hotel take-over, the two US West joint ventures in mobile telephones, the GM engine and assembly plan, etc.). French investors provided USD 90 million investments in Hungary in 1990, USD 120 and 130 million in 1991 and 1992, respectively, and are likely to invest as much as USD 190 million in 1993.[8]

The Threefold Motivation of Foreign Investors

Market Expansion. In several sectors, especially in consumer goods production, Central and Eastern Europe can be the only new market for Western investors. Four central European countries (i.e., Poland, the Czech Republic, Slovakia, and Hungary) constitute a market of 65 million people. According to Bundesbank Research, the annual growth rate of the region will be 6 percent between 1990 and 2020 while, the current members of the European Community will not realize more than 3 percent per year growth in the same period of time.[9] Even more important, from a Central European base, it is much easier to reach Eastern European countries, especially that of the former Soviet Union. It is pretty obvious, if one takes a look at the list of breweries, soft drink companies, chocolate and biscuit producers, sugar and vegetable oil companies, large multinational franchise systems in catering, large retail trade networks, the representatives of household chemicals, and so forth, that almost every important international company is present in the Central European countries, generally in each of them.

Cheap Labour Force. Central European production can be fairly cost effective due to the fact that the labour force is pretty cheap although very well educated, skilled, and experienced, and several other costs, such as real estate prices and fees for public utilities are very much lower than in Western Europe or North America. At the same time, important tax incentives make Central European production even more cost effective. By far the most important item is the cheap labour force.

Taking the productive sectors in 1992, the average monthly wages were equal to DEM 403 in Hungary, DEM 254 in (then) Czechoslovakia, and DEM 218 in Poland. At the same time, fringe benefits took about DEM 259 in Hungary, DEM 147 in (then) Czechoslovakia, and DEM 149 in Poland. Taking the same costs in the former West Germany—DEM 3.575 for monthly average wage and a further DEM 3.000 for fringe benefits—total wage costs in Hungary in 1992 were equal to some 10 percent of that of the former West Germany.[10] Nobody would have expected that the relative productivity of the Hungarian labour force was no higher than one-tenth of the German one. In 1992, hourly average wages were equal to USD 16.25 in Japan, USD 15.5 in Germany, USD 13.5 in the United States, and less than USD 10 in France, while in South Korea (after having tripled in the recent ten-year period), they were equal to USD 5.5. The central European average was approximately the same as that in Mexico. Total production costs (per unit of output) were 35–40 percent lower than in Germany.[11]

There are promising examples of the impact of Western investments on developments in manufacturing. In 1990 the Swedish-Suisse engineering giant Asea-Brown-Boveri (ABB) took over the totally bankrupted Polish Zamech, which had high administrative effectiveness and low quality of production and had suffered continuous losses. As of 1992, ABB-Zamech was profitable and the quality was equal to Western European standards, while costs were about half of that of the German ABB affiliates; therefore production increased no less than 50 percent in two years' time. The French electronic giant Thomson had the same experience in Poland. In order to compete with Asian competitors,

Thomson produces its 14- and 20-inch television screens in its Polish affiliate Polkolor. Hungarian Suzuki planned to export as many as 10,000 Suzuki Swift cars to Western Europe in 1994, out of a 40,000 yearly production; another 10,000 cars were slated to be exported into Eastern European countries. GM considers its Hungarian plant, which produces engines for the Opel Astras and Opel Vectras, to be one of its most effective European plants. And not only are international giants searching for investment possibilities in Central Europe and in Hungary; a medium-sized German manufacturing company has relocated most of its machine tool production to Hungary because of the 35–40 percent lower production costs.[12]

According to the French analysis quoted earlier, Poland, the Czech Republic, and Hungary are "tigers in the courtyard" and can easily become the "new Hong-Kong" since their labour forces are as skilled as that of developed Western European countries, with one-tenth of their wages. Therefore, in the long term, Visegrád countries will likely be specialized in the production of products that require a high degree of skilled and well-qualified labour.[13]

Although pros are important, there are cons too. According to a recent survey made by Deloitte Touche and Tohmatsu, most of the Western businessmen find it too risky to invest in Central and Eastern Europe; half of the sample found the political and social climate inconvenient, and they faced a significant lack of adequate financial services dominated by Germany, France, and Italy. The survey also clearly showed the importance of the pre-war historical relations in the region on the distribution of investments. The most attractive feature of investment in Central and Eastern Europe was business opportunity, which was the very first motivation for 70 percent of the investors. The most attractive country in this survey was Hungary: 55 percent were interested in Hungarian possibilities and about 33 percent were interested first of all in Hungary. Czechoslovakia occupied the second place (with 49 and 29 percent respectively), while Poland was in third place (with 48 and 26 percent respectively).[14]

Major investments based almost exclusively upon a cheap labour force are pretty risky, and superficial comparisons can cost a lot. "Hungary's comparative advantage in its efforts to expand the economy is its relatively cheap labour force. This was also the case with the four East Asian economies (South Korea, Taiwan, Hong-Kong and Singapore) in the initial stage of their development and it is to some extent the case now." But experiences are not necessarily examples to be followed:

The attitudes of workers in the East Asian economies and Hungary differ greatly. The first four [East Asian] countries had no previous experience with organized labour. Indeed, both in Taiwan and South Korea, the violent repression of organized labour was and remains the norm. A more individual, European culture such as Hungary's, however, might more easily result in labour unrest in the case of economic growth, which would diminish any comparative advantage in labour rates. Moreover, 40 years of state ownership in Hungary has resulted in a deterioration in work discipline, which is strong in the East Asian countries.[15]

Major cultural/traditional and organizational differences have caused problems between workers and management at the Hungarian Suzuki Company. Japanese organizational habits seemed pretty strange to Hungarian workers, while Japanese management felt the low level of devotion to work of the Hungarian workers, was strange. Hungarian workers found unacceptable the low level of wages and obligations to put in extra working hours, and so forth.

The Intention to Roll Back the Asian Export Boom in Western Europe

According to Western European economic forecasts, in the second half of the 1990s, newly industrialized East Asian countries will launch a huge and effective export offensive—in both Western European and North American markets. Therefore, developed industrialized countries of those regions must find ways and means to make significant cuts in their production costs. Translocation of a fairly large part of their manufacturing industries to Central and, to a lesser extent, Eastern Europe would be a self-evident solution. "Fortress Europe" can serve as a real fortress against an East Asian export offensive only if Western Europe allows Central European countries to join them. In this case—the most welcome scenario for the interested Central European countries—European car production, electrical engineering, and maybe even electronics would be defended against the East Asian export offensive.

FOREIGN DIRECT INVESTMENTS AND JOINT VENTURES IN HUNGARY: ENGINES OF DEVELOPMENT

Before World War II, 20 percent of the Hungarian domestic assets had been owned by foreigners, but the postwar nationalization process practically ended the operation in Hungary of any kind of foreign working capital.[16]

In 1968 New Economic Mechanisms, that is, a new system for economic direction and management, was introduced in Hungary. And as is well known, it was the very first major economic reform in the so-called socialist countries of Central and Eastern Europe. This New Economic Mechanism represented, so to speak, the first step toward a market economy. But not as much was achieved at that time as had been expected. In the early seventies, the Soviet leadership under Brezhnev curbed the reform process, even though it could not be brought entirely to a halt. A relatively limited private sector began to take shape under the form of working associations of private people and joint ventures. A certain kind of entrepreneurial spirit emerged among the population.

The foundation for joint ventures was first made possible by a decree of the Finance Minister issued in 1972. However, the conditions for such ventures were unfavourable. Every two or three years, some improvements were made in the conditions for establishing joint ventures, and from January 1, 1990, they can definitely be described as attractive. In the seventies, the objectives of Hungarian-Western joint ventures were primarily aimed, from the Hungarian perspective, at the import of modern technologies and at improvement in the balance of payments (the achievement of a positive balance of transactions). Due to internal economic conditions and inflexible regulations, and in view of the emergence of conflicting goals, between 1972 and 1979 only three Hungarian-Western joint ventures were established. From the late seventies and the early eighties, more emphasis was placed on the goal of earning foreign exchange, but what was most important was that legal regulation became more flexible and more facilities were introduced. As a consequence of these more attractive regulations, the establishment of 15 new joint ventures between 1979 and 1982 occurred. Further progress was made in the mid-1980s; more legal relief as well as allowances for the establishment and operation of duty-free zones resulted in the establishment of 36 more joint ventures in the 1983–1985 period. In 1983 the amount of foreign working capital investments totalled about USD 25 million in Hungary, and the corresponding amount in 1985 was more than USD 80 million. Up to December 31, 1987, 130 joint ventures had been established; in 1988 140 new ventures and in 1989 700 more were established. In September 1990, over 2,500 joint ventures and fully foreign-owned companies were on record.

Due to the "hunger" for capital on the one hand and the almost total lack of domestic capital on the other hand as well as the need for major technological improvements and the possibilities of joining the global networks of the world economy, it is a must to attract foreign direct investments in their most common form currently in Central Europe: the East/West corporate joint ventures.

There is a real rush to establish joint ventures, and the increase in capital inflow is fairly impressive: till the end of 1988 no more than 270 JVs were established in Hungary, with a total of USD440 million in capital inflow. The number of JVs increased to 5,370 in 1990. Two years later, as of December 31, 1992, as many as 14,471 joint ventures were already operational. The amount of foreign assets in Hungary was equal to about USD 5.4 billion at the end of the same year. In the first half of 1993, the total amount of foreign investments in Hungary reached USD 6.06 billion, the capital inflow was some USD 650 million and the number of companies with foreign equity participation was more than 16,500. (See Table 7.1.)

Actually, the greater part of the FDIs realised up to 1993 in Central and Eastern Europe went to Hungary. Hungary's advantage is obviously due to its recent two decades of step-by-step development toward a market economy, making it the most developed financial system in the region, as well as to the existing regulatory frameworks that were put into place as early as 1987–1988. This is quite obvious if we take into consideration the decrease of those advantages in 1992–1993—especially compared to Poland and the Czech Republic, which are more and more popular among (mostly West European) investors.

As far as the amount of invested foreign working capital is concerned, in 1993 the United States was the greatest investor (29 percent), with a few but

Table 7.1
Foreign Direct Investments in Hungary

Year	Number of companies with foreign equity participation (at the end of the year)	Average foreign capital invested in foreign owned companies USD	Total amount of foreign direct investments USD million
1972-1984	30	n.a.	40
1985-1986	75	n.a.	70
1987	130	1.0 million	80
1988	270	1.5-1.6 million	430
1989	1.370	500-600.000	550
1990	5.370	240-270.000	900
1991	10.370	300-320.000	1.700
1992	14.471	400.000	1.641
1993 (1st half)	16.564	311.000	651
		TOTAL:	6.062

Source: The author's own calculations—based upon data issued by the Central Statistical Office and the Ministry of International Economic Relations.

large investments (see Tables 7.2 and 7.3), such as the GM assembly plant (USD 275 million), the takeover of the Tungsram Light Co. by the General Electric (USD 225 million), Guardian Glas (USD 100 million), Citicorp Budapest (USD 40 million), Sara Lee (USD 65 million), and the US West investments (USD 55 million in the 450 Mhz mobile telephone and a further USD 48 million concession fees paid already for the Mhz 900 mobile telephone, where USD 100 million in investments was expected). The second largest investor was Germany (20 percent)—second in the amount of capital but by far first in the number of investments. (There have been about 4,000 fully or partly German-owned companies in Hungary.) The third is Austria (14 percent) which is followed by France (7 percent), Italy (6 percent), Japan (5 percent), the Netherlands (4 percent), and Great Britain (4 percent).

As far as the sectorial distribution is concerned (see Table 7.2), 66 percent of the foreign direct investments went to industry (including food and beverage), 11 percent went to financial services, 9 percent to foreign and domestic trade, and 3 percent to telecommunications. Taking the number of JVs, trade and (both productive and personal) services were well ahead in 1993.

ACHIEVEMENTS AND PROBLEMS IN 1993

According to the Central Statistical Office (CSO), in the first half of 1993 as many as 2,093 joint ventures had been established. Since the CSO does not register capital increases (only the initial equity capital), data don't reflect more than trends. As the data show, the greatest number (53.9 percent) of JVs had been established in domestic and foreign trade, but with a fairly low amount (17.1 percent) of initial equity capital. (See Tables 7.4 and 7.5.) Fully 15.7

Table 7.2
Distribution of Foreign Direct Investments (1993)

	According to the investor countries (%)	According to sectors (%)	
USA	29	Industry (incl: food)	66
Germany	20	Financial services	11
Austria	14	Trade (both foreign and domestic)	9
France	7	Hotels and office buildings	7
Italy	6	Transports and telecommunications	3
Japan	5	Others (including agriculture)	4
Netherlands	4		
Great-Britain	4		
Others	11		
TOTAL:	100		100

Source: Author's calculations based on data provided by the State Property Agency, 1993.

percent of new JVs had been established in manufacturing, with a much higher foreign capital involvement (35 percent), while some 21 percent of newly established JVs were operating in services, representing about 36 percent of the total direct investments realized in Hungary in the first half of 1993.

According to the State Property Agency, in the first half of 1993 about USD 160 million came from foreign investors, of which 88.5 percent were invested in manufacturing.

In the evaluation of the Ministry of International Economic Relations, it is a clear sign of the increasing trust of foreign investors that while in 1992 1,531 fully foreign-owned companies were established (representing 37.3 percent of the total of newly established JVs), in the first half of 1993, 957 100 percent foreign companies had been set up—representing 45.7 percent of the total. As of mid-1993, there were about 4,000 fully foreign-owned companies operating in Hungary.[17]

As far as the geographical distribution of foreign investors is concerned (see Table 7.2), we have adequate data since 1992 (prior to that year, CSO hadn't monitored it). In the period from 1992 to the end of 1993, according to the number of newly established JVs, Germany, Austria, Italy, and the United States were the leaders, while according to the amount of invested capital, the United States was the leader, followed by Germany, Austria, France, and Italy. The major investors in 1993 were Audi (Germany), Marriott Hotels (United States), PCA Packaging Co. (United States), Pertodyne (United States), Linamar (Canada), Hantarex (Italy), Daikin (Japan), Totalgas (France), and US West (United States).

It is more and more difficult to monitor FDIs because (1) the share of large multinational corporations is increasing, (2) there is significant reselling of as-

Table 7.3
Major Foreign Direct Investments (more than USD 20 million)
in Hungary (as of 12/31/92)

Investor	Invested amount (USD million)	Further investment to be expected (USD million)	Sector-activity
General Motors	250	25	engines, car assembly
Suzuki	225	25	car assembly
General Electric	200	25	lights
Allianz (Germany)	125	---	insurance
Prinzhorn (Austria)	110	---	pulp and paper
Guardin Glas (USA)	110	---	glas
Siemens	100	---	electronics, engineering
Feruzzi-Unilever	80	20	vegetable oils
Sanofi (France)	80	25	pharmaceutical
Ford Motors	80	---	car spare parts
German syndicate	80	---	Hotel (Kempinski)
Alitalia	75	---	airlines
Elektrolux	60	20	refrigerators
Amilum (Belgium)	60	---	industrial alcohol
Raemsta	60	10	tobacco industry
Messer Griesheim	55	---	industrial gas
Sara Lee (USA)	55	10	cafe and tea trade
Begin Say (France)	55	15	sugar
US West	55	---	mobile telephone
Primagaz	50	---	PB-gas
Daewo	50	---	bank
Alcoa	50	20	aluminium
Atex (Russia)	50	---	bus production
Agrana (Austria)	45	---	sugar & alcohol
Coca-Cola	45	---	soft drinks
Philip Morris	40	---	tobacco
Cofinec (Fr-It)	40	---	printing
CIB (England)	40	---	bank
Wienergraber	35	---	brick
British-America	35	---	tobacco
CP (Britain)	35	---	foreign trade
Interbrew (Belgium)	35	---	brewery
Nestlé	35	---	biscuit
Brau (Austria)	35	15	road construction
Linde (Germany)	35	15	carbonic acid
Voest Alpine	30	---	steel
Henkel	30	---	household chemicals
Citicorp	30	10	bank
Aegon (Netherlands)	30	10	insurance
Stolwerck	25	30	biscuits, chocolates
Strabag (Austria)	25	---	road construction
Zwack (German)	25	---	liqueurs and alcohols
Schwenk (Germany)	25	---	cement
Tetra Pack	25	---	packaging
Holderbank (Suisse)	25	---	cement
Pankl-Hoffmann	25	---	meat
Julius Meinl	25	10	retail trade
Ansaldo (Italy)	20	---	electric engineering
Bran (Austria)	20	10	brewery
Schöller	20	---	dairy
Audi	---	200[*]	car engine
Columbian Chemicals	---	50	chemical industry
Hantarex (Italy)	10	15	electronics

*The contract was signed in late 1992, and the investment was realized in 1993.

Source: Figyelö, January 28, 1993.

Table 7.4

Newly Established Companies with Foreign Equity Participation in the First Half of 1993

Number of companies contribution	Equity capital	Out of which non-cash	Equity capital in hard currency Out of which non-cash contribution	
M i l l i o n H u n g a r i a n F o r i n t s				
Fully foreign owned companies 957	8,962.6	905.1	8,717.5	908.7
Joint ventures with foreign and 1,136 domestic owners	14,181.0	3,012.5	8,252.2	778.4
TOTAL: 2,093	23,143.6	3,947.6	16,969.7	1,687.1

Source: Author's estimates based on information provided by the Ministry of International Economic Relations.

sets, (3) characteristic figures for the investments are generally regarded as business secrets.

From an American point of view,

the major increase of recent years can be attributed to the favourable terms and conditions, of which just a few will be mentioned here: highly favourable profit taxation, full guarantee (including an American OPIC guarantee) on foreign partner's property in Hungary, exemption from duty for physical contributions, possibilities for the firms to acquire real estate, existence of a stock exchange in Budapest, arrangement for the transfer of profits without limitation, activity of the Joint Venture Club aimed at the representation of interests, and last but not least the fact that since 1968 there have been many people with an entrepreneurial spirit in Hungary.[18]

SOME "ADVERSE CONSEQUENCES"

One of the most frequently mentioned "adverse consequences" of the legal authorization for the establishment of relatively small firms has been the spread of so-called phantom joint ventures in great numbers. These are very small ventures that are often established in the private sector in such a way that the Hungarian partner buys the convertible currency necessary for the establishment of the venture on the black market and asks one of his or her foreign partners (or relatives) to enter into a formal association with this money. In this case the Hungarian will be the real and only owner of the firm. The established joint venture receives tax allowances, and it receives part of the profits in convertible currency, irrespective of its hard currency earnings. While there are legal provisions to allow only legal entities as foreign partners, in practice it is very easy to handle this problem. More than half of the joint ventures are small firms with a total capital of USD 20,000 to 30,000, and many of them could be considered

Table 7.5

Newly Established Companies with Foreign Ownership in the First Half of 1993

Sector	According to the number of joint ventures	According to the share of the foreign owner
	(%)	(%)
Agriculture	3.58	3.00
Manufacturing	15.72	35.06
out of which:		
food and beverage	1.62	8.41
textile	2.63	2.53
paper and printing	3.39	3.41
chemical industry	1.48	4.45
machinery	3.68	12.01
Construction	5.54	8.62
Trade (domestic and foreign)	53.94	17.10
Real estate	11.66	19.00
Personal services	1.91	0.27
Others (services)	7.65	16.95
	100.00	100.00

phantom joint ventures.[19] Of course, we can speak about some "adverse consequences," but on the other hand, one of the major goals and incentives of Hungarian economic policy is to promote the establishment and operation of small and medium-size ventures. The former Hungarian prime minister declared a desire to see as many as 100,000 small ventures in Hungary in three to five years' time. Why is the relatively large number of small joint ventures necessarily an adverse consequence of the miscalculated legal regulation, and why do we not accept it firstly as a natural phenomenon, and secondly as a positive improvement in the economic climate in Hungary? In my view, the fact that half of the joint ventures are relatively small is not at all bad or negative. If the Hungarian government intends to promote small ventures in every branch and form, it has to promote small joint ventures too. On the other hand, this phenomenon does not show anything more (or anything less) than that Hungarian entrepreneurs are both eager to find and capable of locating the most advantageous legal form for their personal ventures. As far as the so-called phantom joint ventures are concerned, they are not damaging to the economy at all. The main reason for their existence is related to the lack of full convertibility of the Hungarian currency. Thus, a realistic view about the impact of joint ventures in the Hungarian national economy is a necessity in the government and scholarly assessments.

A second common criticism is that the share of productive JVs is relatively low compared to the share of services. This is totally false in my view. The sectoral distribution of joint ventures reflects global trends fairly well. As András Inotai points out, "FDI started everywhere in the service sector. Low capital requirement and low risk, accompanied by unsatisfied or growing internal demand for the products of this relatively underdeveloped sector motivated investment decisions."[20]

It is quite difficult to obtain any relevant information about the total employment impact of the joint ventures in Central and Eastern European countries. However, it is pretty obvious that FDIs and JVs have not had a positive quantitative effect on employment while taking over or buying into a Hungarian company; more advanced technologies and higher organisational standards require a smaller labour force. On the other hand, green-field investments have had positive effects. According to Professor M. Simai, it is not only the number of people employed in joint ventures that is worth mentioning, since, their skill level was higher than the average of the national firms.[21]

It is not a directly adverse effect but a much less positive effect than expected that "foreign capital appearing in Hungary relies not on Hungarian subsuppliers but on its own home-based subsidiaries and satellites. Appropriate stimulation should lead to foreign capital becoming involved in the development of the Hungarian small-business sphere that acts as a subsupplier for it."[22]

Certainly the most harmful pattern in the foreign capital inflow is that "recently, *foreign capital has liquidated a great part of the social and educational bases of the enterprises taken over.*"[23]

THE LEGAL FRAMEWORK OF FOREIGN DIRECT INVESTMENTS

The former Hungarian government[24] realized that in order to promote foreign direct investment and increase the number of joint ventures, a modern and internationally competitive legal and regulatory framework was necessary. The Bill on Business Organizations and the Bill on Foreign Investments in Hungary, both approved in 1988 and put into effect as of January 1, 1989, intended to fulfill this aim.[25] Beyond these general rules, Hungary has mutual investment protection agreements with the following countries: Austria, Belgium, Cyprus, Denmark, Finland, France, Germany, Greece, Italy, Korea (Republic of), Spain, Sweden, Switzerland, United Kingdom, and Uruguay. Hungary joined the MIGA, and OPIC guarantees were extended to Hungary in 1989.[26] The establishment of the legal framework for foreign investments was so successful that Hungary has become a real "tax haven."

Officials of the Ministry for International Economic Relations declared that although foreign investment activity is dynamic, it would be much more effective to promote not simply the import of capital but the improvement and growth of certain given activities. Therefore, changes are intended to channel foreign direct capital into those fields where the need is the greatest for new technologies and marketing skills as well as for the improvement of management.

Béla Kádár, Minister of International Economic Relations, stressed in an interview that the Hungarian situation is controversial: there are always many bureaucratic obstacles hampering direct capital imports, and on the other hand there are several unjustified legal advantages compared to domestic ventures, which are unsustainable. Kádár emphasized that there is no special branch that

Table 7.6
Joint Ventures with Hungarian Equity Participation Registered Abroad

Till the end of the year	Number of JVs	Equity capital (HUF million)
1989	78	4.329
1990	159	1.422
1991	367	1.998
1992	398	2.176
TOTAL:	1.002	9.925

Source: Ministry of International Economic Relations, April 1993.

should be closed to foreign capital but also that there is no national economy that offers tax reductions or/and other special allowances to foreigners "forever." "We would support those investors who intend to establish a sustained economic partnership with the Hungarian economy, and not those who will simply exploit the special tax reductions in order to make huge profits and to repatriate them out of our country."[27]

As far as improvements in the legal framework for foreign investments in the recent past are concerned, first of all, major allowances have all been maintained: JVs receive a 60 percent tax allowance in their first five years of operation and 40 percent in the second five years, provided that they were registered prior to December 31, 1993, their registered capital is at least HUF 50 million (USD 50,000), and the share of the foreign owner is a minimum 30 percent. Companies granted this tax allowances may not reduce their assets during the following five years.

Beyond December 31, 1993, new JVs to be established are eligible for tax allowances only if they have assets of over HUF 200 million (USD two hundred thousand) or plough back more than HUF 50 million (USD fifty thousand) in dividends. But even in this case, the maximum tax allowance cannot be more than 38 percent.[28]

As far as taxation of foreigners is concerned, in the Appendix No. 6 of the Law on Corporate Taxes (which came into force on July 1, 1992), it is unambiguously defined in the agreements on the avoidance of double taxation, in which case the activity of a firm registered in another country can be considered as a business venture. No taxation obligation applies to a foreign venture that does not engage in trading activity and does not conclude contracts but just conducts promotional activities for the parent company's product. Where there is no agreement on the elimination of double taxation, a foreign firm is to pay taxes according to the relevant Hungarian rules, naturally on the activities carried on in Hungary. As of January 1, 1993, with a view to avoid tax evasions by charging their activities with high costs and producing deficits, the basis of assessment was established at 10 percent of the foreign venture's receipts where its profit is less than that.[29]

Concerning personal income taxes for foreign private persons, agreements on the elimination of double taxation are also to be considered as authoritative. If there is no such agreement, foreigners may enjoy some special advantages thanks to the finance ministers' agreements, which include reciprocal allowances. The foreign employees of foreign companies and JVs are to pay their tax in Hungary even if they don't receive their salaries here, but only part of it is transferred to Hungary. Seventy percent of the income earned from such a company registered in Hungary is considered taxable. Foreigners who are considered self-employed are also obliged to pay taxes to the local authorities.[30]

HUNGARIAN–EAST EUROPEAN JOINT VENTURES AND HUNGARIAN DIRECT INVESTMENTS ABROAD

Hungary, benefiting from its market knowledge, traditional technological links, relatively developed national economy, as well as its good international economic positions, is playing a key role in capital flow to former CMEA countries.

As far as Hungarian–East European JVs are concerned, among those which are registered in Hungary there are two large ones; AREX-Holding from Russia bought a majority share in the large Hungarian bus producer Ikarusz (accompanied by the Central European Investment Corporation, a Hungarian-American JV). This deal is worth about USD 50 million. A Hungarian-Russian consortium bought the Orion Radio and Electronics Company, which was under liquidation. The three buyers are the Hungarian subsidiary of the Russian oil and gas company Yuganskneftegaz, a newly established limited liabilities company founded by the ORION management, and a Hungarian electronics company. The Russian owner has 83 percent of the shares and the Hungarian owners have 8.5 percent each. The new company name is Yuganskorion Ltd. The new firm intends to export to the former Soviet Union but has high hopes of attracting Western partners too as suppliers or—in the longer term—as investors.[31]

As far as Hungarian capital export is concerned, their number and equity capital have increased. As of December 31, 1992, more than 1,000 JVs were operational—with Hungarian equity participation abroad representing a cumulative USD 100 million. The greatest number of JVs were established in the former Soviet Union, but other East European countries were also popular with Hungarian investors. (See Tables 7.6 and 7.7.) It is quite obvious that Hungarian capital export to East European countries is continuously increasing, while capital exports to developed Western countries has declined in the recent past.

Most of these Hungarian enterprises are involved in small-scale trade, in many cases barter trade. Their main assets are knowledge of markets and knowledge of the availability of goods available in exchange for Hungarian products. Given the existing shortages in some of the neighbouring countries, foodstuffs, canned food, fruit juices, fresh fruit, clothing, shoes, and medicines are easily sold there. It is a much greater problem to find the goods to be delivered in exchange. A great advantage to Hungarian businessmen in this matter is the presence of

Table 7.7
Geographical Distribution of Hungarian Capital Exports

Countries	1991		1992	
	Number of JVs	Capital (HUFm)	Number of JVs	Capital (HUFm)
CIS	52	1.191	133	924
Romania	87	92	101	53
Czechoslovakia	64	48	52	37
Germany	45	159	36	122
Austria	31	109	20	100
USA	10	27	8	24
Great Britain	12	95	3	17

Source: Ministry of International Economic Relations, April 1993.

Hungarian minorities in the neighbouring countries. Some of these JVs are using Hungarian machinery and equipment. Because of the fairly different technological standards, Hungarian secondhand equipment is quite often welcomed as useful in the neighbouring countries (as Western secondhand technologies are welcomed in Hungary). In many cases, the secondhand equipment (machinery or personal computers, copiers, and telefax machines) is the noncash contribution of the Hungarian investors (as is the case for a lot of small Western-Hungarian JVs registered in Hungary).

Hungarian capital is important for the neighbouring countries.

• In Slovakia, 1.6 percent of foreign direct investments actually came from Hungary, while 9.3 percent of the JVs have Hungarian owners. In 1992 the amount of Hungarian working capital in Slovakia was no more than USD 1.1 million, but the number of JVs was growing exponentially.
• In Romania, 1.1 percent of foreign direct investments came from Hungary, and there are Hungarian partners in 4.3 percent of the JVs registered. As of the end of 1992, the cumulative value of Hungarian direct investments in Romania reached about USD 5 million.[32]
• In the Ukraine, there were 70 JVs with Hungarian equity participation, and Hungary had HUF 1 billion (USD 10 million) in foreign direct investments in its largest neighbour in the first half of 1993. Hungarian businessmen have been most welcome to the Ukraine; there is no legal or political obstacle at all hampering the development of cooperation, including capital flows.[33]

Although the establishment of companies abroad is subject to an outdated regulation dating from 1975, which prescribes conditions that are virtually impossible to meet by private investors, the Ministry of International Economic Relations in practice does not raise difficulties for FDI outflows. To set up a company abroad, to buy a stake in a foreign company, to increase or decrease the share, or to establish a branch are all subject to ministerial licensing. The Ministry of International Economic Relations weighs factors as to whether foreign investment can be safely invested in the targeted economy, whether foreign investments are guaranteed, and whether profits can be repatriated in full or in part according to the international practice. If all these conditions are met, the licence is automatically issued.

In the three years from 1990 to 1993, significant Hungarian capital export into neighbouring countries took place. Nevertheless, its extent was pretty far from that of the end of the nineteenth century and also far from the high expectations of the late 1980s. Market knowledge, business abilities, and close personal contracts cannot replace capital exports, a capacity which Hungary lacks.

CONCLUSION

In the formerly centrally planned economies in the first half of the 1990s, joint ventures with foreign equity participation had not yet met the final objectives originally set by the partners, particularly to serve as a major instrument to boost economic growth and better incorporate national economies into the world economic system. In most of the Central and Eastern European countries the macroeconomic impact of joint ventures has been much less significant than was expected in 1989–1990. This situation is partly attributable to the international political and economic environment prevailing in the early 1990s—to the lack of market access, essentially.

It is not possible to build up an economy or to privatize an enterprise if that enterprise has no markets. It is not possible to invest, to build market shares, to build networks, to establish a basis of operations without the prospect, even if not the certainty of outlets. Grant aid without market access does not assist recipients in their endeavour to join the world economy. It does not help them produce tradable goods. It only leads to a permanent subsidizing of their consumption—enabling them to buy imports in excess of what they can finance through their permitted exports. This is certainly not development nor integration, and it is costly to tax payers.

If the western half of Europe fails to provide market access for East European exports, these countries will be unable to reimburse or even service their debts, their currencies will not become convertible and this could in turn provoke a financial crisis in the West.[34]

Joint ventures tend immediately to help generate necessary corrections in the legal and regulatory systems in the Eastern European countries and in Hungary. While legislative and regulatory measures in the former socialist countries have made the legal framework more appealing for international joint venture operations, representing an important new phase in East-West relations, it also has become clearer that the framework must be regularly studied and corrected. This form of international cooperation requires sufficient flexibility on both sides due to differences in the working mechanisms of the economic systems and sometimes in the motivations and interests of the partners. In light of all these problems, it is evident that some issues, such as the still complicated and inflexible economic environment, the lack of full convertibility of national currencies, and the rigidity of mechanisms of international economic relations, will have to receive greater attention in the former CMEA countries.

As far as Hungarian partners in joint ventures are concerned, they are generally satisfied, since in the joint ventures established so far, the companies' balance positions have improved and profits have increased in comparison to previous periods. Joint ventures have contributed to technical and managerial modernization, which could not have been financed without such ventures. Total company exports have increased in comparison to the previous export performance of the Hungarian partner alone, and labour productivity has increased on a relatively major scale.

Foreign partners who are involved in Hungarian-based joint ventures can consider the following positive effects and consequences. They can establish market positions in Hungary (and also in the rest of Central and Eastern Europe). Taking this trade expansion into account, longer-term relations, learning experiences, and references can help them to acquire further orders in the near future. By participating in Hungarian-based joint ventures, Western partners can gain experience in the socioeconomic peculiarities of Central and Eastern European national economies.

Despite some adverse effects, the establishment, the large-scale dispersion, and the increasing number and economic importance of joint ventures for the Hungarian economy are evident. Clearly, forming JVs is a potentially advantageous method of development for Central and Eastern European countries. The establishment of joint ventures as a major form of foreign direct investment can successfully contribute to the decrease of foreign debt, to technological improvement of the host economies, importation of badly needed managerial, organisational and marketing skills, and access to the world market. The current political situation and economic reasoning are also favourable for importing working capital to establish large numbers of joint ventures. "Two major questions appear to dominate future discussions. Have extraordinarily generous tax holidays been determined adequately or should these benefits be reduced? Should some sectors be given priority treatment, and if so, which sectors and according to which criteria should sectors be identified as 'priority fields' for FDI?"[35]

Almost every given country of the region can be described as a tax haven for foreign direct investments, due to special laws governing taxation. These laws exist because the region is not attractive enough for massive capital imports and because foreign businessmen here have to face extra difficulties while doing business, such as an infrastructure that is in extremely bad shape. On the other hand, the experience of Hungary shows that not special tax breaks but a sound economic policy, a solid legal framework, and good market expectations could be the decisive factors in attracting foreign direct investment. It is quite obvious that special tax reductions for foreign ventures (including joint ventures) can be economically harmful and politically counterproductive.

As Inotai stresses,

The fundamental point is that domestic and foreign capital should receive the same liberal treatment. Essentially, it is not that foreign capital's possibilities should be restricted, but that domestic capital's chances should be considerably enhanced. A sound, well-functioning, and efficient network of domestic enterprises is also a key factor in attracting international capital.[36]

The flow of foreign working capital is largely influenced and motivated by market considerations. From this point of view, the Central and Eastern European national economies are not attractive enough for Western investors.

Hungary seems to be obliged to share its former leading role in foreign direct investments with the Czech Republic, but remains fairly attractive for foreign investors, due to its solid legal framework and a two-decades-long (although a sometimes contradictory, step-by-step) market-building economic policy. Hungary has the longest experience in establishing and operating joint ventures with developed partners (since 1968). The financial (especially banking) infrastructure is better then anywhere else in the region, the private sector's share of the national economy is 15 percent, there is a growing entrepreneurial community, and the privatisation process is moving ahead. Hungary is in a good position to play the role of "bridge," that is, to act as an honest broker between Western and Eastern partners in order to promote the development of real pan-European cooperation. The advantages that Hungary has vis-à-vis other Central and Eastern European countries can be maintained only if a stability-oriented, market-based macroeconomic policy remains, the privatization process moves ahead, the entrepreneurial mentality is strengthened, economic policy is stable and transparent for both foreign and domestic investors, a growth-oriented (and at the same time world market–based economic policy) is run, and the necessary infrastructural development is realized.

In order to promote the further development of joint ventures, foreign partners need much more fair and credible information about their potential Hungarian partners. It is extremely hard to negotiate and conclude agreements with Hungarian partners. The Hungarian economy badly needs an efficiently functioning banking system; the tax system is complicated, sometimes even confused; and currency exchange restrictions need to be lifted.

Hungary is not yet an "investment haven." That is, business is more difficult than in a well-functioning market economy. An American businessman, Fred Martin, published his experiences in the United States, and the article was reprinted in Hungary.[37] According to Martin,

Budapest is a marvelous, dynamic city with two million inhabitants. In spite of all its charm it is very difficult to arrange our affairs, and that is true for both foreigners and residents. Most of the Hungarians do not have a phone, and if they do then there is no free line. It takes hours to buy a railway ticket and to change a plane reservation is even a torture. . . . To establish a joint venture you need six months; the approvals of two Ministries and the registration of the Court is also needed. And even taking into account all the above difficulties and inconveniences, Hungary is by far in first place concerning the legal framework of foreign investments in comparison to the other Eastern European countries.[38]

Without quoting all the interesting examples of his difficulties, I want to quote one further statement by Martin:

Paradoxically, the larger the business is, the easier the negotiation is. If you contact the top of the hierarchy, you can more easily cross the jungle of bureaucratic legislation and regulation. . . . The Hungarian system is no more a communist one, but it is not a capitalist one either. It is in a transitory period, therefore, it is more difficult to conclude an agreement than a year ago.[39]

Concerning industrial development and foreign direct investment in industry, another Western analyst, C. Boffito, states that

in 1988, average industrial investment in Eastern European countries was over 40 per cent of total investments. After the productive restructuring, which will give greater importance to investing outside the industrial sector, this percentage can drop to 30 per cent. Under the hypothesis that private foreign capital contribution is significant if its flow equals ten per cent of industrial investment, industry's need for foreign investments would be USD 9 billion in 1993 and USD 11 billion in 1997. On the basis of recent experiences in this field from Greece, Portugal and Spain, this seems easily obtainable.[40]

He further states that "support for private investments in Eastern Europe can take two forms, in various combinations: concessionary credit through interest account contributions and credit and capital conferment insurance for foreign enterprises and joint ventures."[41]

To set up a joint venture, joint motivation is needed. Although there is a fairly great interest in the West in further investment possibilities in Hungary and in Central and Eastern Europe, the economic and political risks and uncertainties deter major potential investors from investments. The honeymoon of 1989–1990 is obviously over. It is obvious that Western governments might and should offer much more concrete and effective support and guarantees to their investors than they have so far. In Central and Eastern Europe, the current task is to establish a market economy; however, these countries are in a pre-market-economy situation. In this situation, the support cannot be either an educative activity or a simple granting of further credit. More concrete governmental support is needed to surmount the gap between the current economic conditions and a real market situation. If the investors have to wait for the emergence of a Western-type market economy, the lack of investments will hamper the emergence of a market economy in Hungary and in the rest of the region. Only a mutual governmental and internationally institutionalized cooperation can resolve this problem.

NOTES

1. Nicholas Denton, "Hungary Builds Capitalism without Capital," *The Financial Times,* November 1, 1993, p. 13, italics mine.

2. Giles Keating and Jonathan Hoffman, "Privatisation Theory: Hold Back for a Swift Advance," *Central European,* April 1991, p. 34.

3. Denton, p. 13.

4. OECD, *International Direct Investment Statistics Yearbook, 1993* (Paris, 1993), p. 14.

5. Ibid.

6. This is not taking into consideration, of course, the former GDR, the now "five eastern Landers of the Federal Republic," which absorb the bulk of German investment possibilities.

7. *East European Investment Magazine,* different issues and data bank.

8. See "A Round-Table of Foreign Economic Attachés in Budapest," *Invest in Hungary,* June 1993.

9. See *Osteuropa-Themen,* December 29, 1992.

10. "Europe de l'Est: la stratégie des firms allemands," *Problemes Economiques,* no. 2.343, September 29, 1993, p. 27.

11. György Gonda, "A nyugati tőke Kelet-Europában" (Western capital in eastern Europe), *Magyar Hirlap, Pénz-Plusz-Piac,* September 18, 1992, p. vii.

12. "Az érem három oldala—mit keres a tőke Kelet-Európában?" (Three sides of the coin—what does the capital search for in Eastern Europe?), *Figyelö,* October 15, 1992, p. 32.

13. "Europe de l'Est," p. 29.

14. "Kelet-Európai befektetések: még nagyok a kockázatok" (Investments in Eastern Europe: Risks are always high), *Figyelö,* October 8, 1992, p. 21.

15. Károly Okolicsányi, "Lessons from the East?" *Banks & Exchanges,* February 4, 1993, p. 12.

16.

There were some isolated examples of joint ventures which were not nationalized after the political changes. In Hungary, a small railway line connecting a Hungarian and Austrian region, (the Györ-Sopron-Ebenfurt Railways Ltd.), and two firms in industrial services, IBM Ltd. and SKF Ltd., remained joint ventures on the basis of two pre–Second World War laws related to joint stock companies (the Laws of 1875 and of 1930). As far as IBM Hungary is concerned, it is a fully owned subsidiary of the IBM World Trade Corporation, and traces its origins to 1936 when it was established as "Elektromos Könyvelőgépek Kft" (Electrical Accounting Machines Ltd.) and renamed in 1939 to Watson Electric Accounting Machines Ltd. IBM Hungary assumed its present name in 1947. During the following 40 years of the Cold War it maintained the banner of free enterprise despite overwhelming odds. It has been one of the extremely few Hungarian fully owned companies that was not nationalized, and remained the only IBM subsidiary in the COMECON-countries that did not close down in the last forty years. A large firm in vacuum technology (Tungsram Ltd.) also remained an international joint stock company with foreign minority interest. The experiences of these ventures were not considered as precedents concerning the overall situation, they were "islands" isolated from the rest of the economy.

Mihály Simai, "New Dimensions of Joint Ventures in the Socialist Countries of Eastern Europe during the 1980s," unpublished manuscript, Institute for World Economics of the Hungarian Academy of Sciences (IWE-HAS), Budapest, 1989, p. 3.

17. An interim report of the Ministry of International Economic Relations, Budapest, July 21, 1993.

18. István Toldi-Ösz, "Working Together: Joint Ventures in Hungary," *Tözsde Kurír,* October 11, 1990, p. 17.

19. Mihály Simai, "Foreign Direct Investments in the Hungarian Economy—1990 (The Legal and Economic Environment)," unpublished manuscript, IWE-HAS, Budapest, 1990, p. 17.

20. András Inotai, "Foreign Direct Investments in Reforming CMEA Countries: Facts, Lessons and Perspectives" (Paper presented at the Conference "Multinationals in Europe and Global Trade in the 1990s," organized by the American Institute for Contemporary German Studies and the Johns Hopkins University, Washington, D.C., September 4, 1990), pp. 5–6.

21. Simai, p. 51.

22. Sándor Maka, "Main Trends in Foreign Investment Flow," *Banks & Exchanges,* September 17, 1993, p. 17.

23. Ibid., italics mine.

24. That is, the last communist government of Hungary.

25. Accompanied by a Cabinet Decree on the possibilities of foreigners buying real estate and by several regulatory decisions concerning the exchange mechanism.

26. See Simai, p. 33.

27. "Kádár Béla a kül- és belföldi tőoke egyenjogúságáért" (Mr. Béla Kádár stands for the equal rights of the foreign and domestic capital), *Világgazdaság,* November 28, 1990, p. 5.

28. *Banks & Exchanges,* August 6, 1993, p. 16.

29. Ibid.

30. *NAPI Gazdaság,* August 3, 1993, p. 3.

31. See *Banks & Exchanges,* August 13, 1993, p. 12, and *Heti Világgazdaság,* October 23, 1993, pp. 109–10.

32. Árva, László, "Magyar tőkekivitel a környező országokba" (Hungarian capital exports into the neighbouring countries), *Magyar Hirlap,* July 23, 1993, p. 15.

33. Béla Dajka, "Egymilliárdos tőkekivitel Ukrajnába" (One billion worth capital exports to Ukraine), *Magyar Hirlap,* October 30, 1993, p. 15.

34. Jacques Attali, Preface in Albert Bressand and György Csáki, (eds.), *European Reunification in the Age of Global Networks* (A joint publication of *Promethee* [Paris] and *IWE* [Budapest]), 1993, p. 8.

35. Inotai, p. 15.

36. Ibid., pp. 16–17.

37. Fred Martin is the president of Bancroft Group, a New York–based consulting firm that intended to set up a relatively small venture in Budapest. In February 1990, he decided to open up a shop for copying machines. He published his experiences in the *New York Times Magazine,* December 16, 1990. A shorter version was published in the Hungarian daily *Népszabadság,* December 22, 1990.

38. *Népszabadság,* p. 9.
39. Ibid.
40. Carlo Boffito, "The East on the Rise from the Rubble of the Wall," *Cooperazione,* Supplement to no. 98, p. 14.
41. Ibid.

8

Investment Policy and Privatization in Bulgaria

Georgi Smatrakalev

The development of the modern world with all its shifts and reforms has been influenced a lot by the changes in the postsocialist economies. The striving in these countries for rapid change of the system and the establishment of a free market economy has been closely connected with the investment policy.

This chapter will try to clarify the contemporary policy of the Bulgarian government for increasing the investments in the country and for privatizing the state sector. To this end, the chapter will briefly examine the investment decision-making process during the period when the economy was centrally planned and the imbalances it has created. Some light must be thrown also on the structural policy as the prerequisite for investment and future privatization. The methods for privatization in Bulgaria depend a lot on the political structure and interests in the country.

It is necessary to examine also the tax policy as one of the major components in the future privatization and investment policies. Changing the taxation policy in Bulgaria is one of the basic objectives in the economic reform, a prerequisite for other changes. Changes in property relations are of great importance for improving the economic activity and attracting foreign investments.

GENERAL VIEW OF INVESTMENT POLICY IN THE PAST

In Bulgaria, for the whole period of totalitarism (1944–89), investment, as all other activities in the economy, was strongly centralized. The allocation of the resources was not made according to economic considerations, but according to the single-minded ambition of a government or party official. The struggle between the leaders on national and local levels became a struggle for gaining funds for the development of their native places. This was the main way of making investment decisions concerning place allocations.[1]

Allocation of Resources

As far as sectorial allocation is concerned, things were not much different except that what mattered was the knowledge of the leaders or, much more accurately, the different types of information they gathered from their subordinates. For example, when some of the policy advisors wrote on the gains in chemistry or electronics, this suddenly became the priority branch in the next five-year plan and attracted almost all the investment funds. In reality, these investment decisions also depended a lot on the people among the leadership in the socialist bureaucracy. If they were convinced about the importance of certain directions, the same directions followed the investment decisions.

Investment Regulation

It was only in the last decade that the bureaucracy started considering the investment policy and its regulation more carefully.

Through the regulation of investments, much better conditions can be achieved, from the economic point of view, for allocation of the funds and expansion of the production unit. Investment is a compound, comprehensive, and significant process for any economy. In the contemporary world, its direction is of vital importance for achieving efficient terms of growth. Underestimation of the investment policy can lead to imbalances in the economy.

Clearly, the set of investment objectives defines the economic structure of the country and its future development.

The dynamics of investment activity are defined by two types of factors: first, long-term relatively fixed necessities of the economy, and second, the short-term requirements of the economy.

The impact of these factors influences at different rates the components of the investments. For instance, investments for expanding the scale of production can react very quickly to every change in the economic situation. On the other hand, investments in reconstruction, the dynamics of which are defined by the accumulation of fixed assets, cannot be influenced by ups and downs in economic activity.[2]

CHANGES IN THE ECONOMIC POLICY

All these considerations are made in relation to the change in the economic policy in the country. After the initial stage of reform (1991–92), which found expression in active monetary policy directed at financial stabilization, should come the so-called structural stage.

Unfortunately, it is quite clear that very little has been done in this field,

Figure 8.1
Types of Investments

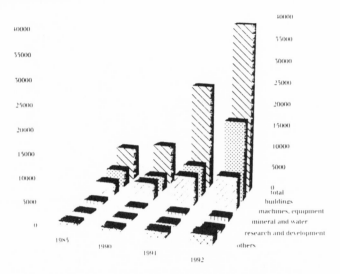

though some of the principal laws for economic restructuring were voted in by
the Parliament in 1991—for example, the law for foreign investment, the anti-
trust and trade legislation, and the Commercial Code. But these laws suffered
the political influence of the Communist-majority (now called Socialists) Parliament, and this made them ineffective and to some extent a burden on the
reform process. All this has caused a lag in structural reforms and further de-
teriorations in production.

In February 1991, industrial production (in constant prices) fell by 12.4 percent and gross output by 20.4 percent, from February 1990. In March 1991, the
decline was 10.7 percent and 15.8 percent respectively.[3] The poorest results have
been manifested in the chemistry, oil-processing, food, wine and tobacco, and
machine-building industries. Drops in production have been registered by 61
percent of enterprises, whereas others don't function at all and their labor forces
are in a state of compulsory holidays.

The Investment Process

Investment activity dropped to a dead level. The raised interest on credits—
imposing the reverse on former credits—has actually frozen the investment
process.

A general view of the development of the investment in the country[4] would
give the impression of a great boom in the investment policy in recent years
(see Figure 8.1) but this is a false impression. In reality, things are much worse;
there is a real decline in the investment activity in the country[5]—considering
the almost double increase in real inflation.

Figure 8.2
Investments in Different Sectors

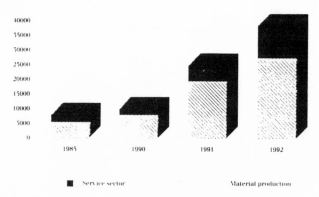

The increase of investment is in the service sector, where most of the private undertakings are (Figure 8.2). In the production sector the investments in the building industry are rising (Figure 8.3). The share of building activities in the service sector (dwelling, urbanization) is also high (Figure 8.4). This is explainable by two main factors: the existence of the very old material base in most of the industries, premises that private businesses do not want to buy, and the enormous demand for dwellings in the industrial sites.

Steps in the Economic Reform

In early 1991, the continuous slowdown of production was accompanied by the first steps of economic reform, connected with rigid budget restrictions and sharp interest rates raises. The financial restrictions concerning budget-subsidized entities have caused serious reductions, mainly in the spheres of science, culture, art, and state administration. At the same time, high interest rates and the expected privatization hinder the opening of new jobs. Thus the unemployment–labor demand scissors opened widely, and at the end of 1991 the unemployed reached the number of 414,342 people (one-tenth of the total active labor population), while vacancies were almost twelve times less. Perhaps the number of unemployed is higher than that registered in labor bureaus, as these bureaus have emerged recently and lack experience; besides, many of the unemployed haven't asked for the bureaus' help in job seeking.

The negative tendencies apply also to the sphere of foreign economic relations. Regardless of the Bulgarian Lev devaluations toward hard currencies, the balance of payments remains negative. Exports growth is rather insufficient due to the relatively low competiveness of Bulgarian products on Western markets and the slow and even negative economic growth in Bulgaria's traditional CMEA partners. At the same time, the net compressible import capacity and imports in general cannot be reduced considerably because of their high degree

Figure 8.3
Share of Investments in Production Sector

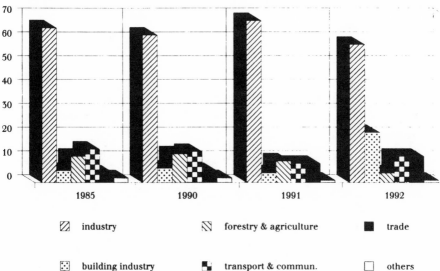

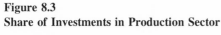

of complementarity in domestic production. In 1991, imports exceeded exports nearly four times.

The only favorable circumstance by the end of 1990 has been speeding up the relations with international financial institutions. Bulgaria became a member of the IMF and received the right to 450 million Special Drawing Rights (SDR) credits, some of them compensatory due to the raised prices of import materials. Moreover, the EC Commission has allowed a 290 million ECU medium-term credit, which is part of the OECD financial assistance for East European reforms. From the EU PHARE program, Bulgaria will obtain 160 million ECU credit, which is to be applied to privatization and to encourage private business, agriculture, energy-saving programs, education, and job training. Some credits are already available but are not being used due to the lack of appropriate allocation and settlement mechanisms.

Tax Policy

Tax policies are important tools of short- and long-term macroeconomic adjustment. They influence savings and investment decisions of households and firms as well as the supply and demand for labor. However, little progress (the only exception being the introducing of VAT in 1991) has been made in defining new tax policy and creating new tax administration in Bulgaria.

As privatization proceeds, with the number of private enterprises growing and revenues no longer being taken from captive state enterprises, tax collection is

Figure 8.4
Share of Investments in Service Sector

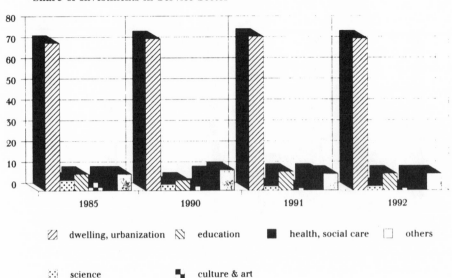

▨ dwelling, urbanization	◲ education	■ health, social care	☐ others
▦ science	▪ culture & art		

likely to become more difficult. The tax evasion is obviously a result of weak
tax administration and a lack of experience with mass taxes. As Kornai notes:
"Taxes should be collected where they are 'seizable,' giving preference to the
technically simplest forms of taxation."[6] For example, pending the development
of improved taxpayer morale and auditing, it is important to utilize withholding
to the extent possible and to design the system in such a way as to facilitate
this.

The role of taxes in the market economy, one that we are striving to build,
is also to regulate it. What is more, such a category as tax law does not exist
in a pure form. On the contrary, tax principles are connected with phenomena
and operations that can be carried out even without any taxation, but the tax
principles form these phenomena and operations in a different way. A tax law
is based not only on logic but on experience as well, because every tax has an
inevitable regulation effect in the economy. To implement a tax on a certain
operation may mean to a great extent to discourage its accomplishment. Tax
relief will have the opposite effect.

Disincentives for productive economic activity should be avoided, especially
in investment decisions. Taxes must not interfere in the decisions of households
and firms. The tax rates must correspond with the achievement of the major
goals of the transition—privatization and restructuring of the economy.

Investment tax credits, accelerated depreciation, and other tax credits may
encourage savings and investments. But tax relief is one of the main levers that
can put the economy into action again. The smaller the tax base, the bigger the

tax rates needed in order to accumulate a certain amount of money in the budget. Higher tax rates have a negative impact on investment and savings, hamper innovations and inventions, encourage unproductive investments in tax shelters, and so forth.

Tax systems are not static models but dynamic ones, and in order to be effective, they need to be relevant to the conditions in which they are implemented.

THE LAW ON FOREIGN INVESTMENTS

Some of the laws voted in by the old Parliament have been sent back for additional elaboration and amendments with regard to the requirements of a free market economy. One that requires special attention here is the Law on the Business Activity of Foreign Persons and on the Protection of Foreign Investment.

After the amendment passed, Bulgaria has had one of the most liberal laws on foreign investment in the whole of Eastern Europe, according to both businessmen and politicians from East and West. There are no longer any obstacles for the flow of foreign investments into the country. Most of the restrictions have been abolished. "The size of a foreign interest in newly formed or existing partnerships shall not be restricted," states Article 3 (3),[7] because the country definitely needs productive and effective investment and also because it is believed that foreign investment will bring new technology, new management, and know-how and thus will improve the economic situation as a whole.

Any foreign person shall have the right to carry on business in Bulgaria and to acquire shares or interests in commercial partnerships according to the procedure provided for Bulgarian citizens, and juristic persons and shall be equal in rights to the latter. Joint-venture partnerships shall have same rights as non-joint-venture partnerships. The size of the share in newly formed or existing partnerships is not restricted.

Any foreign person shall have the right to open commercial agencies in Bulgaria, which shall have to be registered at the Bulgarian Chamber of Commerce and Industry.[8]

However, some of the pre-1989 restrictions are preserved. These are connected with the fact that no foreign person may acquire the right of ownership of land, including such acquisition through a branch and in a single-merchant capacity. No partnership wherein a foreign person holds an equity exceeding 50 percent may acquire the right of ownership in agricultural land.

It is a necessity to obtain permission for:

- manufacture of and trade in arms, ammunition and military equipment;
- carrying on of banking and insurance and acquisition of interest in banks and insurance societies;

- acquisition of immovable property in geographical areas designated by the Council of Ministers;
- exploration, exploitation and extraction of natural resources from the territorial sea, the continental shelf or exclusive economic zones;
- acquisition of interest which will secure a majority in decision making or will block decision making in a partnership carrying on business or owning property pursuant to the preceding subparagraphs.[9]

All this does not mean that these spheres are forbidden; for example, Texaco has several platforms in the region of Kavarna, and not long ago they found natural gas.

Foreign persons are obliged to register any investment in Bulgaria and the changes therein within thirty days of making the investment except for bank deposits that are not subject to registration. Foreign investments must be registered by declaration at the Ministry of Finance.

The transfer of revenues and compensation are also settled by this law. Any foreign person shall have the right to buy foreign currency from Bulgarian banks or Change bureaus for the purpose of transferring the currency abroad, where he converts:

- revenue in leva, derived from his investment;
- compensation received for a compulsory purchase of his investment for purposes of State;
- a liquidation quota where the investment is wound up;
- proceeds from the sale of the investment;
- the proceeds in leva from the sale of goods, securing a receivable in foreign currency.

Any foreign person shall have the right to transfer abroad the foreign currency he has bought upon presentation of receipts for taxes due and paid.[10]

There are also requirements concerning labor and insurance relations and foreign exchange regulations. The fine for not complying with that law is equivalent to twice the amount of the profit made in Bulgaria but not less than 50,000 leva.

All these changes resulted for three years in only two major deals with foreign investments—the sale of a cereal plant to an international firm, and the sale of a magnetic heads factory to an American company.[11] The investment credentials of the country have still been very low. According to the annual classification of *Institutional Investor*, we were somewhere behind Iraq in 1992, with a fall of −2.3 from the previous year.[12]

PROPERTY RELATIONS—PRIVATIZATION

The establishment of private firms by physical persons was allowed in 1989. By early 1993, they numbered over 250,000,[13] most of them engaged predominantly in transport services, trade, catering, education, tourism, and other services. In the beginning, the private sector faced considerable difficulties and restrictions related to registration rules, tax regulation, raw material supplies, building production capacities, pricing mechanisms, labor hiring, foreign-trade activities, and so forth. All this has forced private entrepreneurships to turn their efforts toward spheres allowing easy transformation of private property into business capital as well as giving opportunities for activities outside working time in regular jobs.

The demolution of the totalitarian system after 1989 and the new political climate has lifted the barriers to private business, and it started developing under more favorable conditions compared to state-owned enterprises. First of all, there are certain tax facilitations, for example, that decrease the rate for corporate taxation and the possibility that the reinvested private firm's profit is to be free of tax. The salary growth in private business is also tax free, thus encouraging the attraction of highly qualified specialists.

The rent practice and private activities represent important elements of the preparatory stage of privatization. They have awakened the enterprising abilities of Bulgarian people, favored private capital accumulation, created alternative and profitable economic agents, and legalized some of the incomes in the shadow economy.

At the same time, private sector dynamics suffers from a certain meagerness and unevenness. That's why it won't be able to reduce immediately the expected high unemployment level caused by privatization. The restrictive financial policy reduces the free funds available both to private firms and to households, and this will hamper privatization.

State ownership has been transformed into private firm ownership through the so-called "quiet privatization." After the law amendment of 1991, firms began trading in their movable property without any governmental supervision or auction regulations. Some of the administrative staff members took advantage of the situation and transferred the state property into their own private firms.

Another form of "quiet privatization" was carried out through transformation of actual state enterprises into cooperatives. More than 20 years ago, the established labor-production cooperatives were nationalized de facto but retained their legal entity status. With state supervision liberalization, the personnel engaged declared themselves successors who should receive the state and cooperative property. This implies that in exchange for 300 or 400 leva individual shares, the personnel of these enterprises will obtain ownership rights to a million leva funds.

In Bulgaria, as in the other East European countries, "spontaneous privatization" has not been avoided. It seems that these processes cannot be overcome. In spite of their inappropriate realization, the positive side of this process is that the sale of state property to private firms contributes to the establishment of a new ownership structure and emergence of an entrepreneurial class.

Dimitar Popov's government (1991) took over economic control under the preliminary declared intention to implement large-scale privatization prior to financial stabilization; this, however, proved to be a rather unrealistic and unfeasible statement. In order to overcome the lagging parliamentary support, the government decided on so-called small privatization through normative acts and decrees. The Agency for Privatization was established, and small privatization programs are being developed. It turned out that selling procedures suffered serious imperfections due to inappropriately formulated normative acts. It became clear that large-scale privatization would prove impossible without a stable legislative basis.

The (only post-1989) government headed by the anti-communist opposition leader Philip Dimitrov (1992) passed a bill for restitution and privatization with the belief that this would help establish a middle class in the country. The need for a middle class is crucial for the future development of the country.

In fact, the whole process stopped with the restitution of big urban properties and rapid increase in rent prices, which has caused a lot of problems for the newly organized private businesses.

Ljuben Berov's socialists (former communists)-backed government (1993–94) proclaimed itself a "government of privatization."[14] It initiated a type of project for mass privatization—a strategy that has failed to be realized during the term it was in power.

The Agency for Privatization prepared a list of about 90 enterprises that had to be open for privatization by the end of the year 1994. Up until March 1995 there were just two tenders and nothing actually sold. Now the agency is preparing another set of enterprises for privatization, but the result probably will be the same.

The most advanced government body in the privatization business is the Ministry of Trade. Not long ago the names of about 27 firms and enterprises for privatization were published, and most of them are connected with services—garages, stores, and so forth. Having in mind the tenders already undergone, I am not very optimistic about the results.

The future of privatization in Bulgaria faces some major problems. The first problem emerges as a result of the lack of a more complete notion on the new social economic model. The state and desired ratio between governmental interference and the "invisible market hand" remain undetermined. Future privatization is very likely to affect some public goods that would better remain—at least in the beginning of the transformation process—under state ownership because of former traditions or lack of experience.

The second problem is related to the lack of large financial resources for the process of privatization. This requires the development and application of different privatization schemes and methods. The variety of schemes and their creative and flexible adaptation in each individual case must be reflected in the major privatization rules. Besides, it is not the "iron" legislative regulations that will lead to privatization but rather the administrative bodies who will set, develop, and implement privatization schemes.

The third problem emerges from the lack of large and efficient private firms that could become the main shareholders and proprietors of privatized enterprises. In this situation the attraction of foreign investors represents another possibility.

There are some difficulties connected with the lack of qualified managerial staff for carrying through a management buyout, or even improving the performance of enterprises; when one adds to these the problems of bad debts of state enterprises, it is obvious that there will be an excess of supply in the upcoming privatization.

CONCLUSIONS

The Bulgarian economy as a whole and the investment activity and property relations in particular face many difficulties in the process of transformation toward market. Most of the financial flows from abroad are still coming in the forms of credits and other support programs—PHARE, TEMPUS, and the like—and not in the form of foreign direct investments.

In 1980 in an open letter, Mrs. M. Thatcher (then prime minister in Great Britain) said: "The foreign investments in the UK are of great importance for this country. The foreign companies bring in capital and open new jobs for the country. They import also new technology, innovations in the management and modern productive techniques, that contribute to the development of our own industrial base."[15] This concept is valid for the contemporary situation in the Bulgarian economy. Foreign direct investment in the production field is of crucial importance for the development of the national economy.

The coming privatization should be interconnected with the flow of foreign investments without the spreading socialist (communist) fear that foreign capital will buy out the national economy. The existence of a law for foreign investments is not the only guarantee that they will pour into the economy. There must also be well-developed legal and economic structures—modern tax laws, an efficient banking system, easy credit facilities, and, above all, a modern and well-organized infrastructure in every field of economic activity. As far as privatization is concerned, all these unsophisticated forms of mass privatization and the like should be ignored, and we should find a new, more effective way of transforming the economy.

Bulgaria has the potential, the ability, and the manpower to overcome the existing recession and face the challenges of the 1990s, but it won't be fully accomplished without active (not only consultative) support from Western countries.

NOTES

1. See also Janos Kornai, *The Socialist System: The Political Economy of Communism* (Oxford and Princeton, NJ: Princeton University Press, 1992), chapter 9.

2. Georgi Smatrakalev, "State Regulation of the Investment Process in UK," *Journal of Economic Studies,* Sofia, vol. 1, 1991, pp. 3–23.

3. "The Bulgarian Economic Reform (Estimates, Analysis, Prognoses)" (Report for an International Conference, "Alternative Development of the East European Countries"), Sofia, June 3–6, 1991.

4. All the graphs are based on the *Statistical Yearbook 1993,* National Statistical Institute, Sofia, 1993, pp. 87–88.

5. The data in the graphs must be judged keeping in mind a rate of inflation about fifteen times higher than that in 1985.

6. Janos Kornai, *The Road to a Free Economy: Shifting from a Socialist System: The Case of Hungary* (New York: W. W. Norton, 1990), p. 73.

7. "Business of Foreign Persons and Foreign Investment Protection Act," *Bulgarian Economic Review,* January 29–February 11, 1992, p. 4.

8. Ibid., p. 4.

9. Ibid.

10. Ibid. p. 5.

11. The latter was not paid as of 1993, and there was no activity in that direction on the American side. There was a real fear that the deal would not come to a desirable end. See *Novinar,* September 2, 1993, p. 6.

12. *Institutional Investor,* New York and London, June 1993.

13. Author's estimates based on data provided by the National Statistical Institute.

14. One of the then deputy prime ministers, Valentin Karabshev, was a coauthor of the Bill for Privatization.

15. A. Hewer, "Manufacturing Industries in the Seventies," *Economic Trends,* London, June 1980, p. 8.

9

Privatization and Foreign Investments in Bulgaria

Daniela Bobeva and Alexander Bozhkov

PRIVATIZATION AND FOREIGN INVESTMENTS IN BULGARIA

Bulgaria has made its choice and continues along the path of speedy and radical reforms despite the enormous difficulties—the painful social and political implications of the transition and the enormous external strain on the economy. Bulgaria sustained losses amounting to approximately U.S. $1.2 billion from the Gulf War and about U.S. $1.4 billion by the end of August 1993 due to the UN embargo against Serbia and Montenegro. In the absence of compensation, with each day the embargo against Serbia is increasingly turning into an embargo against Bulgaria.

Notwithstanding numerous problems, Bulgaria is effecting the transition to a democratic market economy peacefully and remains one of the few countries among the Southern Europeans without ethnic tension and with democratic political institutions. This creates a favorable environment for the expansion of the private sector and the opening up of the economy for foreign investments. The first positive results in this direction are beginning to emerge.

THE ECONOMIC SITUATION ON THE WAY TO STABILITY

The basic indicators of the positive changes are to be found in financial stability—the reduction of overliquidity in the economy, curbing inflation (Figure 9.1), and stabilization of the BLV (Bulgarian lev) (Figure 9.2).

In 1992, the gross domestic product (GDP) dropped by 7.7 percent, and was likely to decrease in 1993 by 4.5 percent in comparison with the 1992 GDP. The GDP underwent substantial structural changes. The share of industry and

Figure 9.1
Annual Consumer Price Indexes (percent)

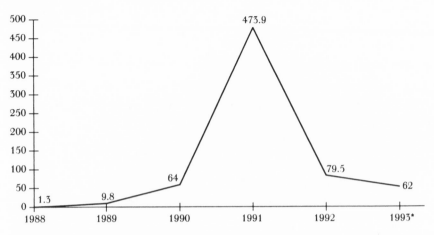

*The first half of 1993 price index compared with the same period of 1992.

Source: Author's estimates based on data provided from Bulgarian National Bank, September 1, 1993.

agriculture is decreasing, while that of services as discussed earlier in Smatrakalev's analysis, is expanding. Despite the ongoing restructuring, Bulgaria remains a largely industrial country, with the share of industry and manufacturing exceeding 40 percent (cf. Figure 9.3).

The servicing of the external debt will affect most severely the economy and foreign investment penetration. In 1992, the debt service ratio (principle and interest payments on medium- and long-term debt to exports) was 29 percent and the ratio of gross debt to GDP 152 percent. These two important creditworthiness indicators point to the liquidity difficulties of the country after 1989. The domestic credit policy is still restrictive (the annual interest rate in September 1993 had dropped to 48.0 percent), which limits the domestic investment potential and impedes the restructuring of the economy. That is one of the reasons for the slow progress of privatization and the increasing leaning toward mass privatization schemes. In 1992 investments amounted to 18.8 percent of GDP.

Since 1990 the private sector has undergone the most substantial and rapid changes. For the three years from 1989 to 1992, its share in GDP increased from 7 percent to 18.8 percent (it should be pointed out that the methods of evaluation of the private sector and its contribution to the GDP are still quite unsatisfactory, leading to its considerable underestimation), as shown in Table 9.1.

Figure 9.2
Exchange Rate (1 US dollar for BLV)

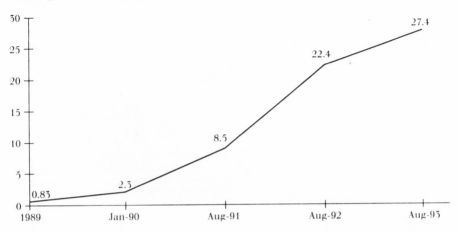

Source: Author's estimates based on data provided from Bulgarian National Bank, September 1, 1993.

Employment constitutes an indirect indicator of the role of the private sector. Bulgaria is the only one among the former communist countries where employment in the public and cooperative sectors rapidly fell by 34 percent over a period of three years, that is, approximately 1.5 million workers left the public sector. But this bad record in public sector employment was accompanied in the 1989–1992 period by a considerable surge of entrepreneurial interest on the part of the population, resulting in a rapid increase in the number of private companies, which reached 250,000. The expansion of the private sector as discussed in the previous chapter by Smatrakalev is also due to the property transformations realized over the three years from 1989 to 1992, through the adoption of the laws regulating three crucial aspects of the economic reforms—the agrarian reform, restitution, and privatization. Even if still of quite limited scope, foreign investment is also an important factor in the growth of the private sector.

The reform in agriculture began in 1992 with the amendment and revision of the Ownership and Use of Farmland Act, which had been adopted in 1991. Despite the difficulties in the implementation of the law, more than 35 percent of the available farmland had been restored to the former owners as of 1944. The restitution laws guarantee the reinstatement of property and real estate of the rightful owners prior to the nationalization in 1947.

Figure 9.3
Structure of GDP

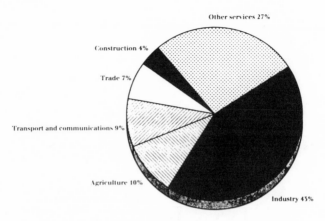

BULGARIAN PRIVATIZATION AND ITS APPEAL FOR FOREIGN INVESTORS

Advantages of the Legal Framework

On the 23rd of April 1992, the National Assembly passed the Law on the Transformation and Privatization of State-Owned and Municipal Enterprises. With this act, privatization opened for foreign investment. Let me add the following points in this regard to the analysis of Smatrakalev in the previous chapter. The main principles of the law of 23rd of April 1992:

- All physical and legal Bulgarian and foreign persons have equal rights to take part in the privatization process. There are three exceptions to this principle. Employees are entitled to buy on preferential terms up to 20 percent of the shares of each company at 50 percent discount, with the total amount of the allowed discount per employee not exceeding the annual income. These shares are nonvoting for a period of three years. Only Bulgarian citizens, after a lengthy procedure that includes obtaining permits from the Privatization Agency and the Ministry of Finance, may buy shares of the companies by an installment payment scheme, and in the case of small-scale enterprises sold through auction or tender, the employees are entitled to a 30% discount of the price if they have won the auction or tender. (These privileges are minor and would not have a serious effect and preclude the access of foreign investors to privatization.)

- The shares of the company can be sold by public offering, public auctioning of Bulk of shares, and publicly invited tender and through negotiations with potential buyers. Direct negotiations would be the most appropriate procedure for foreign investments. This was the case in the first two transactions with foreign companies conducted by

Table 9.1
Private Sector Developments

	1989	1990	1991	1992
Share of GDP (%)	7.2	9.5	11.9	18.8
Share of employment (%)	5.5	5.9	9.4	16.5

Source: Author's estimates based on data provided by the Ministry of Labor.

the Privatization Agency like in the Czech Republic, as discussed in Mejstrik's chapter, tendering is used only when a number of equivalent offers is available. Public offering of shares is still only a theoretical possibility, since there is no developed capital market in the country.

Foreign investors may obtain up to almost 100 percent of each company, as the 20 percent allocated for employees in most cases remains unsold. Basically, there is no problem with foreign investors immediately acquiring 80 percent of the shares and subsequently buying the remaining shares that have not been sold to the employees within the three months provided by the law.

Privatization procedures are simple and relatively short. The law requires an annual privatization program to be approved by Parliament. It includes the minimum privatization goals, the expected revenues and expenses, and a list of the companies not subject to privatization. The procedure allows for a company to be included in the privatization program on an ad hoc basis. The privatization process in Bulgaria is internally decentralized. The Privatization Agency coordinates the process and directly acts on behalf of large-scale enterprises. A limited number of the very large state enterprises need an approval by the Council of Ministers to be privatized, whereupon the agency takes over the transactions. Small-scale enterprises are privatized by the branch ministries. Each ministry has its own privatization department responsible for the privatization. Municipal enterprises are to be privatized by the local municipal councils regardless of their size.

Privatization may be initiated by the Privatization Agency, the corresponding Ministry, or the management and employees of the company. The decision to initiate the privatization procedure is published in the *State Gazette*. Table 9.3 illustrates the conducted privatization transactions by the institutions involved. The legal audit is carried out by qualified lawyers and the valuation of the company by licensed appraisers. There were more than 1,500 appraisers and 50 companies in 1993, including KPMG Peat Marwick, Price Waterhouse, Arthur Andersen, Ernest & Young, Deloite & Touch, and so forth, that have set up offices in Sofia. The valuation serves as a basis for the formation of the initial price, but the actual price of the shares is established through negotiations. The procedures for tenders in Bulgaria follow internationally established principles.

Table 9.2
Restituted Property

	Submitted applications	Restituted objects	Total area (thous. sq.m)
Total	54,426	30,772	16,843
Plots of land	25,536	11,090	9,916
Housing	11,484	6,775	1,228
Shops	9,003	7,452	382
Storehouses	1,201	882	275
Others	7,202	4,573	5,052

Source: Author's estimates based on data provided by the National Statistical Institute.

As in Poland and the Czech Republic (see Jermakowicz's and Mejstrik's chapters), a specific characteristic is that the tender conditions often involve certain commitments on the part of candidates related to the preservation of the company's profile, workplaces, planned investments, protection of the environment, and so forth.

A major advantage of the Bulgarian privatization framework is that once the decision for privatization has been made, the Privatization Agency (or the respective ministry) does not need any subsequent approval of the contract terms by the government, Parliament, or any other authorities. This simplifies and shortens the procedures.

THE PACE AND RESULTS OF PRIVATIZATION

Privatization started even before the formal adoption of the Privatization Law, under other legislative acts. Fifty-eight privatization objects—of which the largest were four petrol stations—were sold through public auctions in 1991. Privatization in banking has been progressing at a relatively fast pace. By mid-1993, private capital in the banks with state participation reached 16.6 percent of their assets, and in three relatively large banks this share has exceeded 51 percent. In the agricultural sector a powerful mechanism for privatization is the selling off of the property of the former cooperative farms under the Ownership and Use of Farmland Act. This property includes buildings, machinery, and small factories. By the end of 1993, the property sold in this way amounted to a total of BLV 3 billion.

A year after the adoption of the Privatization Law, its achievements were evaluated as quite modest by public opinion, political circles, and experts alike. State property totalling only BLV 630 million had been sold under the Privatization Law by the end of July 1993.

The Privatization Agency conducted three transactions. Two of the enterprises were bought by foreign investors. The sale of Maize Products Ltd. took four months. A Belgium-based company, Amylum, bought 80 percent of the enter-

Table 9.3
Number of Privatization Transactions by Institutions Conducting Them

State Institution	Enterprises in privatization procedure	Sold enterprises
Privatization Agency	23	3
Ministry of Agriculture	17	2
Ministry of Construction	12	1
Ministry of Trade	51	9
Ministry of Industry	27	0
Ministry of Transport	68	0
Tourism Committee	3	0
Energy Committee	1	0
Municipalities	387	26

Source: Author's estimates based on data provided by the Center for the Study of Democracy.

prise for U.S. $20 million. A debt-equity swap was performed with United Bulgarian Bank, which made the bank owner of 19 percent of the company. The Belgian company contractually assumed the obligation to invest another U.S. $20 million over a period of 24 months. A Nevada-based engineering company, Design Review International (DRI), bought 80 percent of the shares of Magnetic Heads Ltd. for U.S. $1.6 million. The company agreed to invest U.S. $1.85 million within one year and to create 1,000 jobs.

Despite expectations for rapid privatization, so far the process has not managed to make up for the delay. It is facing a number of practical problems. It has proven difficult and time consuming to establish the real estate property rights that remain uncertified due to the frequent administrative changes and the unshakable belief in the perpetuity of communism of the former administrators. Another difficulty arises in establishing the shares of privatized enterprises in other companies. The indebtedness of the enterprises also poses a major problem, as it reduces the appeal of the privatization objects and complicates privatization procedures. The settling of the enterprise debts incurred up to 1991 and thereafter has been expected to give an impetus to the privatization process. Other obstacles are posed by the great accumulation of unfinished products and the existence of nondurable assets and separate nonproducing parts of enterprises that are not of interest to prospective buyers. The crucial problem, however, remains finding buyers. For average and small-scale privatization objects buyers are typically local investors, the employees, or smaller foreign companies. The transactions concluded by the Privatization Agency indicate that foreign investors remain the only potential buyers of large enterprises. In this sense, attracting foreign investments is of vital importance to the further course of privatization.

Only a year from the enactment of the Privatization Law and the beginning of its application, without waiting to see the first effects of the adopted market-oriented methods of privatization, the government embarked on the elaboration of a new mass privatization project. The project adopted by the government in 1993 provided for the parallel realization of a mass privatization involving a limited number of enterprises. The implementation of the project would require certain changes in the Privatization Law which, provided the idea is accepted at all, would take a rather long time. Under the mass privatization project, foreign persons gain access to the management of the investment funds.

FOREIGN INVESTMENT PENETRATION

Legal Framework

Bulgaria opened for foreign investment in 1980. Under Ordinance 535, foreign persons were allowed to invest in Bulgarian enterprises up to 99 percent of the assets upon approval by the Council of Ministers. The regulations limited the access of foreign capital. As a result, only 31 joint ventures were created up to 1989. Despite their small number, the joint ventures brought in high technology, know-how, and large investments. In 1991, a Law on Foreign Investment was adopted; this was replaced in 1992 by a new Law on the Business Activity of Foreign Persons and on the Protection of Foreign Investment in Bulgaria. As stressed in Smatrakalev's analysis in the previous chapter, the law created some of the most liberal legal conditions for foreign investment in Central and Eastern Europe.

Foreign investors can hold up to 100 percent of the company's capital. Unlike countries like the Ukraine, Lithuania, Kazakhstan or Belorussia, in Bulgaria, authorization is not required in the case of large-scale foreign investments and there are no fixed minimum investments (this was one of the changes in the new foreign investment law).

Foreign investors enjoy equal rights as domestic investors. Concerning the legal forms of investments, Bulgaria is more liberal than Hungary, Poland, or the Czech Republic. In contrast to those countries, where only companies whose head offices are located in the host country and which have been established under the legislation of the host country (except in a few special sectors) can do business, Bulgarian legislation allows the setting up of branches and commercial agencies. This practice accounts for the fact that the number of commercial agencies and branches is almost the same as that of joint ventures. These forms of foreign economic activity provide a number of advantages to trade companies and to foreign investors in the initial phase of their investment. From a purely financial point of view they do not bring direct investments.

Bulgaria is among the countries offering the broadest variety of forms of investment. There are no restrictions regarding the forms of business activity that foreign legal persons may carry out. Foreign physical persons are required to have a permit for permanent residence in the country in order to register as sole proprietors and to become members of cooperatives or of a general partnership and members with limited liability of a limited partnership or a company limited by shares. The formalities involved in setting up a business are transparent and generally the same as those applying to domestic business. The only additional obligation is to register the investment at the Ministry of Finance.

In Bulgaria there are no regulations prohibiting foreign investment in certain areas. Only three cases are subject to authorization:

• Banking and insurance

• Production and trade in arms, ammunitions, and military equipment

• Development or extraction of natural resources from the territorial sea, the continental shelf, or the exclusive economic zone

A special permit is required in these cases if foreign participation is sufficient to secure majority in decision making. The permits are issued by the Bulgarian National Bank in the field of banking, and in other cases by the Foreign Investment Commission. The fact that by the end of 1993 eleven permits were issued to foreign persons for carrying out business activity in these spheres confirms their accessibility to foreign investments. A foreign person may acquire ownership over buildings and limited material rights over real estate.

Foreign investments are protected against expropriation. The repatriation of the profit is subject to the most liberal regulations as compared to the other Central and East European countries. In addition to Smatrakalev's analysis in the previous chapter, the following points should be made. Foreign persons may buy foreign currency from all Bulgarian banks for the purpose of transferring it abroad in the cases of income from an investment, the liquidation quota in the event of termination of the investment, and some other cases. The only requirement is to present a certificate that all due taxes have been paid.

A special commission was established in May 1993 at the Council of Ministers to promote foreign investment. The commission is a policy-coordinating body. It provides information about the investment environment in the country and information on the various branches and sectors of the economy. It organizes promotion campaigns abroad and in Bulgaria.

An important factor in attracting foreign investments is the relatively low tax level in the country and the uncomplicated procedures for buying foreign currency and for the repatriation of profits. The profit tax is 40 percent. Profits made by foreign investors within the territory of the nine free trade zones are exempt from taxes during the first five years and thereafter are taxed at a 20 percent rate. There are some other forms of tax relief, but they are currently subject to parliamentary discussions.

Table 9.4
Does the Country Need Foreign Investment?

%	December 1990	November 1991	March 1992	April 1993
Yes	65.9	62.0	63.0	65.1
No	18.0	19.5	16.9	16.9
Do not know	16.1	18.5	20.1	18.0

Source: D. Bobeva, "The Best Buys," *The INSIDER*, June 1993.

VOLUME AND STRUCTURE OF FOREIGN INVESTMENT

Liberal legislation is not enough to attract foreign investment. Only a few hundred U.S. million have been invested in Bulgaria over the three years of reforms (1990–93) in the form of direct investments (this is the minimum estimate of foreign investments, as it includes only the registered investments of 451 companies with foreign participation, while the remaining 1,260 have not registered any investments). The largest investors in the country are American Standard, Shell, Coca-Cola, and Amylum.

The correlation between foreign loans and foreign investments for Bulgaria is in favor of the former. The role of foreign investments in the financial stabilization of the country and the restructuring of the economy is underrated, and even though public opinion is extremely favorable to their penetration, pledging support and incentives for domestic business is politically profitable. As indicated by data from the surveys of the Center for the Study of Democracy, foreign investments have enjoyed public approval throughout the years of reforms (see Table 9.4).

Bulgaria finds itself at the initial stage of foreign investment penetration when the conditions favor small investments in trade and services, realizing quick and easy profits. There are as yet relatively few investments in industry and manufacturing. Electronics has recently proven to be one of the most attractive sectors for foreign investment. There is not a single company in electronics that has not drawn foreign investments. (See Table 9.5.)

Investments of less than BLV 50,000 (US $2,000) make up 65.4 percent of all foreign investments (this is the minimum fixed capital required for LTD company establishment), and only 14.6 percent of registered investments are above U.S. $20,000 (see Table 9.6). The reason for the substantial share of small investments in the country lies above all in the fact that Bulgaria is largely unknown to foreign investors. Unlike Hungary, for instance, where a considerable number of joint ventures were created even before 1990, in Bulgaria their number before 1990 was merely 31. The process of market liberalization in the country began later, and this sent Bulgaria to "B Division" in the ratings concerning economic and political reforms—lagging behind Hungary, Poland, and the Czech Republic. The political risks to foreign investment are frequently

Table 9.5
Distribution of Foreign Investment by Sectors

	Number of foreign investment companies
Trade	279
Industry	44
Services, tourism, housing	40
Construction	10
Finance, insurance	11
Electronics	16
Transport and communications	10
Agriculture	3
Education and culture	5
Others	33

Source: Author's estimates based on data provided by the Foreign Investment Commission.

exaggerated, in contrast to the achievements of the economic reforms, which are typically underrated. Serious investors are still reluctant to invest in Bulgaria due to the unsettled problem of the country's foreign debt. Even if its size per capita is smaller than that of Hungary, Bulgaria's production and export possibilities for debt servicing are quite limited, particularly under the present trade embargo against Serbia. The granting of credits by Western Banks and export/ credit agencies for large and long-term investments in Bulgaria is one of the major problems of foreign investment in the country. A serious obstacle to attracting foreign investment (like in the Central European countries) is also the lack of long-term priorities and strategy of the economic reform—something that none of the political forces or governments in Bulgaria has so far been able to propose. And this despite the fact that Bulgaria has had four different governments in the period (1990–93). It has to be stressed, however, that the general course and nature of the market-oriented reform and the supporting legislation have not changed. This only confirms the fact that regardless of political strife, Bulgaria is following the path of reforms like in the Central European countries, with privatization and foreign investments being crucial milestones in this process.

In contrast to the other countries of Central and Eastern Europe, the distribution of foreign investments by country of origin is quite dynamic. While German investments held first place in number and size in 1990–1992, at the end of 1992 and the beginning of 1993 there predominated investments from neighboring countries, mainly Greece and Turkey. Greece is investing actively in Bulgaria, which is favored not only by the geographic proximity but also by the numerous programs of the EU and the Greek government that encourage investments in Bulgaria.

154 Privatization in Eastern Europe

Table 9.6
Distribution of Foreign Investment by Size

Up to US$ 2,000	65.4
US$ 2,000–20,000	20.0
Over US$ 20,000	14.6
Total	100.0

Source: Author's estimates based on data provided by the Foreign National Commission.

The still modest amount of foreign investments is primarily due to the small number of joint ventures. Unlike all other countries in the region, where foreign investments were drawn mainly through the setting up of joint ventures, merely 1,900 such ventures have been created in Bulgaria, of which only 51 are between a state-owned enterprise and a foreign partner. The problem with the indebtedness of the enterprises and the frequent change of their management make green-field investment and investment through privatization the most adequate and widely favored mechanisms for investing in Bulgaria.

Portfolio investments have been slow to make their way into the country, due mainly to the belated start of the banking system reform and creating of capital market. Nevertheless, the reforms in this sphere are making some progress. Following the consolidation of the banks and the passing of the Law on Banks in 1992, the adoption of the Law on Insurance Activities will further facilitate the inflow of investments in this sphere. A stock market is currently emerging in the country, and the process is accelerating and will speed up in the course of privatization.

Prospects

Some recent developments are expected to have a positive effect in encouraging foreign investments:

- Following several months of parliamentary debates in 1993, the last laws of the comprehensive tax legislation package, in line with the European tax system and Bulgaria's association with the EU, were adopted by the Parliament.

- A year from the enactment of the Privatization Law, considerable experience had been gained and many transactions had been prepared, which guaranteed a good number of privatization deals till the end of 1993 and in 1994. This allowed greater opportunities for foreign investments and particularly for investments in industry, communications, transport, and so forth.

- The government has elaborated a project for settling the debts incurred by the enterprises up to 1991, this facilitated at some point the privatization and the inflow of foreign investments in state-owned enterprises.

• The explorations of the seven petrol companies that obtained concessions for prospecting for petrol and natural gas in the Bulgarian continental shelf had made good progress. Natural gas reserves have been discovered in the Bulgarian continental shelf by Texaco Exploration Off Shore Bulgaria Ltd., with a capacity of 960 thousand cubic meters per 24 hours, and there are continuing explorations for petrol.

10

New Regional Developments in Post-Communist Europe: Free Trade Zone in Central Europe?

Gabor Bakos

After the collapse of the Council for Mutual Economic Assistance (COMECON) we can witness the formation of new regional groupings in Central Europe in a shift toward more integration in the region. Before and after the war the small countries in Central Europe were always tied to some greater power outside the region and could not develop significant mutual cooperation even if they had wished to. Now that in East Europe systemic changes have begun and CO-MECON has collapsed, the question arises: will these countries develop cooperation or will they swing again to one side? As to the answer, this chapter tries to provide the historical and economic background and then a discussion of the problems of the recently established the Central European Free Trade Association (CEFTA).

HISTORICAL BACKGROUND

Plans about a Danube confederation date back as early as to the late eighteenth century, when the stability of the Habsburg empire began to erode and national movements emerged. The first drafts envisaged within the Habsburg empire a federative pattern of territorial units with equal rights. Among such a drafts, for example, were the Jacobins' constitution plan for an Austro-Slavic federation from 1794 and later the Wesselenyi conception, which suggested in 1843 a federation under the Habsburg leadership. After the Hungarian revolution was defeated in 1848, the emigrated politicians agreed to create a confederation for the small Central European countries. Their idea maintained that an alliance of independent states was necessary for the survival of these smaller states and for their protection against the great powers.

Kossuth, the father of the Hungarian revolution, being already in exile, worked out his proposal in two steps. First he drafted a plan for a new constitution in Kütahya in 1851; this he later developed into the so-called Danube-Alliance published in 1862.[1] According to his plan, the confederation would have included Hungary, Transylvania, Romania, Croatia, and the southern Slavic provinces. The alliance was to be governed by the federative parliament, and the federative council was to have the executive power. The following affairs were to be jointly managed: defence, foreign affairs, trade, customs, transport, currency, and weights and measures. The federative parliament and the council was to meet alternatively in Belgrade, Bucharest, Budapest, and Zagreb. The national and cultural rights of every nation would have been scrupulously guaranteed, and within the given autonomous territories the language of the given nationality could have been used in administration and education.

A similar conception was developed by Oszkar Jaszi, published on the eve of the collapse of the Austro-Hungarian monarchy. He suggested a confederation of Austria, Hungary, Czechoslovakia, Poland, and the southern Slavic nations in which some affairs would have been conducted commonly.

A new chance was offered after World War II, when Central European countries, freed of the German war economy integration and not yet under Soviet influence, began to establish new cooperation among themselves simultaneously with the ambitious reconstruction of their economies. A series of agreements provide the benchmark for this period. In December 1946 Yugoslavia and Albania agreed to coordinate their plans and establish a customs union. The year 1947 was especially rich: in May the Hungarian-Yugoslavian bauxite-aluminum agreement was signed, in July Czechoslovakia and Poland concluded an agreement on economic cooperation, and further, also in July Bulgaria and Yugoslavia declared they would form a customs union. In January 1948, Romania and Bulgaria formed a customs union. After these bilateral agreements, it seemed quite probable that the next step would come, the multilateral declaration of a customs union by the Central European countries. This concept is known as the Dimitrov plan, named after the Bulgarian prime minister Geogri Dimitrov. History, however, decided otherwise. At the end of the same month, January 1948, a short communiqué in the Moscow *Pravda* (28 January) informed readers about the establishment of the CMEA (COMECON) and claimed that "the young democratic countries do not need a customs union for their efficient development."[2]

ECONOMIC BACKGROUND

Now, let us see how strong economic cooperation was among Central European countries between the two world wars and after.

Between the two world wars, the majority of total trade was internal trade among these countries. If we take, for example, Hungary, in the beginning of the period 80 percent and later over 50 percent of its total trade was with neighboring countries: Austria, Czechoslovakia, Germany, Romania, and Yu-

Table 10.1
The Share of Five Countries in Hungary's Total Exports (percent)

	1922–1925	1926–1929	1930–1933	1934–1937
Austria	36.8	33.9	28.7	29.0
Czechoslovakia	20.0	18.1	10.2	1.2
Germany	9.0	12.5	12.5	27.5
Romania	6.4	4.6	3.4	4.8
Yugoslavia	7.5	5.6	5.7	2.4
	79.6	74.7	60.5	57.9

Source: J. Buzas and A. Nagy, *Magyarország külkereskedelme 1919–1945* (Hungary's Foreign
Trade between 1919–1945), KJK Budapest, 1961, p. 53.

goslavia. Of these, three countries are important: Austria, with its gradually
decreasing share; Germany, with an increasing share; and Czechoslovakia,
whose share shrank and fell below 10 percent by the mid-1930s (see Tables
10.1 and 10.2).

Germany's strongly increased share indicates the expanding influence of the
German military economy. The German economy centred economic flows and
caused a radial arrangement, thereby decreasing the internal trade among the
other smaller countries. Thus, for instance, Hungary's trade with Czechoslovakia
and Poland also experienced a severe setback (Table 10.3).

After World War II, as a result of applying the Stalinistic economic model
in the smaller Central European countries, the radial arrangement changed its
direction for the East, with a Soviet centre, while trade among the smaller countries remained insignificant. The trade with the Soviet Union was decisive and
even after 1989 remains important at some point for these countries. Its share
amounted after the war to two-thirds of total trade, for example, in the case of
Hungary, Czechoslovakia, and Poland. After 1989 trade with Russia, in the case
of Hungary, accounts for some 30–35 percent, as a result of the large energy
component on the import side.

It is less known that in addition to the Soviet-centred pattern, there was a
wider economic triangle system among the Soviet Union, Eastern Europe, and
China, which existed until the early 1960s.[3] In this wider context, the Soviet
Union exchanged its surplus of lower-level machinery with China for food and
textiles, whereas it bought high-level machinery from Eastern Europe in
exchange for raw materials. Finally, China exported to Eastern Europe food and
textiles and imported machinery. As a result of the political break between China
and the Soviet Union, by the early 1960s the Soviet Union had accumulated a
domestic machinery surplus, since exports were suspended to China; nevertheless, the Soviets tried to sell these machines to Eastern Europe. However, Eastern European countries also faced a machinery overproduction because their
exports to China had been similarly cut off. This machinery overproduction was
the starting push to specialization in CMEA from the 1960s onward. This spe-

Table 10.2
The Share of Five Countries in Hungary's Total Imports (percent)

	1922–1925	1926–1929	1930–1933	1934–1935
Austria	24.7	16.0	13.7	19.1
Czechoslovakia	24.4	22.7	14.4	5.8
Germany	14.8	18.5	21.8	27.0
Romania	8.2	8.0	10.1	11.4
Yugoslavia	3.3	4.5	5.8	4.9
	75.4	69.7	65.8	68.2

Source: J. Buzas and A. Nagy, *Magyarország külkereskedelme 1919–1945* (Hungary's Foreign
    Trade between 1919–1945), KJK Budapest, 1961, p. 53.

cialization helped Eastern European countries to make their parallel industrial
structures more complementary, but nevertheless the bulk of their trade was
with the Soviet Union.

In the 1970s, and especially in the 1980s, as Soviet oil became high priced
and deliveries fell back, internal trade among the smaller Eastern European
countries suffered a slight decline. Toward the late 1980s the CMEA began to
erode and countries turned more to the West, as shown in trade data (Table
10.4). Particularly in 1990 the decline in Soviet oil deliveries caused problems,
and Hungary, Czechoslovakia, and Poland had to import several million tons of
oil from other suppliers. In 1990 internal CMEA trade decreased on the average
by 20–25 percent, and so did trade among Eastern European countries. In 1991
further trouble was caused by the introduction of U.S. dollar accounting, which,
together with other circumstances, resulted in a further trade decline of 40–50
percent. The pattern of trade between Hungary, Czechoslovakia, and Poland
signifies, however, their established cooperation, as we shall show later, and so
the considerable decline might have been prognosticated as temporary.

To sum up the picture, before and after the Second World War, Hungary,
Czechoslovakia, and Poland were drawn into trade with the West (Germany and
Austria) and the East (the Soviet Union) respectively, and their mutual trade
could not accrue to a level of significance. And at present, after Soviet and
Russian dominance has ended, a new reorientation toward Western Europe,
more precisely, toward Germany, becomes evident. The trade shares of Germany
alone with our three countries amount in 1993 to a share equal to that of the
former Soviet Union in 1991. With a further decline in trade with Russia and
the other former Soviet republics and the expansion of German capital exports
to Eastern Europe, the German influence will soon become dominant, and trade
among the smaller countries may be of secondary importance, as in the pre-war
years and for four decades in 1949–89.

THE DILEMMA OF THE PRESENT

At present two tendencies are at work.

Table 10.3
Hungary's Trade with Czechoslovakia and Poland

	Czechoslovakia	Poland
Export 1928 millions of Pengö	145	27
share in percent	18	3
1938 millions of Pengö	22	5
share in percent	4	1
Import 1928 millions of Pengö	272	49
share in percent	22	4
1938 millions of Pengö	22	6
share in percent	7	1

Source: Statisztikai Adattár, Zsebkönyv (Statistical data), 1946.

First Tendency: Toward the West

The tendency of a renewed radial orientation toward the West seems to be probable, first, because of the desired European Union (EU) membership, and secondly, because of the problems of restructuring these economies.

As to the first, Hungary, Czechoslovakia, and Poland applied for (then) EC (European Community) membership, and in December 1991 they became associate members of the EC. Also, the three countries made steps to join the European Free Trade Association (EFTA). Czechoslovakia has signed an agreement for industrial products, effective from July 1992; Hungary signed one in March 1993, which went into effect in July 1993; and Poland signed in 1992.

These countries could redirect their trade surprisingly rapidly from Eastern European markets to the West. The share of EU countries in their total exports has come up by now to over 50 percent, and another 15–20 percent is accounted for by EFTA countries. In 1992 the agreements with the EC resulted in the full abolition of quantitative restrictions on industrial products exported by these countries. In the three years 1993 to 1995 the EU should liberalize over 60 percent of the trade in agricultural products coming from Hungary, the Czech Republic, Slovakia, and Poland. The agreements with the EFTA abolished both tariff and nontariff trade barriers for 85–90 percent of the exports from the four countries. The agreements with both the EU and the EFTA were so-called asymmetric agreements, freeing imports from the four countries from the beginning, while stipulating that the EU and EFTA countries would liberalize their imports from Eastern Europe within five to ten years.

Cooperation with EU countries is progressing well, and although the time for full membership is not fixed, it may be expected that these countries will be accepted before the year 2000.

All the Eastern European economies very much need capital to carry out privatization and to obtain high technology in order to modernize. They cannot

Table 10.4
Hungary's Trade with CMEA, Poland, and Czechoslovakia (millions of forint, trade accounted in rubles)

Year	CMEA Import	CMEA Export	Poland Import	Poland Export	Czechoslovakia Import	Czechoslovakia Export
1985	188,944	200,684	......	......	......	.....
1986	209,301	213,247	....	......	......	.....
1987	205,504	210,656	18,385	15,453	24,979	22,624
1988	196,654	203,727	19,194	16,650	23,695	27,020
1989	198,519	214,892	17,222	18,091	26,966	28,980
1990	158,606	158,072	13,028	10,044	25,383	25,002
1991	.....	.....	17,108	16,275	37,493	17,013

Source: Külkereskedelmi Statisztikai 'Evkönyv (Statistical Yearbook for Foreign Trade), 1988, 1989, 1990.

obtain these resources from each other but must depend on the West, and every joint venture and Western investment will contribute to the process of binding these countries to the West. Since liberalizing capital imports, most direct investments have come from EU countries, especially Germany, and from the United States. On the other hand, however, the experience gained so far indicates an opposite tendency as well. Western investors often request that their Eastern European partner not to abandon Eastern markets, especially the former Soviet markets, but even to boost sales there.

Second Tendency: Toward New Regional Groupings

Central European countries are not yet ready to join the EU. They need to reshape their economies: to develop the market elements and to introduce compatible institutional structures.

Another impulse in favor of strengthening cooperation among Central European countries comes from the deepening crisis situation in the CIS. The reliance of Central European countries on the CIS for imports of energy and raw materials is an imbalancing factor in their economies, especially in the case of unstable oil deliveries. Beginning in 1991, when CMEA countries adapted dollar payments and world market prices, the former Soviet Union and Russia exhibited strong one-sided endeavours to acquire maximum dollar incomes from Central European countries. This aim has been the most important point in foreign economic policies of the Russian Federation, as demonstrated when it says that "it is necessary to accumulate sufficient currency reserves which are at present exhausted" and that Russian exporters must sell 40 percent of their foreign currency earnings to the Central Bank in order to create currency reserves for the Russian Federation.[4] These strong goals make it necessary for Central European countries to cushion themselves from harmful impacts, possibly through joining the West European energy system or through creating a payment union.

After the collapse of COMECON, the former member countries, including the republics of the former Soviet Union, are seeking their identity and new ways to cooperate. It is interesting to look at the new regional groupings:

1. The Trilateral Cooperation (Visegrad Treaty)
   The grouping was established in February 1990 with the participation of Hungary, Czechoslovakia, and Poland. The agreement was signed in the Hungarian city Visegrad, which is why it is called the Visegrad Treaty. The main motive was to cooperate in democratic transformation after the Warsaw Treaty Organization was disbanded. After a free trade agreement was signed in December 1992, it was renamed CEFTA (Central European Free Trade Association).
2. Central European Initiative (Pentagonale)
   The CEI was formed in August 1990 by five countries: Austria, Czechoslovakia, Hungary, Italy, and Yugoslavia. At that time its name was Pentagonale. After Poland joined in 1991 and the Ukraine in 1992, it was renamed CEI.
3. Black Sea Economic Cooperation Scheme
   Established in 1992 with Albania, Bulgaria, Romania, Moldova, the Ukraine, Russia, Georgia, Azerbaijan, Armenia, Turkey, and Greece.
4. Economic Cooperation Organization (the Izmir Treaty)
   Established in 1992 by five former Soviet republics (Kazakhstan, Azerbaijan, Kyrgyzstan, Turkmenistan, Uzbekistan) and Iran, Pakistan, and Turkey.

In the following discussion, we shall confine ourselves to the Trilateral Cooperation, which consists of the three countries that are the most advanced in democratization and marketization, and the CEI.

TRILATERAL COOPERATION (THE VISEGRAD TREATY, OR CEFTA)

The trilateral grouping was established in February 1990 with the participation of Hungary, Czechoslovakia, and Poland. The domestic conditions for this act were created by each country's revolution toward democracy and a market economy. But the decisive push to realize it came from outside, when the Warsaw Treaty Organization (WTO) declared its disbanding. It was the work of the Consultative Committee of the WTO (June–November 1990) that brought the three countries together, when they recognized their common needs for security and sovereignty.[5] Economic cooperation came to the forefront in 1993, when the respective countries agreed on a free trade association.

According to the establishing document, the three states agreed to strengthen their cooperation in the following fields:

1. Security policies and relations with European institutions
2. Transportation, highway infrastructure and telecommunications

Table 10.5
Population, Territory, and GDP of Hungary, Czechoslovakia, and Poland (1988)

	Population in millions	Territory 1000 sq km	GDP US$ billion	GDP per capita
Hungary	10.6	93,030	32	3,000
Czechoslovakia	15.5	127,870	54	3,500
Poland	37.9	311,700	76	2,000
Total	64.0	532,600	162	

Source: Author's estimates based on data provided by *National Statistical Yearobok*, individual
countries, 1988.

3. Subregional and microregional projects

4. Enterprise to enterprise cooperation

5. Cooperation among the private sectors in tourism and retail trade

6. Cultural, education, and youth exchange

7. The establishment of bilateral foundations to promote cultural, historical, and scientific cooperation

Let us consider the main economic features of the cooperation among the three countries. The market of Hungary, Czechoslovakia, and Poland consists of 64 million people and more than half a million square kilometers, as shown in Table 10.5.

The share of mutual trade is not very high, as seen in Table 10.6. In Hungary's total trade, Czechoslovakia figures some 5 percent; Poland, some 3 percent; and their added share, still under 10 percent. Data on the partners' side indicate a similar weight in mutual trade, that is, Hungary's share in their trade is similarly low, as shown in Table 10.7.

The pattern of mutual trade, however, is interesting. Hungary's trade with Czechoslovakia is dominated by manufactures (machinery, industrial consumer goods) both in exports and imports (Table 10.8). Raw materials and energy have a share of some 14–27 percent. Within the generally balanced turnover, there are two structural discrepancies: first in raw materials and energy, the share of which is bigger in Czechoslovakia's exports; and second in food, with a share bigger on the Hungarian export side. The trade pattern shows a stability also in time; during almost one decade, between 1980 and 1988, no considerable structural shift can be observed. But during the past two years alone, in Czechoslovakia's exports the share of machinery dropped to half, while raw materials increased to a major position. Considering Czechoslovakia's industrial economy, it is interesting that during the 1980s not only the food balance but also the machinery balance is negative for Czechoslovakia.

The structural stability suggests that during the 1980s, in spite of lacking a market mechanism, this trade was based on intensive intrasectorial specializa-

Table 10.6
The Share of Czechoslovakia and Poland in Hungary's Trade (percent)

Year	Czechoslovakia		Poland	
	Export	Import	Export	Import
1988	5.4	5.1	3.3	4.1
1989	5.1	5.2	3.1	3.2
1990	4.1	4.6	1.7	2.4
1991	2.1	4.1	2.0	1.8

Source: Author's estimates based on data provided by *National Statistical Yearbook*, various years, Budapest.

tion, as V. Benáček states, and the level of specialization was equal to that among developed Western market economies.[6] This means that inter-industry trade was dominant and the products of companies within the same industrial branch were exchanged against each other. The trade of semifinished goods (parts) was relatively high. Further, both countries could make use of their comparative advantages. Hungary has a comparative advantage, that is, a relative surplus in labor force; Czechoslovakia is a net importer of this factor. Capital intensity is indifferent for trade. In natural resources, Czechoslovakia possesses a comparative advantage, which is shown in the trade pattern by its net export of energy and materials to Hungary. As for human capital, the picture is paradoxical. Generally, in Czechoslovakian exports, production wages are lower than in the production of potential import substitutes. But paradoxically, in exports to Hungary, the products require advanced technology and high skill levels, that is, products associated with higher wages are exported.

Hungary's trade pattern with Poland is shown in Table 10.9. The share of materials and energy is higher than in the trade with Czechoslovakia, amounting to some 46 percent of total imports in 1988 and more than 77 percent respectively in 1991. The share of manufacturing is high, with 45 percent both in exports and imports. Structural asymmetry is relevant in materials and energy, with Hungary being a net importer; this surplus is counterbalanced by Hungary's net exports of manufactures and food.

A striking phenomenon in the trade with the two countries is the great share of manufactures both in exports and imports. This is a fundamental difference from the trade with the former Soviet Union, where raw materials and energy were changed for manufactures. The high share of manufactures is a sign of intrasectorial specialization, which, under market-type cooperation, may soon become an intensive inter-industry cooperation. It can be concluded, then, that the pattern of internal trade among the three countries, that is, the high share of manufactures, is a favourable condition for developing their mutual cooperation.

In the data for 1991, the collapse of the Soviet market is reflected in Hungary's increase in imports of energy and materials from the two other countries

Table 10.7
Hungary's Share in the Trade of Czechoslovakia and Poland (percent)

Year	Czechoslovakia		Poland	
	Export	Import	Export	Import
1988	5.5	5.5	2.8	2.7
1989	4.0	4.8	1.6	1.6

Source: Külkereskedelmi Statisztikai Évkönyv, Budapest Statistická rocenka, Praha, Rocznik Statystyczny, Warszawa, various years.

Table 10.8
The Pattern of Czechoslovakia's Trade with Hungary (percent)

Groups of items	Export				Import			
	1980	1989	1990*	1991*	1980	1989	1990*	1991*
Machinery	55.4	47.6	24.8	14.1	55.1	57.6	42.4	25.4
Raw materials, energy	27.8	27.8	39.9	65.1	14.1	12.6	24.0	38.1
Cattle and animals	5.5	0.1 }	8.9	7.1	0.9	0.4 }	14.3	21.5
Food		4.4	25.9	13.7	17.0	15.1 }	19.3	15.0
Industrial consumer goods	13.3	20.1	25.9	13.7	12.9	14.3	19.3	15.0
Total	100	100	100	100	100	100	100	100

Source: Statistická rocenka CSR, 1989, Praha, p. 478.
Author's estimates based on data provided by Külkereskedelmi Statisztikai Évkönyv, Budapest.

Table 10.9
The Pattern of Hungary's Trade with Poland (percent)

Groups of items	Export				Import			
	1987	1988	1990	1991	1987	1988	1990	1991
Energy	1.1	1.0	3.2	0.0	8.7	7.3	4.0	27.7
Materials	28.2	28.3	27.1	21.8	35.0	39.0	43.7	50.7
Machines	43.5	37.4	29.7	9.5	36.1	31.8	25.7	5.3
Industrial consumer goods	20.5	20.3	20.2	26.8	14.8	15.6	13.5	9.6
Food	6.7	13.0	19.8	41.9	5.4	6.3	13.1	6.7
Total	100.0	100.0	100.0	100.0	100.0	100.0	100.0	100.0

Source: Author's estimates based on data provided by *Külkereskedelmi Statisztikai Évkönyv*, Budapest, various years.

and its increased exports of food. This is also a sign that these countries have moved toward redirecting their energy imports away from Russian sources.

CENTRAL EUROPEAN INITIATIVE

The Central European Initiative (CEI) was formed in August 1990 by five countries: Austria, Czechoslovakia, Hungary, Italy, and Yugoslavia. At that time its name was Pentagonale. In 1991 Poland joined and in 1992 the Ukraine, so in the same year it was renamed Central European Initiative. Further, Bulgaria and Romania requested participation in various pentagonal projects. Germany's Bavaria and Baden-Württemberg also expressed their interest in some projects.

In contrast to trilateral cooperation, where countries as whole entities are participants, CEI is intended actually as a means of cooperation between bordering provinces of the respective countries. Thus, for instance, the main participants are the northern republics of Italy, the northern republics of Yugoslavia, the southwestern prefectures of Hungary, and the southern *Länder* of Austria. In this sense, CEI seems to be a system of microregional cooperation. Probably this will also better favor cooperation between countries with so different statuses, ranging from EU member to former CMEA members.

The participants decided to foster cooperation in the following fields:

- Transport and telecommunication
- Environment
- Small and medium-size enterprises
- Scientific and technical research
- Culture and tourism
- Information
- Energy
- Migration

In these fields, the working groups established have made concrete progress already. Many studies have been carried out and projects in the above mentioned fields have been implemented.

PERSPECTIVES

Concerning the international reaction, probably the most important point to mention is that the two cooperative formations were not criticized by the former Soviet Union or recently by Russia and were positively received by the West. International financial institutions also expressed their interest. For example, the World Bank was positive about cooperating with the CEI, and there are good chances that Pentagonale projects may further enjoy some World Bank's financial support. Also, the G–7 1990 meeting in Houston welcomed regional co-operation initiatives in Central and Eastern Europe that would make a contribution to economic progress and stability in the region.

As to the area, the new groupings embrace Central Europe in a wide sense. The limits extend from Italy to the Ukraine and from the Baltic to Southern East Europe. In September 1991, the Baltic republics gained independence, they have been developing intensive contacts with the Nordic countries, and through Poland the very center of Europe will be connected with the North. Romania and Albania also want to open to the world. Their way will lead through Central Europe, so it is no wonder that they declared their intention to cooperate with CEI. Bulgaria and Romania signed a cooperation agreement with EFTA in December 1991. In any case, the core members remain Hungary, the Czech Republic, and Poland, and that is the trilateral cooperation on which the success of the whole Central European cooperation seems to depend. This is so for two reasons. First, these three countries are essential in the geographic sense. Second, their transition to democracy and market economies and their new market-type cooperation sets the standard for other Eastern countries.

A third formation was inaugurated in June 1992, providing a framework for the cooperation between southeast European countries and adjacent Asian countries. This formation is called the Black Sea Economic Cooperation Scheme (BSECS), and has the participation of Albania, Bulgaria, Romania, Moldova, Ukraine, Russia, Georgia, Azerbaijan, Armenia, Turkey, and Greece. The fields envisaged for cooperation are: environment, transportation, communications, energy, information, science and technology, agriculture, tourism, health, and the establishment of free trade zones. In order to create a free trade zone, the free movement of labor, goods, capital, and services is targeted. To ease the capital need and payments problems, the Black Sea Trade and Investment Bank was proposed.[7]

A brief look at the fields of cooperation suggests that there are two main aims of the new groupings. First, as far as the political aspect goes, Eastern European participants, now free from Soviet dominance, want to stabilize their sovereignty and security, while Western participants, especially Italy, don't hide their aim of outweighing the increasing German influence in the region. Second, concerning the economic side, participating countries want to pool their potential in order to develop an Eastern "Common Market" after the Soviet markets have collapsed and until the EU single market is open for their exports.

In the economic realm, there seem two major tasks. One is the energy supply, and another is restructuring the manufacturing industry.

As Soviet energy supplies are dwindling, Eastern European countries should redirect their energy imports. Countries are already negotiating on joining the West European energy system. A further way might be to create a North-South transit access from the Polish ports down to the Adriatic to provide energy transportation. The Adria oil pipeline (Hungary-Yugoslavia), if extended to Italy, would provide a connection down to Sicilia. A North-South transit access could also connect the industrial regions of Silezia, Moravia, Hungary, and Croatia, enabling further cooperation among them.

In manufacturing, Hungary, Czechoslovakia, and Poland developed a considerably large machinery industry in which automobile production is common, and Hungary has the largest bus factory in Central Europe. For some time cooperation in the car industry was not free from frictions. Each country established joined ventures with Western firms to modernize: Poland with Fiat; the Czech Republic's Skoda with Volkswagen; and Hungary with Suzuki, Opel, and Ford. These separate actions are, on the other hand, quite understandable, if we remember that these factories neither by themselves nor jointly could have raised capital or acquired technology for developing and that there has been no coordinated industrial policy among the new governments, as there is no industrial policy in the individual countries. A further important branch of manufacturing is the textile industry, which should be restructured following the pattern of industrialized Western economies, again requiring new capital.

Agriculture is nonetheless important, especially in Hungary's and Poland's exports to the West. As privatization in agriculture, mainly in the case of Hungary and the Czech and Slovak Republic, will result in a restructuring from large cooperatives toward farms, these countries will need diverse machines for efficient farming. This presents a good opportunity to develop agricultural and food processing machinery in Hungary and the Czech and Slovak Republics. Food production and agribusiness will continue to have good markets in the East, but joining the EU will increase the competition coming from the Western European producers.

A special field is research and development (R&D). Central European countries possess highly skilled human capital, including engineers, mathematicians, chemists, and biologists. Their knowledge is essential to developing modern branches like electronics, biotechnology, and ceramic technology. Hungary, former Czechoslovakia, and Poland have established a wide academic network, but since 1989, huge state budget deficits have been forcing the governments to cut expenditures; thus, research institutes are seriously endangered and researchers are seeking jobs abroad or in production, which is to the detriment of fundamental research. Central European countries should develop more cooperation in R&D; they should also invite foreign capital into capital-intensive research fields, for example, in the form of joint laboratories. For Western investors, the advantage would be the access to highly skilled research potential at lower wage costs and a ready-made infrastructure, also at a lower cost. Some Western firms have already realized this chance and taken actions. For example, the Japanese Furukawa Company bought up a certain part of the Hungarian Chemical Research Institute in 1990, and it also located some of its production in Hungary based on the available human capital, that is, the Hungarian researchers.

The institutional aspect is twofold: first, domestically, in each country a market economy must be promoted; second, the external institutions of coordination must be developed.

After the radical systemic change, all three core countries (Hungary, former Czechoslovakia, and Poland) declared their intention to introduce the liberal version of a market economy, with only the speed of implementation being different in these countries. The main elements of this process are privatization, mostly with foreign capital; liberalizing domestic prices and imports; drastic cutbacks in budgetary spending (leading to a deterioration of the social-cultural environment); and monetary restrictive policy. As prices were freed and earlier centrally planned methods abandoned, high inflation developed. The stabilization policy, operating with monetary restrictions, maintains that subsidies to production should be stopped, on the one hand, and, in order to keep the surplus money from consumption triggering inflation, price increases should be held until they hit the limit of demand, on the other hand. At this moment inflation would stop, price ratios would stabilize, and the expansive phase of monetary regulation could begin to boost the demand. However, after the initial euphoria of experiencing the free market, governments increasingly recognized the need to boost the supply side and began applying sober guidance to help restructuring.

Privatization is going on and is advancing in the three core countries, and simultaneously, the capital market is also developing. In 1990, in both Hungary and Poland, the stock exchange was opened. At present, however, all these countries suffer from capital shortages, which also retards privatization. Therefore, even if the countries made capital flow free among themselves, it would hardly be probable that, for example, a Hungarian company would buy up a Polish one. Rather, the future development will be such that joint companies with Western partners will grow, and after they fill in the gaps in domestic markets, will expand over the borders. Then they would expand not to the intensive and demanding Western markets but to the Eastern markets, and so the capital flow among these countries will acquire new dynamism.

The external institutions are forming. In the following section we will take up two such issues, the system of payments, and free trade.

The System of Payments

After the breakdown of the special intra-CMEA trading and accounting system, as mentioned earlier in this chapter, from January 1991 the countries applied current world market prices and dollar payments. National banks suspended the quotation of Eastern European currency rates. As convertible currency is scarce in these countries, payment became a serious problem and kept back trade transactions. Even if there were some other impacts on general economic restructuring, it is no exaggeration to declare that the unresolved payment problem was the main reason for dwindling trade.

Since 1990 there have been several propositions to establish a Central European payment union. The first was raised by Hungary in early 1990; it suggested a payment union for Hungary, Czechoslovakia, Poland, and the Soviet Union. Its main aim was to alleviate the burden of introducing the dollar payment system among these countries. At that time the Soviet Union opposed this plan.[8] The next, presented in May 1990, was the so-called Dienstbier proposal (named after the Czechoslovakian minister of foreign affairs), which envisaged a stabilization plan for Eastern Europe plus the Soviet Union. The proposal connected stabilization with the introduction of a multiclearing system. It estimated that $16 billion in aid would be necessary for stabilization. The multiclearing, it was suggested, should be realized through the assistance of the European Bank for Reconstruction and Development (EBRD). Third, a similar proposition was prepared by Jozef van Brabant, who also suggested a simultaneous solution to aid and payment problems. According to his plan, the new convertible payment system was to be assisted by the Bank for International Settlements (BIS) using the ECU as key currency, and the aid program was to be supported by the EBRD.[9] He included a total of seven countries, with the former Soviet Union, and calculated the starting capital at a surprisingly low level of $2.5 billion, because he conceived the payments union taking the earlier EPU (European Payments Union) as a pattern. That is, the member countries would also contribute their quotas to the base capital.

According to the Hungarian approach,[10] a multilateral clearing center would be set up. The EBRD or the BIS could also be entrusted to take this function. In this clearing system, payments would be settled with the clearing center and effective payments would be due only to the balance, according to agreed time and credit conditions. This payment union could serve as a basis for receiving aid from the West through establishing its own base capital, providing payment guarantees, and supporting the convertibility of national currencies. As key currency, the ECU was suggested because it provides connections with European Monetary System and thus prepares for the future monetary integration of Eastern Europe into the EU.

Later, although not for the purpose of a payments union, the German mark was suggested as the key currency. Helmut Schlesinger, then president of the Bundesbank, proposed that Hungary, for instance, peg the rate of the forint to the deutsche mark. (At present the Hungarian currency basket is shared half and half by the dollar and the ECU.) The proposal may be considered by the Hungarians in the future, since over 50 percent of Hungarian exports are paid for in marks or other currencies based on the mark.[11]

As we can see, the proposals were aimed at solving the following problems:

- The shortage of convertible currency stocks: the clearing system would reduce the need for effective payments to the balance.
- Instability: the ECU as key currency could provide a firm base for the new payment system and would also necessitate the adjustment to the EU monetary system.
- Allocation of Western aid: it seems probable that the EBRD will continue to keep this function.
- Convertibility of national currencies: financial support was expected to help currency convertibility.

According to J. van Brabant, the main functions of the payment union should be:

- A clearing payment facility among member countries that would arrange mutual payments among countries belonging to the circle
- A credit facility that would help overbridge payment imbalances due to trade fluctuations
- Trade liberalization through a coordination mechanism, which would lead to free trade among countries within the circle without causing disturbances in domestic economies of the member countries
- Macroeconomic policy surveillance, facilitating structural adjustment with the aim of redirecting exports from Eastern markets to the West

At the time when van Brabant wrote his book, the currencies of the three countries were not convertible, and he maintained that they would not be in the near future, either. Therefore, he attributed to the payment union a strong economic-policy harmonization role. Thus, in his understanding a structural adjustment would endogenously establish the convertibility of national currencies. However, in the meantime, as a matter of fact, the Hungarian forint, the Czech and Slovak koruna, and the Polish zloty became (non-fully) convertible. The reason for this sudden change is that these countries were able to redirect their trade to Western Europe surprisingly quickly, within one year after the COMECON's collapse. Thus, they haven't suffered severely from the shortage of convertible currency stocks.

How can van Brabant's reasoning be assessed now that these countries have introduced limited convertibility? It seems that the credit function together with the need for regional development harmonization make the proposal for a payments union still relevant. (If this is still politically feasible is a topic which goes beyond the scope of the present paper.) Other functions, like trade liberalization and macroeconomic policy surveillance, usually go beyond banking competence and belong to the governments or their trade missions in the member countries. But even if so, the idea of the payments union remains relevant, for it could considerably help trade and other cooperation activities.

Furthermore, and this is our main point, the currency convertibility achieved by the three countries is a limited convertibility, meaning it allows:

- The legal right of residents to acquire and maintain domestic holdings of foreign currency
- The right of domestic enterprises to import freely and to acquire the necessary foreign exchange from their banks
- The right of joint ventures or entirely foreign-owned firms to repatriate their profits and capital withdrawal in foreign currency

The currencies of the three Central European countries are not used for making international payments. Therefore, the task of extending the convertibility also on the capital account remains to be achieved. This is the field where a payments union could help considerably, since it would contribute to the stability of payments and the stability of national currencies.

When devising a payments union, stability especially should be stressed. Actually, stability has a twofold meaning: as a condition of underlying factors resulting in the stability of the exchange rate, and as a beneficial effect on the total economy coming from a stable exchange rate. These two aspects are sometimes difficult to harmonize, requiring a compromise between the level of the exchange rate and the monetary policy. At present, as to the three Central European currencies mentioned, the rate of inflation and the monetary policies are of utmost relevance. A compromise between these two, for example, in the Italian case was reached by considering the stability of the national currency as a priority requirement through adopting the European Monetary System (EMS), but this led to giving up the autonomous domestic monetary policy. In the case of Hungary, the Czech Republic, Slovakia, and Poland, the real rate of inflation in 1993 was kept within the 20 percent limit, and provided the tight monetary policy continues, the rate of inflation could be even less and devaluations may not exceed 10–15 percent (in the case of Hungary, Poland and Slovakia). Usually in these countries, nominal devaluation is less than the rate of inflation; hence, the real rate of devaluation is negative, indicating, in fact, a gradual appreciation of national currencies. In other words, galloping devaluation is not a real threat to the stability of exchange rates. Since in shaping their monetary policies, these countries are considering the International Monetary Fund (IMF) recommendations, the inflation and the future devaluations will be kept under lower limits, and thus the countries could comply with the requirements of a possible payments union.

One of the barriers to a payments union is the question of whether to include the Commonwealth of Independent States (CIS) or not. Since the CIS still suffers from a considerable shortage of convertible currency stocks, if it became a member in the new payments union, it would pose the biggest danger of destabilization. Therefore, the three core countries seem to be unwilling to accept the CIS. For Western Europe, however, it is much more convenient to treat Eastern Europe together with the CIS as one bloc; this also serves Western Europe politically, as a gesture to showing that it is helping to overcome the former isolation of the CIS. This difference between the Central European and Western European stands is the main reason for the delay in establishing the payment union.

The intention of the countries is also ambiguous. Several specialists are of the opinion that such a payments union would be merely an artificial institution and in fact would not contribute to expanding trade, or, reasoning more generally, they maintain (especially the Czech specialists, after establishing the CEFTA) that any regional grouping would only conserve the "waiting room status'' of Central Europe for EU. Instead, they claim that what is really necessary would be to dismantle tariff and nontariff barriers.[12] Thus, the idea for payments unions in Eastern Europe may become only a topic for economic historians.

The Free Trade Area

In 1991 the Visegrad treaty countries decided to form a free trade area. Establishing a free trade area means in the classical sense to abolish trade barriers among member countries while toward third countries each member maintains its own regulations (e.g., EFTA).

Why did the free trade area become necessary, once these countries had liberalized their trade during 1990–1991? What, then, did the liberalization mean? Actually, liberalization meant the abolition of the administrative import regulations called the "licensing system." Earlier, both export and import deals had been subject to central licensing. Then the export regulations became more liberal, and finally import controls were lifted. Freer imports posed difficulties for the producers of similar commodities of the importing country, since prices were not market clearing prices and customs tariffs, though existing formally, did not provide a shield for them. The only exception was probably Hungary, where freeing of prices and bringing them closer to world market prices began prior to 1990. In the other two countries, however, budgetary subsidies continued to exist and prices remained distorted. In the light of these considerations, it is no wonder that the three countries began introducing tariff and nontariff regulations.

In order to protect the domestic producers, former Czechoslovakia restructured its tariffs in January 1992, so that import duties on imports from Hungary increased by several times, and introduced adjusting customs for agricultural products, which are prohibitive for whole product groups among Hungarian exports. Poland increased import tariffs in August 1991, followed by another customs increase in January 1992. Hungary was also forced to react, and imposed import quotas for imports from the CIS and former Czechoslovakia and also introduced a customs surcharge for cement, restricting imports from Czechoslovakia. The CIS also increased its import tariffs. Hungary introduced car import quotas in 1992, and this measure is interesting because it has also been suggested actually by the then EC in order to protect the EC market.

Thus by 1992, the necessity to remove trade barriers became urgent. It was also necessitated by the EC associate membership of the three countries, because the three countries stated to the EC in 1991 they would reduce tariffs. At the same time they maintained among themselves the restrictions; this contradiction could not continue. Therefore, they decided to provide among themselves at least the same treatment that they granted separately to the EC.

After hasty preparation, the three countries tried to declare the free trade area in July 1992, but it was delayed because of disagreement on several issues. Finally, the agreement was signed on 21 December 1992. It envisaged free trade

Table 10.10
Lists of Tariff Dismantling in Trade between the Czech and Slovak Republics and Hungary (based on trade figures from 1991)

For Czech and Slovakian exports (total exports: US$ 387 million)

Lists	Export value (US$ million)	Share of the respective list (%) in manufacturing exports	in total exports
A	62.5	17.8	16.1
B	101.2	28.8	26.1
C	72.8	20.7	18.8
0	114.7	32.7	29.6
Total	351.2	100.0	90.6

For Hungarian exports (total exports: US$ 194 million)

List	Export value (US$ million)	Share of the respective list (%) in manufacturing exports	in total exports
A	55.9	38.7	28.8
B	52.0	36.0	26.8
C	13.9	9.6	7.2
0	22.7	15.7	11.7
Total	144.5	100.0	74.5

Source: Author's estimates based on data provided by Ministry of International Economic Relations, Budapest, 1993.

between member countries by 2001. However, the members also agreed to intensify negotiations about an earlier removal of the tariffs, within five years. The agreement is different from the EC-type agreement (that is, from the agreement that the three countries signed with the EC), because here the basic principle for tariff removal is symmetry (e.g., Hungary provided a greater tariff cut for industrial products imported from the partners but also received from them the same greater tariff cut for Hungarian agrarian products). The agreement was actually concluded bilaterally among the countries, so it contains three bilateral lists of commodities (each country with the other two). The tariff removal, depicted in Tables 10.10 and 10.11, began in March 1993 and will continue to be implemented in three steps:[13]

1. List "A": immediate dismantling. This applies to industrial raw materials like Polish copper, salt, and sulphur and Hungarian bauxit and aluminium. Also, some industrial manufacturers are included, for example, Polish agricultural machinery and Hungarian pharmaceutics.

2. List "B": dismantling by the end of 1996. Most industrial products belong to this category. Import tariffs were cut only from 1 January 1995 by less than one-third, to be followed by another one-third cut in 1996; the remaining one-third is to be abol-

Table 10.11
Lists of Tariff Dismantling in Trade between Hungary and Poland (based on trade figures from 1991)

For Polish exports (total exports: US$ 212.5 million)

List	Export value (US$ million)	Share of the respective list (%) in manufacturing exports	in total exports
A	46.8	23.4	22.0
B	76.3	38.0	36.8
C	9.6	4.8	4.5
0	67.9	33.8	32.8
Total	200.6	100.0	94.5

For Hungarian exports (total exports: US$ 201.3 million)

Lists	Export value (US$ million)	Share of the respective list (%) in manufacturing exports	in total exports
A	54.6	47.6	27.1
B	43.6	38.0	21.7
C	15.3	13.4	7.6
O	1.2	1.0	0.6
Total	114.7	100.0	57.0

Source: Author's estimates based on data provided by Ministry of International Economic Relations, Budapest, 1993.

ished on 1 January 1997. Thus, by 1997, 80 percent of industrial trade with the Czech Republic and Slovakia and 90 percent of the trade with Poland should be free.

3. List "C": dismantling within eight years. Included are industrial sectors in which production and employment require degressive protection. These are the most sensitive fields. Such sectors are the automobile industry in Poland, textile production in former Czechoslovakia, and the steel industry in Hungary. But actually, the list is wider for these countries, for example, the list for imports from the Czech Republic and Slovakia to Hungary contains textiles, apparel, shoes, metallurgy, selected machines, automobiles, and furniture; while the list for the opposite direction, that is, restricting Hungarian exports, contains chemicals, plastics, rubber, wood and paper products, textiles, apparel, shoes, ceramics, glass, metallurgy, machines and equipments, automobiles, weapons, and furniture.

However, ongoing machinery cooperation is being promoted by special exemptions. Hungary provided a tariff-free contingent of $5 million for Polish car parts beginning in 1993, so the figures for Poland must be accordingly increased by $2.6 million in List "A" (while it decreases by the same amount List "C"). Similarly, Poland granted free treatment for the import of Hungarian-made bus parts up to a contingent of $14 million (so List "A" should be increased by $4.3 million, and Lists "B" and "C" decreased by the same amount). Tariffs should decrease beginning in January 1995, by a 15 percent cut each year thereafter.

Finally, there is a List "0" (zero), containing positions the trade of which was also free before the agreement. These positions will be added to List "A," showing the total of free trade from 1993. Thus, for example, the Czech Republic and Slovakia free their imports from Hungary to 54.4 percent of the total industrial imports (38.7 percent of List "A" plus 15.7 percent of List "0"), while in the opposite direction trade will be free to 50.5 percent.

A special category is agricultural products. Four lists exist:

1. Tariff reduction within two years, by a total of 20 percent (10 percent each year), and within this, maintaining an import quota for some products, and not keeping an import quota for other products.

2. Tariff reduction within five years, by a total of 50 percent (10 percent each year), and within this, maintaining an import quota for some products, and not keeping an import quota for others.

As we can see, even by 2001 mutual trade will not be totally free. Especially difficult is the dismantling of tariffs on agricultural products.[14] In this area, the protective policies of Slovakia and Poland for their domestic producers do not favor Hungary, which has large agricultural surpluses.

SOME CONCLUSIONS

Will the century-long dream of a confederation of the countries along the Danube be realized?

As we saw, during the postwar period trade between Hungary, former Czechoslovakia, and Poland was low in volume, but its pattern indicated a high level of cooperation. Now that CEFTA has been created, most trade barriers should be cleared by 2001, and in the meantime the change to a market economy will progress. CEFTA left, however, two main areas for further resolution. One of them is the system of payments, including the full currency convertibility, and the other is regional coordination of economic policies. A certain coordination will be needed to harmonize industrial restructuring and to help harmonize financial and banking structures.

The criticism against the CEFTA that the new grouping, similarly to the COMECON, is just an "integration of the 'poor-club' countries" lacking competitive forces, seems in my judgement, not well founded. The new grouping is an open formation, in several ways. Member countries are open toward the EU; the problem is that toward each other they remain less open than toward the EU. They are also open to foreign capital, which together with privatization is boosting competitive markets. That is, there is not an absolute lack of new technology and new capital. Until the new products achieve a level sufficient to enter West European markets, they can find a good outlet on the Eastern market, enlarged through CEFTA.

In the sense of time, CEFTA is also open: it seems to be a temporary grouping, since even if the time for its acceptance into the EU has not been set, the three or four countries will be accepted eventually. The EU may give exceptional treatment to these four countries as it did in the case of Greece; namely, even if structurally and institutionally the country is not fully prepared, membership will be granted in order to help the democratic transformation in the joining country.

Openness, however, should be assessed with two limiting considerations. One is the need for transitional protection for some products against Western competition, which was strongly recognized by the countries after they had generously liberalized their imports.[15] This consideration could and should lead to a transitional customs union. Another consideration is that the new grouping might not be open to the former Soviet Union, since its crisis economy would destabilize the region.

Looking at the situation from another angle, while these countries await acceptance by the EU, they obviously continue to exist as neighbouring countries with a good geographical, economic, and political reason to develop cooperation. Further, they may well remember the experience of the past decades, when a close tie with a great country, be it in the East or in the West, was not always to their benefit.

NOTES

1. *Magyarország története* (Hungarian history), Budapest: Academic Publisher, 1987, vol. 6, pp. 513–519, 709–713.

2. Iván T. Berend, "A közép- és kelet-európai gazdasági integráció kérdéséhez" (On the economic integration of Central and Eastern Europe), *Közgazdasági Szemle,* 5, 1968, pp. 550–554.

3. S. Najima, "A szocialista nemzetközi munkamegosztás rendszerének változásai 1950–1981 között" (Changes in the system of socialist international division of labour between 1950–1981), *MTA KTI Közlemények* (Bulletin of the Institute of Economics), Budapest, no. 34.

4. "Memorandum ob ekonomicheskoi politike Rossiyskoi Federatsii" (Memorandum on the economic policy of the Russian Federation), and "Instruktsiya o poriadke obyazatelnoi prodazhi predpriyatiyami, obedineniami, organizatsiyami i grazhdanami valuty v Respublikanskiy valutniy rezerv Rossiyskoi Federatsii, valutnie fondi resplublik, krayev i oblastei v sostave Rossiyskoi Federatsii, stabilizatsionniy valutniy fond Banka Rossii" (Instruction on the regime of compulsory currency selling by enterprises, trusts, organizations and citizens for the Republican Currency Reserve of the Russian Federation, currency funds of republics, prefectures belonging to the Russian Federation, and stabilization funds of the Russian Bank), *Ekonomika i zhizny,* 10 March 1992.

5. L. Kiss, "The Erosion of the Post-War European Order and Hungary's Foreign and Security Policy Perceptions," in *Searching for a New Security Structure in Europe,* ed. H. Clesse and L. Ruhl, Baden-Baden: Nomos Verlagsgesellschaft, 1990.

6. V. Benáček, "Komparace determinant a struktúry specializace československého a madařského zahranicního obchodu" (Comparing the factors and structure of specialisation in the trade between Czechoslovakia and Hungary), *EÚ ČSAV,* Praha, 1989.

7. G. Winrow, "Eastern Europe and Japan: Political Risks and Economic Prospects" (Paper for the Second Fukushima International Symposium, July 1992).

8. I. Illés, K. Mizsei, and I. Szegvári, "Válaszúton a közép-európai gazdasági együtt-müködés" (Central European economic cooperation at crossroads), Europa Fórum, October 1991.

9. J. van Brabant, *Integrating Eastern Europe into the Global Economy: Convertibility through a Payments Union,* New York: Kluwer Academic, 1991.

10. Illés, Mizsei, and Szegvári.

11. "Márkához kötött forint" (Forint pegged to the mark), *Népszabadság,* 2 April 1993.

12. "A Hármak kétes egysége" (The doubtful unity of the three), *Figyelő,* 7 May 1992.

13. "Januártól szabadkereskedelem" (Free trade from January), *Népszabadság,* 3 November 1992.

14. "Visegrádi szabadkereskedelem 2000-től" (Free trade among Visegrad countries from 2000), *Népszabadság,* 22 December 1992.

15. Richter, S., and Tóth, G. L., "Szabadkereskedelem-avagy "felzárkózás" Európához" (Free trade or catching up to Europe), *Figyelő,* 24 February 1993.

PART II

PRIVATIZATION AND FOREIGN INVESTMENTS: WESTERN PERSPECTIVES

11

Japan's Foreign Direct Investment in East European Countries

Ken Morita

The main purpose of this chapter is to examine Japan's stagnated presence in East European countries. The so-called Daihatsu-FSO case, a planned project for medium-sized automobile production between FSO (Fabryka Samochodow Osobowych, a Polish passenger car company) and foreign automobile companies, will be analysed in particular. Throughout the 1980s, Japanese Daihatsu and other Japanese companies were in keen competition to obtain a contract for the project with Polish FSO.

During the course of this keen competition, the Japanese consortium played second fiddle to an Italian competitor, although until the spring of 1988, it was said that compared to the Italians, the Japanese offered both a better credit policy and a superior technology transfer policy.

This chapter focuses mainly on the reasons for European superiority over Japan in such competitions,[1] for the purpose of investigating the stagnated presence of Japan's foreign direct investment in East European countries.

THE STAGNATED PRESENCE OF JAPAN'S FOREIGN DIRECT INVESTMENT IN EAST EUROPEAN COUNTRIES

Although Japan's foreign direct investment has been reduced since its peak in 1990 of US $48.0 billion in the flow base (about 21 percent of the world total), the flow amount of Japan's foreign direct investment in 1991 equaled US $30.7 billion (a reduction of 36 percent from the previous year), which represented the largest single position (around 18 percent) in the global total amount in the flow base. In the stock base, in 1991 Japan accumulated US $231.8 billion, which represented about 15 percent of the world total and put it in second position after the United States (US $450.2 billion or 29%).

As for Japan's foreign direct investment in East European countries, until the end of 1991, the stock value amounted to US $5 million in Poland, US $221 million in Hungary, US $9 million in Romania, and US $1 million in Bulgaria. Of the total stock value of Japan's foreign direct investment, the ratios were 0.002 percent (Poland), 0.1 percent (Hungary), 0.004 percent (Romania), and 0.0004 percent (Bulgaria).[2]

Needless to say, Hungary has received almost all of Japan's foreign direct investment into East European countries. In 1990 and 1991 Hungary received US $29 million and US $181 million respectively in internal direct investment from Japan. The dramatic increase principally came from the Magyar Suzuki case (automobile production of the Japanese Suzuki Motor Corporation with a Hungarian partner).[3]

My estimates, based on statistics from the State Foreign Investment Agency in Poland, indicate that the overall equity and loans value of 100 major foreign investors in Poland as of 1992 equaled US $1.79 billion (although the overall investment commitment of the same major investors was several times bigger), of which US $1.6 million (or only a 0.089 percent share) represented Japanese investment held by three major Japanese investors. According to data from the Japanese government, at the end of 1992, there were approximately 9,000 internal direct investors into Poland, with an overall equity and loan value of US $1.7 billion.[4] Japanese direct investments in Poland equaled only nineteen, with a value of about US $4.5 million, or a 0.21–0.26 percent share.

Although the statistics vary from one source to another as shown also in the introduction chapter and in the Jermakowicz chapter, whichever statistics are used, the Japanese position in foreign direct investment in Poland is quite small. In the following sections, we would like to try to explain why.

The Daihatsu-FSO Case

A summary of the essential facts of this case study follows.

It is easy to speculate about confidential information regarding the tough negotiations that extended over many years. This discussion will rely on information coming from several journals published in West Europe and Japan.

Since 1982, FSO has been in the process of modernization. In 1983 it began discussions with foreign car producers, mainly in an effort to lead economic development in Poland. It considered sixteen foreign automobile companies as candidates for its partner. Potential Japanese candidates included Japanese Daihatsu, which offered its plan to the company through Itochu (a Japanese general trading company) an exporter of FSO's automobiles to third countries, as well as Sumitomo (another Japanese general trading company), which had imported Daihatsu's passenger cars into Poland. Daihatsu, Itochu, and Sumitomo joined together to form a consortium.

The first article to announce this project in West European journals, as far as the author determines, was in *East-West* (March 27, 1984). According to this article, Poland was considering a new model passenger car to be manufactured in cooperation with a Western automobile company. The new model was to be a five-seat, 1,200cc engine type, manufactured at the rate of some 120,000 units per year, with 25 percent of output allocated for export. It was also announced that the total amount of this project was to be about 300 billion zlotys.

However, in 1985, an article in *Business Eastern Europe* (April 12), for example, said that launching of the project had been delayed, mainly due to Poland's economic problems and the lack of Western company interest.

A fairly long article under the title "Development Plans for Polish Car Industry" in *East-West* (September 26, 1985) reported on a talk by Jan Raczko, technical director of FSO, that indicated it was expected that a contract with a Western partner would be signed before the end of 1985. An article in *East European Market* (October 18, 1985) mentioned that the various Western candidates were Daihatsu, Nissan, Toyota, Fiat, Renault, and Spanish Seat. This article said that Daihatsu was favoured to be the winner because of its diesel engine, which offered considerable fuel economy.

According to Japanese sources of information, Japanese interest in this project had become stronger as a result of linking the Japanese consortium, through MITI (the Japanese Ministry of International Trade and Industry), with the Japan-Poland Economic Committee initiated by the chairman, Toshikuni Yahiro, president of Mitsui (a Japanese general trading company), which had joined the consortium. On May 28, 1986, a document under the name of the Minister of Metallurgy and Machinery Industry in Poland, Janusz Maciejewicz, requesting cooperation with a Japanese automobile company, was received by Mr. Yahiro.

In 1986, *East-West* (September 11), in the article "Daihatsu in Poland," announced that Daihatsu was likely to make a final decision by the end of the summer of 1986 on the assembly of cars in Poland. And an article in *Ost-West Handel* (October 29, 1986) entitled "Polen: Lizenzverhandlungen mit Daihatsu und Fiat," mentioned a talk by Edward Pietrzak, FSO general director, at a press conference in Warsaw on October 25, 1986, saying that the financial arrangements would play a role in the negotiations.

On November 27, 1986, the Worker's Council of FSO announced their analysis of the case and supported Daihatsu, claiming that Daihatsu was offering a more advanced type of car and better financial conditions, including lower licencing costs, more favourable terms of loan repayment, and better conditions for the export of cars made in Poland (*East-West*, February 24, 1987). The same article also mentioned the interesting opinion that *the Polish authorities apparently favoured Fiat* but that their decision was made more difficult because the FSO Workers' Council supported the Japanese offer.

The first article that we could find mentioning difficult points in Daihatsu's offer to Poland was in *East-West* (December 19, 1986). This article said that Poland claimed that Daihatsu had demanded a very strict system of quality control, which was not enforceable in Poland.

Prime Minister Yasuhiro Nakasone visited Poland on January 16 and 17,

1987, and his visit had an influence on these negotiations. (Before his visit to Poland, a program on Polish National Television took the position that the visit was expected to be important for Poland in selecting its partner.) In his talks with the then First Communist Party Secretary, Wojciech Jaruzelski, and Prime Minister Zbigniew Messner, Nakasone did not commit to giving Poland official financial credit to promote Daihatsu's cooperation with FSO. However, it was said that the mere fact that the summit talks included this very project, initiated mainly by private companies, was very important, and the inclusion led to optimistic expectations.

Another influential visit concerning the project was Jaruzelski's trip to Japan from June 28 to July 2, 1987, which followed his visit to Italy. According to a Japanese source of information, in the summit talks, Jaruzelski declared a plan for allocating the medium-sized car production project to Daihatsu and the small-sized production project to Fiat. In addition, Jaruzelski mentioned that he had not accepted any request from Italy on this particular project and that he had rejected an Italian proposal for setting up a committee of third countries to mediate the tough negotiations. The Japanese stance on giving official financial credit to Poland did not change.

It seems to the author that the leaders' visits (including Jaruzelski's visit to Italy) helped to strongly promote Japan's economic relations with Poland. This resulted in a very pessimistic statement by Govanni Agnelli, the president of Fiat. In his statement, Agnelli said that Fiat apparently had lost a contract to Daihatsu in a bid to build a modern car plant in Poland and that the Japanese had offered superior technology and better financial terms. (*International Herald Tribune* and *Financial Times,* July 1, 1987; *East-West,* July 6, 1987; *Business Eastern Europe,* July 13, 1987).

It was said that in his talks with Jaruzelski in Japan, Nakasone noted that he looks positively on the Japanese consortium's stance on considering a "bridge loan," that is, a loan on a private basis, to fill in the time lag before being given financial credit on a government basis. The Japanese consortium, however, did not actually view the bridge loan with enthusiasm.

The Japanese consortium was also in sharp conflict with MITI concerning whether or not MITI would give a definite written promise of export insurance for the project. I think we can assess the inner negotiations in Japan as follows: MITI thought that the private companies had to take the risk that the business would be profitable; in contrast, the consortium thought that official financial support for this project was a fairly easy burden for the Japanese government budget when compared to the expected benefits.

On August 20, 1987, an article in *Radio Free Europe Research* (RFER) said that Daihatsu would produce a medium-sized car in Poland. In the same article, RFER specifically announced the following three points: First, the Polish government had exploited the competition to obtain progressively better terms for its own automobile industry. That explained the lengthy period needed to complete the agreement. Second, the adaptation of Japanese work methods and style to Poland might be a problem. Third, while the Japanese were steadily pursuing the Polish contract, they did not seem particularly enthusiastic about investing on such a large scale in Poland. In any event, RFER recognized that the Japanese were in a strong position to win the contract.

According to information coming from a Japanese source, in mid October 1987, officials of the Polish Ministry of Foreign Affairs and Polish Ministry of Foreign Trade gave their opinion, from a diplomatic perspective, that Daihatsu would win against Fiat.

On November 13, 1987, *East European Markets,* in an article entitled "Daihatsu Decision Expected Soon," announced that as of the summer of 1987, Poland thought Daihatsu was offering better technological and trade terms than Fiat. However, the same article also mentioned that the Japanese companies were unable to come up with the necessary financing and said that an already completed Polish agreement with Fiat for the FSM (Fabryka Samochodow Malolitrazowych, a Polish small-sized passenger car company) small-car plant gave the edge to Fiat. In addition, it reported that the Italian government had given Fiat the go-ahead to purchase one million cars from these modernization agreements, on condition that the machinery and equipment for FSO and FSM came from Italy.

On January 29, 1988, an article called "FSO Looks Ahead" in *East European Markets* announced that Edward Pietrzek said he expected that the long-running negotiations with Fiat and Daihatsu on the future of the plant were coming to an end.

While these negotiations were proceeding, Poland was engaged in multilateral and bilateral negotiations on its outstanding debt. Although the rescheduling negotiation in the Paris Club reached agreement, bilateral negotiations between Poland and Japan were far from complete agreement at the beginning of 1988. Around this time the Japanese side apparently recognized Fiat's strong activity favouring "roll back."

On August 6, 1988, bilateral negotiations between Poland and Japan concerning the third and the fourth debt rescheduling agreements finally resulted in agreement to make interest rates 6.5 percent in Japanese ¥ and 7.95 percent in U.S. dollars. Objectively viewed, this constituted a Japanese concession. It was thought that after many years of tough negotiations, the most serious obstacle for successful talks between the two parties had been eliminated.

Just after reaching the agreement, however, on August 19, Tomohiro Eguchi, the president of Daihatsu, declared at a press conference his pessimistic expectations concerning the keen competition with Fiat (*Nihon Keizai Shimbun,* August 20, 1988). Eguchi actually visited Poland at the end of July 1988, so we can readily speculate that some high-ranking Polish officials who favoured Fiat told him on a confidential basis their decision on the project.

On September 8, 1988, also just after the successful agreement on the rescheduling talks, the Polish government requested that the Japanese government start renegotiation of interest rates in the first and second rescheduling agreement (around 9 to 10 percent), which had already been completed. Needless to say, the Japanese Ministry of Finance immediately rejected this unprecedented request.

Only five days after this request by Poland, on September 13, Pietrzek announced that Fiat was the winner for the contract (*Zycie Warszawy,* September 14, 1988; *Rzeczpospolita,* September 15, 1988; *Ost-West Handel,* September 19, 1988).

However, on December 6, 1988, after the reshuffle in the Polish cabinet, Jerzy Urban, the then Polish government spokesman, announced a new Polish decision. This decision, led by Mieczyslaw Wilczek, the new Minister of Industry, was to stop medium-sized passenger car production. Also, Pietrzek resigned as FSO president. Since the change toward a market economy in Poland that began in 1990, this project has remained uncertain, but with European in the lead.

Based on the facts mentioned, I think we can find some crucial points that explain the reasons for Italian better position over Japan up to the end of 1980s, even though Agnelli had officially recognized Fiat's loss in 1987. These can be viewed in a conceptual framework relating to foreign direct investment.

This chapter intends to interpret the reasons for European superiority from the viewpoint discussed and implicitly tries to reconsider the theory of foreign direct investment in light of these findings.

INTERPRETATION

The Daihatsu-FSO case could be considered from the perspective of economic behaviour relating to export and import of technology and materials for manufacturing passenger cars. However, I wish to emphasize the aspect of foreign direct investment observed in this case, using Japan's official definition of direct investment, "long-term credit not accompanied by equity ownership is included in outward direct investment, if a certain close relationship exists between the lender and the borrower."[5] This definition is, I think, rather easily applied to the case under consideration. As applied, this case should be interpreted as an instance of Japan's foreign direct investment.

In addition, the historically close relations of Poland with Italy in the fields of economy, culture, diplomatic relations, and so forth, seem to have played a crucial role in Fiat's success over Daihatsu. This means that this case should not be interpreted as involving only export-import behavior between the two parties. Rather, it should be viewed in terms of foreign direct investment behaviour along with several other factors not involving export-import behaviour.

Some Polish experts emphasize several beneficial factors that make foreign investment in Poland attractive. Some of these are as follows (mainly from *Polityka,* June 10, 1989):

1. Poland is the biggest country in Central Europe (area, 312,000 sq. km; population, 38 million; per capita national income, US $2,000–2,500) and has the biggest market.

2. Poland is in a very good geographical situation, in that Warsaw lies halfway between Moscow and Paris and Stockholm and Budapest, or, in other words, Warsaw lies between the East and West as well as the North and South of the continent.

3. Poland has a very well developed railroad network, with one-third of the 27,000 km of railway line electrified. The density of the railroad network in Poland is greater than that in France, Great Britain, or Italy.

4. Poland has 250,000 km of roads, including 150,000 km with an asphalt surface.

5. Planes belonging to 35 airline companies land at Warsaw airports, while the Polish Airline LOT provides regular flights to and from 40 countries.

6. The merchant marine consists of 250 cargo vessels, with a combined capacity of over 4 million deadweight tons. The Polish Baltic ports have a handling capacity of over 50 million tons a year.

7. Poland has substantial mineral resources, compared to other European countries.

8. Poland has a large and skilled labour force.

9. Direct investment into Poland provides a production base that spreads business into other West and East European countries.

Among these benefits, the last was considered the most advantageous by Daihatsu because, according to the plan, some 120,000 passenger cars would be manufactured in Poland, of which 25 percent would be allocated to West European markets. On the other hand, because Fiat had played a major role in the Polish automobile industry for many years, it would have been a very serious blow to Fiat if Daihatsu had been the winner.

For Poland, the main purposes of negotiating with foreign automobile companies were (1) needless to say, to modernize their outdated automobile industry, and (2) to attract foreign capital in order to develop its economy. Some Polish experts have particularly stressed the benefit that Poland has a large and skilled labour force in comparison with labour costs (see item 8 on the list) as the most attractive advantage for foreign investors.

Considered on the basis of the facts mentioned in the previous section, I think we can conclude that Poland has attached great importance to capital inflow as well as to traditional diplomatic relations with West European countries. We can also speculate that one of the important issues that caused the keen competition between Fiat and Daihatsu was the West European market, taking into account both the global automobile market and EU economic integration.

There was a big difference concerning the unity between government and company on the Japanese side as compared with the Italian rival. The Italian government and Fiat had formed a strong united front against the Japanese rival to block the rival's presence in the European market. The Japanese side, on the contrary, experienced differences between the government and the companies and between the Japanese Embassy in Poland and the Ministry of Foreign Affairs (MOFA) in Japan.

It seems to the author that the Japanese Ministry of Foreign Affairs held to the view that close and stable diplomatic relations between Japan and West European countries such as Italy and France were more important than relations with East European countries such as Poland. From the Japanese MOFA's point of view, in a diplomatic sense, giving priority to the West is plausible. From the consortium's point of view, in a business sense, their behavior in adopting a very cautious attitude toward joining the big-scale project was also plausible.

Regarding the behaviour of the Japanese side, I would like to explicitly mention in the next sections three points that help interpret the facts in the previous section.

Characteristics of Japan's Foreign Direct Investment

The first point concerns the characteristics of Japan's foreign direct investment. As mentioned previously, in 1991 Japan had the largest position of all countries in foreign direct investment measured by the flow base. However, Japan's position in the direct investment area has not always been so strong. The flow was decreasing in 1991 compared with 1990 principally because the profit rate in the manufacturing sector was lower than both the profit rate from domestic investment by Japanese companies and foreign investment by other countries' companies. It is easily seen that the dramatic increase in Japan's foreign direct investment in the 1980s was coming from (1) the appreciation of the Japanese yen and (2) avoidance of trade conflict—not from superiority of managerial resources in the global market.

Along with Komiya [7] we note the following characteristics of Japan's foreign direct investment. First, Japan is the latest arrival in the field of foreign direct investment, and is still in its early stage of development as a direct investor country. The fact that Japan is far from a state of maturity as a direct investor country is indicated in many statistics. For example, in an international comparison of the ratio of the outstanding value of foreign direct investment to GNP, Japan's ratio is the lowest among the major investor countries, which include the United States, Great Britain, and Germany. Second, the Japanese share of manufacturing industries in foreign direct investment is substantially smaller than the shares of the United States, Great Britain, and Germany. Third, in the regional breakdown of Japan's foreign direct investment, the shares of developing countries used to be relatively large in comparison with foreign direct investment by major developed countries. Fourth, as mentioned in the discussion of the recent decrease in Japan's foreign direct investment, the profitability of Japan's foreign direct investment has been lower than the profit rate in Japan. In addition, the profit rate earned by Japanese-owned subsidiaries in the U.S. manufacturing sector is much lower than the average rate earned by all foreign-owned subsidiaries in the same sector. The fact that there are very few examples of Japanese-owned large-scale and well-established subsidiaries in foreign countries is closely connected with these characteristics.

These facts and characteristics are very adequately explained as being based on the fact that Japanese companies have not yet accumulated the managerial resources necessary for running factories abroad as efficiently as those at home. In this regard, "managerial resources" simply means "organizational know-how and expertise necessary to run a firm efficiently."[6] In other words, such resources amount to the ability to make profit by correctly accepting and excluding factors (economic, cultural, political, sociological, etc.) that are inseparable from host countries. It probably takes many years to accumulate such scarce resources. This is especially so in the case of running subsidiaries in East European countries, which still have somewhat different economic adjustment mechanisms. Accordingly, running factories in such countries as efficiently as in the home country seems to be extremely difficult. Italian Fiat, as I mentioned previously, has a long tradition of working with East European countries. This experience is rare among Western companies.

Therefore, taking into account this general characteristic of Japanese foreign direct investment, namely, the lack of managerial resources, I think we can understand the differences between Fiat and Daihatsu when it comes to accumulating managerial resources within the East European region.

Characteristics of Risky Foreign Direct Investment

In the previous section, we applied foreign direct investment theory to interpret the case with which we are concerned. In addition to general theory, this case has a specific important factor that must be taken into account, that is, the huge amount of foreign debt in Poland. As mentioned earlier, better financial terms have been a crucial point in the tough negotiations.

Also, the lack of accumulated managerial resources seems to make Japanese companies in general more risk averse in foreign direct investment. The issues raised in this and the next section are, therefore, deemed to be more appropriate to Japan's foreign direct investment behaviour.

In light of certain aspects of specific factors applicable in this case, I think we can correctly interpret the reason for the long negotiation period in this case. In fact, negotiations were never actually concluded because of the after-1989 change that occurred in Poland. As was mentioned earlier, some Polish experts emphasize that the most attractive feature in Poland, as is the case also in Bulgaria, the Czech Republic, and Hungary, for foreign investors is the existence of a large and skilled labour force compared with labour costs. If Poland were free from its foreign debt, it would, as Polish experts emphasize, be an attractive country for foreign investors. However, foreign investors are not free from the risk that arises from the huge amount of Polish debt, and they believe that Poland is a very risky country.

Therefore, we should investigate the distinctive features of risky direct investment along the lines used by Frey [3]. Frey [3] statistically examines political and economic determinants of foreign direct investment in 54 cases involving less developed risky countries, comparing four competing models. He concludes that the "politico-economic" model he presents performs relatively the best with respect to goodness of fit. In his investigation, eleven economic and political determinants are statistically considered and the standardized regression coefficients are calculated. Among the eleven determinants, the most influential economic determinants are real per capita GNP and the balance of payments. Frey wrote that "the higher the per capita income and the lower the balance of payments deficit, the more foreign direct investment is attracted."[7] Two very interesting findings in Frey's research that impact on the subject of this chapter and the points emphasized by Polish experts are as follows: first, "among the less important economic influences are the growth of GNP and *the worker's skill level*" (emphasis added), and second, "among the political determinants, the amount of bilateral aid coming from Western countries has the strongest stimulating effect."[8]

Frey's research was done with the data of 1979, but I think the findings are applicable even to the latest cases and, needless to say, the case under discussion. First of all, as mentioned earlier, Poland has a large and skilled labour force with cheap labour costs; as established, this factor has been emphasized by some experts in Poland. However, as long as Poland is a risky country for foreign investors, workers' skill level has a less important influence on decisions for FDI by Western companies. I think this reality explains the huge difference in viewpoint between the Polish officials and the foreign automobile companies that led to the lengthy and tough negotiations. In addition, the Polish level of skilled labour is far from adequate, from the viewpoint of the requirements of Daihatsu and Fiat, especially Daihatsu. The workers' skill level in Poland has not only a noninfluential effect on foreign direct investment's decisions, but also might deter such investment, even if the level of the Polish workers' skill is higher than that in most developing countries.

The dominating negative influence of the balance of payments problem, that is, the huge amount of foreign debt closely connected with the amount of bilateral aid from Western countries, should be interpreted as playing a crucial role in this case. The difference between the lack of unity on the Japanese side and the unity existing on the Italian side mentioned earlier should also be considered a crucial factor in determining the winner of the contract with Poland. This is because official aid plays a very important role when private companies invest directly into risky countries.

Concluding Thoughts: Toward Establishing an International Regime

As mentioned previously, in the case discussed, uncertainty and risk, closely related to the lack of accumulated managerial resources in Japanese companies and the difference between Japan and Italy as to government-corporation unity, played important roles. In this section, we approach and examine the issues solely on the basis of the international regime theory.

This section concentrates upon rational political and economic measures designed to make the extremely weak economic presence of Japan in East European countries stronger.

Concerning the stagnated presence of Japan's foreign direct investment in East European countries, it seems that social costs have played crucial roles hindering capital movement. The main cost factors come, I think, from (1) lack of a clear legal framework establishing liability for actions, (2) information imperfections, and (3) positive transaction costs. These three cost factors, understood to be market failures, are conditions indicated by Coase [2]. By inverting the Coase theorem,[9] we see that if at least one of the factors exists, international regimes are of value in facilitating agreements among governments.

I think it is useful to examine the concept of international regimes with a view to overcoming serious cost factors. Generally speaking, where there are orderly, stable, and active relations between countries, social scientists usually call the situation a regime. Such a regime has certain features.

According to Keohane [5], to reach a situation of international regime, we have to distinguish "harmony," "cooperation," and "discord." This means that if each actor's policies (pursued without regard for the interests of others) are perceived by others as facilitating the attainment of their goals, no communication is necessary and no influence need be exercised, that is, no international regime is necessary. On the other hand, if each actor's policies are regarded by others as hindering the attainment of their goals and if their policies are adjustable and become significantly more compatible with one another, cooperation takes place. (If their policies are not adjustable, or incompatible even in adjustable cases, discord ensures.) As Keohane correctly indicates,[10] a major function of regimes is to facilitate specific cooperative agreements among governments.

In accordance with Keohane [4] and Krasner [10], we define international regimes as sets of implicit or explicit principles, norms, rules, and decision-making procedures around which actors' expectations converge in a given area of international relations. Also, we agree with Keohane that international regimes should be comprehended chiefly as arrangements motivated by self-interest. We should emphasize, at the same time, that because international regimes reflect patterns of cooperation over a long time, regimes can produce shared interests for actors, as institutionalists maintain.

In focusing upon the economic relations of Japan with East European countries, generally speaking, the following four factors are understood to be shared interests: (1) decreasing uncertainty, (2) decreasing the costs of collecting information, (3) making relations more stable, and (4) decreasing transaction costs.[11]

Considering the application of international regime theory to more orderly, stable, and active economic relations, we should particularly emphasize that Japan and East European countries have just embarked on an attempt to establish such a regime. Japan has never had any principles, norms, rules, or decision-making procedures in common with East European countries. This was clearly reflected in the Daihatsu-FSO case mentioned earlier.

Therefore, we indicate that the stagnated presence of Japan's foreign direct investment into East European countries has been due to the nonexistence of a regime producing shared interests.

Also, as many experts correctly stated,[12] the Japanese business community is more risk averse than the American and West European business communities. That means Japanese companies will make fewer agreements under potential market failure conditions than less risk-averse companies, and Japanese companies will make fewer agreements than they would under conditions of perfect information. Needless to say, cost factors arising from market failure conditions make economic mechanisms inefficient through moral hazard and adverse selection.

Therefore, eliminating asymmetric information, decreasing transaction costs, creating a clear legal framework, and having more certainty through establishing an international regime can produce a more efficient mechanism and make Japanese risk-averse companies more active in post-communist Europe.

NOTES

This chapter is based upon papers originally presented at the 33rd and 34th ISA Annual Meetings. The author is thankful for helpful comments given him by a number of people, including Dr. Gabor Bakos, Professor Wojciech Bienkowski, Professor Masumi Hakogi, Professor Bartlomiej Kaminski, Professor Carl H. Mcmillan, Professor Steven S. Rosefielde, and Dr. Iliana Zloch-Christy. Any remaining errors are the author's responsibility.

1. As of October 1993, as a matter of fact, Italian Fiat was concentrating upon producing small-sized automobiles in cooperation with FSM. In the field of medium-sized automobile production with FSO, GM (Europe) has the biggest advantage. Our attention is mainly focused on the period from the beginning till the end of 1980s, when Japanese players joined the competition.

2. Statistics for the former Czechoslovakia were not available.

3. See Bakos [1].

4. Needless to say, this amount was less than the US $1.79 billion from 100 major investors contained in data from the State Foreign Investment Agency in Poland.

5. See Komiya [7], p. 222.

6. See Komiya [7], p. 261.

7. See Frey [3], p. 83.

8. See Frey [3], p. 83.

9. See Keohane [5].

10. See Keohane [5], p. 62.

11. See, for example, Morita [12].

12. See Bakos [1].

REFERENCES

[1] Bakos, Gabor. "Japanese Capital in Central Europe." *Hitotsubashi Journal of Economics*, vol. 33, no. 2, December 1992, pp. 149–168.

[2] Coase, Ronald H. "The Problem of Social Cost." *The Journal of Law and Economics,* vol. 3, October 1960, pp. 1–44.

[3] Frey, Bruno S. *International Political Economics.* New York: Basil Blackwell, 1984.

[4] Keohane, Robert O. *After Hegemony.* Princeton: Princeton University Press, 1984.

[5] Keohane, Robert O. "The Demand for International Regimes." In Krasner [9], pp. 141–171.

[6] Komiya, Ryutaro. "Direct Foreign Investment in Postwar Japan." In Peter Drysdale (ed.), *Direct Foreign Investment in Asia and the Pacific.* Canberra: Australian National University Press, 1972.

[7] Komiya, Ryutaro. *Gendai Nihon Keizai* (Contemporary Japanese Economy). Tokyo: Tokyo University Press, 1988.

[8] Komiya, Ryutaro. *Gendai Nihon Keizai Kenkyu* (Scientific Papers on Contemporary Japanese Economy). Tokyo: Tokyo University Press, 1975.

[9] Krasner, Steven D. (ed.). *International Regimes.* Ithaca, NY: Cornell University Press, 1983.

[10] Krasner, Steven D. "Structural Cause and Regime Consequences: Regimes as Intervening Variables." In Krasner [9], pp. 1–21.

[11] Morita, Ken. "An Economic Analysis of Japan's Foreign Direct Investment into Poland: The Daihatsu-FSO Case." Paper presented at the 33rd ISA Annual Meetings in Atlanta, Georgia, United States, 1992.

[12] Morita, Ken. "Economic Relations between Japan and East European Countries." Paper presented at the 34th ISA Annual Meetings in Acapulco, Mexico, 1993.

12

Magyar Suzuki: Case Study of Japanese Investment

Gabor Bakos

The liberalization attempts in the early 1980s in Eastern European countries attracted Western car manufacturers. As discussed in the previous chapter written by K. Morita, the Japanese company Daihatsu began negotiations in Poland, while Suzuki targeted Hungary. However, owing to the longer local involvment of Fiat and stronger governmental backing behind it, Fiat won and Daihatsu failed to get the deal. On the other hand, Suzuki, though after long negotiations, established a joint venture car assembly factory in Hungary which remains the largest Japanese direct investment in Eastern Europe. During the first year of its operation, Magyar Suzuki successfully developed a network of Hungarian subcontractors by inviting Suzuki's Japanese partners to help them upgrade. Exports were also started in 1993.

THE MARKET

Although the potential Hungarian automobile market may seem small because Hungary's population is only 10 million, it is really quite substantial as a result of the need for a quick renewal of Hungary's aged car stock. The average age of Hungarian cars is roughly 10 years. Roughly 1 million of Hungary's 3 million cars ought to be immediately replaced, because they are more than 10 years old or have a high-polluting two-stroke engine. In 1990 about 40 percent of all Hungarian cars, including the Trabant and Wartburg made in the former GDR, had a two-stroke engine, and their share did not decrease substantially even after many Western used cars were imported as a result of car import liberalization in 1989–1990.[1] As the government started in 1993 an action to exchange the two-stroke cars for new models, Western car makers may be keen to win this business chance.

Table 12.1
Shares in the Magyar Suzuki Joint Venture

Total project value: US$ 70 million	
Japanese share:	51%
of which	
Suzuki	40%
C. Itoh	11%
Hungarian share:	40%
International Finance Corporation	9%

Hungary's high demand for automobiles is also demonstrated by import data. In 1989, car imports totalled 204,345, of which 136,280 (67 percent) were imported by state car trading companies and 68,065 (33 percent) were imported by private individuals. In 1989, imports by private individuals were particularly high as a result of the temporarily low import duty of only 10 percent. However, even in 1990, when the import duty rose to 35 percent, 30 thousand cars were imported by Hungarian tourists.

In 1992, 36,000 new cars were sold in Hungary; by the end of 1993 this figure reached some 45,000.

According to latest estimations, there is a market in Hungary for 120 to 140 thousand cars yearly. Suzuki's management is considering boosting production to 50 thousand cars by 1995, of which half could be sold in Hungary and half in Western Europe.

Suzuki's world marketing strategy is to establish regional manufacturing and marketing centers for its various products. Three categories of cars are in play. The minicar Maruti is produced in India. The subcompact category Swift and the bigger sedan version have been made in Hungary. The third type, an off-road vehicle, is the product of the Santana factory in Spain.

THE MAGYAR SUZUKI JOINT VENTURE

The Basic Agreement and Capital Sharing

The agreement was negotiated for almost ten years before finally signed in 1990. The basic agreement with Suzuki specifies that the five-door model of the Suzuki Swift, with either a 1.0- or 1.3-liter engine, will be produced starting in 1992. An output of 15,000 was planned for 1992, with production reaching 50,000 by 1995 and eventually reaching a maximum of 100,000 per year thereafter.

The Magyar Suzuki joint venture was founded in April 1991 with shares broken down as shown in Table 12.1. In the figures Suzuki's share is somewhat overrepresented because in reality 20 percent of its share is contributed in the form of foregone license fees.

The total value of the investment is, however, $240 million. The additional

$170 million is financed through credits with international financial market interest rates. For example, a significant amount of the production machinery is imported from Japan, for which the Japan Eximbank extended a credit. The Eximbank demanded a guarantee from the National Bank of Hungary. The National Bank provided this guarantee, but as the whole transaction will later be transferred to commercial banks, the National Bank charged the guarantee fee to Magyar Suzuki as if it had already paid to a commercial bank. Further, the International Finance Corporation (IFC) holds a mortgage on the site and the buildings.[2]

The Hungarian government has decided to promote the joint venture by granting a series of preferences to participants. In the Suzuki project, land upon which the car factory is constructed was sold to the joint venture at a price considerably below its market value. The joint venture will also enjoy a full exemption from income tax during the first five years, after which a preferential reduced taxation rate will be applied. As for import taxes, the agreement envisaged an exemption for imported machines, equipment, and parts to be used on cars for export, while parts used on cars to be sold domestically would be subject to an import tax of only 5 percent. Later this was reduced to 3 percent, and at present there is still no import tax, since a zero tax import car parts quota was granted jointly to Suzuki and General Motors (the total value of the quota is 10 billion forint).

As the joint venture approached completion, the government's support was felt less. Mr. Shinohara, general director of Magyar Suzuki, claimed that in the beginning the Hungarian government promised financial support to the car industry but that Suzuki's subcontractors were suffering from a shortage of capital. Also, full-fledged import liberalization left the developing car industry without any protective umbrella. Therefore, in his opinion, a consequent industry policy was necessary.[3] On the other hand, it must be mentioned that Suzuki tried to involve Hungarian authorities as much as possible by requesting that they take over additional (external) costs associated with the plant. One example is the infrastructure, where Suzuki wanted the Hungarian side to build a special service road to the site. In another case, Suzuki found the local environmental norms too severe and negotiated a compromise that resulted in reducing the costs of environmental protection.

Economic Benefits

The Suzuki project requires wide cooperation with the Hungarian supply industry. While Suzuki provides the important engine and gear-box components, within the first year of operation, 50 percent of all work on the project—25 percent in assembly and 25 percent in parts supply—have been contributed by Hungary. In future years, the Hungarian share should rise to 55–70 percent. As can be seen from the following draft of the value composition (Table 12.2), the Hungarian share consists of two parts, that of the base assembly factory (Magyar Suzuki, Esztergom) and that of other subcontractors. According to the draft, the

Table 12.2
Subcontracting as Value Composition of the Car (percent)

	1992	1993	1994
Suzuki Japan (imports)	70	60	40
Hungarian share	30	40	60
consisting of			
Magyar Suzuki (Esztergom)	20	20	20
Other subcontractors	10	20	40
Total	100	100	100

Source: Author's estimates based on data provided by the Ministry of Industry, Budapest, 1994.

share of the base plant is not going to increase, therefore involving more sub-contractors will become a crucial issue when increasing the total Hungarian share.

Originally about fifty Hungarian companies were targeted as subcontractors. During the project's realization, Suzuki had to face mainly two problems when trying to involve subcontractors. One was that the ambitious program of pri-vatizing state companies was started, which generally made the legal status of enterprizes uncertain. The second was that the government struggled with an aggravating budget deficit and thus was unable to give the financial support needed for restructuring. Potential subcontractors need an investment in the range of Ft 15 to 100 million ($180 thousand to $1.2 million) for restructuring and modernizing in order to supply Suzuki parts of the quality required. At the beginning, Suzuki could contract only slightly over 20 subcontractors. Accord-ing to a tender survey, 130 companies would be able to supply parts provided they could obtain restructuring financial support. It is in the interests of Suzuki to increase the Hungarian share to over 50 percent as soon as possible, because in this case the joint-venture-made car could be qualified as of Hungarian origin and be exported to the EU, thus surmounting the EU's car import quota imposed on Japanese-made cars. During almost a year, the number of subcontractors increased up to 35 (to October 1993), but owing to some shadows in marketing, partly because of the increasing competition on the Hungarian market and partly because of the depressed Western European markets, Suzuki still does not en-visage a dramatic increase in the number of subcontractors.

Several subcontracting deals are successfully being implemented. For exam-ple, the Precision Instrument Factory of Eger and Showa of Japan signed a license agreement to manufacture shock absorbers. The Hungarian firm bought the necessary license and expertise and began production in June 1992. Bakony Works of Veszprem has also formed a joint venture with Suzuki to buy the license for windshield wipers and wiper motors. The Sumitomo Wiring System signed a technical cooperation agreement with the IMAG factory of the Ikarus bus factory. The Japanese partner provides the manufacturing technology and helps to train the workforce. IMAG has several contracts with Magyar Suzuki for supplying wire harnesses and seat frames. In early 1993, a subcontracting joint venture of a larger scale was concluded. The Daikin Company, being one of the largest suppliers for Suzuki in Japan, established a joint venture in Hungary for the production of transmission compartments. The base capital is ¥ 115 million, with a participation of 50 percent for Daikin, 10 percent for Itochu, and 40 percent for Bakersz (a Hungarian private company). While at the beginning the elements have been imported, within some two years all of them should be produced in Hungary.[4]

However, the present state of affairs in subcontracting cannot be judged satisfactory. There are two reasons for this, coming mainly from Suzuki's approach. One is the inflexibility in the cooperation of Suzuki with the Hungarian government, the other is the lot size problem.

First, as for the inflexibility, Suzuki never disclosed its feasibility study to Hungarian governmental organizations. There was a general study made regarding the possibility of an assembly plant in Esztergom, but it lacked main indicators such as the development of production, profitability, and so forth. No estimations were drawn up for the subcontracting background. Suzuki never turned to Hungarian officials to consult on these issues; only before the plant's opening did it present a rough calculation of investment needs in order to upgrade subcontractors. According to information from the Ministry of Industry, in order to reach a subcontracting share of 20 percent of the car's value in 1993, a total of 25 subcontractors that had been suppliers for the Ikarus bus factory would have needed a total of a Ft 2.8 billion ($35 million) capital support. Of this, Ft 1.8 billion should be in credits. In order to help, a special credit construction was arranged with a 15 percent interest rate, which is only half of the usual domestic rate. The Industrial Development Bank (Budapest) informed all 25 subcontractors about the credit line, and twelve of them sent in their applications; four remained after screening, the rest not being able to prove credibility. These latter subcontractors could be upgraded either by Suzuki through Japanese bank credits or by joint ventures with other Japanese companies. The joint venture solution seems be a good opportunity, since a new joint venture can get the so-called job-creating credit, amounting to a maximum of Ft 100 million. (Likewise, when Ford's subcontractor came to Hungary in 1992, it also used the joint venture option and could immediately enjoy the Ft 100 million credit line.) Therefore, efforts would be needed on Suzuki's side to attract other Japanese companies to boost subcontracting in Hungary.

Second, the lot size problem was obvious from the beginning, but became prominent again in the subcontracting. That is, the maximum output volume pegged at 50,000 cars yearly is in fact much lower than the generally accepted optimal level of over 100,000 cars. Suzuki states that the minimum is 10,000 cars for the assembly plant in Esztergom, below which production would be unprofitable.[5]

The present relatively low output level might be a result of a compensation Suzuki probably receives from the Japanese government through some "behind the scene'' arrangement. There are already several new parts manufacturers in Hungary supplying mirrors, plastic parts, wires, and so forth to Western European car makers. As they are supplying in large enough lots to be profitable, Suzuki's low-volume orders would be disadvantageous, and they cannot be combined with Western European ones because of Suzuki's standard specifications. Only there has been a breakthrough in this problem, since Suzuki finally agreed to accept Hungarian-made parts as supplies for other Suzuki assembly factories. Further, in the case of Western European carmakers, the maker usually helps the subcontractor by providing the initial equipment free of charge, a practice that could likewise be adopted by Suzuki.

Magyar Suzuki will inevitably contribute to employment and labor skill. The Suzuki factory in Esztergom employs 1,200, almost all of whom are inexperienced. Quite interestingly, Suzuki assembled a totally new labor force, even though in Hungary there were already skilled workers in bus production and related factories. Two requirements by hiring were important: young persons with no record in the car or machine building industry; these persons were not communists before 1989. Suzuki took the harder road by bringing Hungarians to Japan for training. (This was also the case in the United States, where Japanese car manufacturers such as Honda and Toyota hired totally inexperienced workers at their facilities in Ohio and Kentucky, even though many GM employees and others were available). This was usually theorized as a move by the Japanese companies to avoid having to retrain workers, who may have poor work habits, and so forth, or may not do things ''their'' way. Also, average age was lower (males in their 20s), thus the workers were hired at lower salaries for high productivity production. Both managers and workers were trained in Japan for several months, with about half of the starting staff receiving training. The other half has been trained successively in Japan. Trainees had to sign a contract with Suzuki obliging themselves to repay the training costs if they quit within two years. Experience showed that only a modest number of fifteen trainees left complaining of working conditions. It is interesting to compare employee benefits at Suzuki and Hungarian Opel. For example, managers at Opel, both foreign and Hungarian, are provided with an Opel car at their disposal, while at Suzuki only the Japanese managers are given a car. Another special feature in Suzuki is the equality between blue-collar and white-collar employees. For example, they wear the same uniform, make the same morning gymnastics, dine in the same cafeteria and executives share the same large room with their subordinates.

Suzuki introduced the so-called sandwich pattern in management, appointing alternately Hungarians and Japanese to managerial posts. Thus, the president was a Hungarian, the vice executive president Japanese, vice president of engineering Hungarian and the plant manager Japanese. This pattern helps the smooth adaptation to the Hungarian environment.

There is no labor union at Suzuki. As the work council is merely a consultative body, the management acquired a dominantly powerful position. Because

Table 12.3
Production and Sales (number of cars)

	1992	1993	1994	1995*
Production	740	22,300	42,300	50,000
Sales in Hungary	740	20,300	24,300	26,000
Exports	–	2,000	18,000	24,000

*Estimates.
Source: Author's estimates based on data provided by the Ministry of Industry, Budapest, 1994.

of the lack of an interest-harmonizing mechanism between management and workers, the opposition of workers being discontent with low wages mounted to serious tensions in 1993. Through subcontracting, Suzuki might generate an additional 17 to 18 thousand jobs in other companies. In the subcontractor companies, Suzuki might be willing to help installing new machines and to introduce effective work methods that increase the labor skill and productivity.

As far as marketing is concerned, the Suzuki agreement leaves most of the marketing responsibility to the Hungarian partners. Although the joint venture company is given the exclusive right to sell the assembled cars and parts on Eastern European markets, Suzuki is required only to advise the venture and promote sales through its marketing network. No specific obligations are imposed on Suzuki. Furthermore, although Suzuki is required to recommend the parts made in Hungary to Western buyers, it is under no obligation to sell the joint venture's products on Western markets.[6] Probably because of such stipulations of the funding agreement, among Suzuki's Japanese management staff the engineering orientation dominates while the marketing side is not strong. After initial production increases, however, it seems probable that Suzuki will target both Eastern and Western markets, helping increase sales through its West European network. Such a change in marketing approach is necessitated by the competition in the Hungarian market, which is stronger than Suzuki could have anticipated (see later section).

According to the project draft, during the first two years marketing was to target Hungarian consumers, and only starting in 1994, when production substantially increases, were exports to be activated, reaching nearly 50 percent of total production by 1995 (see Table 12.3).

A sign for a new sales strategy came when in the spring of 1993 Suzuki unexpectedly launched on the market a third new type, the Suzuki Sedan, with the obvious aim of acquiring a greater portion of market through type diversification. The composition of production according car types is depicted in Table 12.4.

As for Eastern export markets, Suzuki set up a sales office in Moscow and began exporting to Russia and the Ukraine toward the end of 1993. Also in 1993, exports to China began. Suzuki's main target is, however, the EU market.

Table 12.4
Composition of Production According to Car Types

	Share in Production
Hatchback 1.11	50%
Hatchback 1.31	30%
Notchback (Sedan) 1.31	20%

Source: Magyar Suzuki, 1993.

Since Hungary has already become an associate member of the EU and has been granted practically tax-free imports for manufactured industrial goods, Suzuki can use this opportunity when the Hungarian made share in the car exceeds 50 percent. In April 1994 Suzuki exported the first few hundred such cars to Italy and the Netherlands. The fact that Suzuki prefers entering the EU market from a third country to direct exports is further illustrated by its decision to export 20,000 Marutis from its factory in India to the EU.[7]

A further problem is linked with payments. Since the joint venture took a considerable amount of Yen credits soon after its funding, the recent appreciation of the Yen poses a new burden for the management. The stronger Yen necessitates on the one hand that the repayment become bigger, and on the other, that parts imported from Japan become substantially higher priced. In order to solve the difficulty, Suzuki was seeking in 1993 a capital increase of $80.7 million shared between the owners in the same proportion with that of the base capital. In addition, Suzuki was considering engaging in counterbalancing trade, that is, developing exports from Hungary like wine, chicken, and other foodstuffs, some of which would be exported to Japan and the rest to third countries.

Finally, competition should be mentioned. Since the initial years when the Suzuki project was devised, market conditions have changed considerably. On the one hand, another joint venture car factory opened production in Hungary in 1992, while on the other, several Western carmakers began operating sales outlets.

The other joint venture car factory is that of General Motors, for production of Opel cars and engines. This contract was signed at the same time as the one with Suzuki.[8] General Motors invested DM 80 million into an assembly factory and DM 440 million into an engine factory. Yearly 15,000 cars will be assembled and 200,000 engines manufactured (the maximum capacity is targeted at 400,000 engines). The cars will be sold partly in Hungary and partly in Western Europe, while most of the manufactured engines will be exported to other Opel plants in Western Europe for use in assembly. The Hungarian supply share is 15 percent. After a three-month experimental run, the joint venture started production in July 1992.[9] Furthermore, the U.S. manufacturer Ford is also present in the Hungarian market, with a car-parts factory that opened in April 1992.

The German company Audi decided to set up a fully German-owned daughter company in Gyor for the production of a new engine family. The total value of the investment is going to be DM 320 million, and opening was scheduled for

1994. The new factory will provide jobs for over 1,000 Hungarians. The Hungarian government encouraged the investment by granting a full tax exemption for the first five years and a 60 percent tax cut for a further five-year period thereafter.

In addition, in the past two to three years several Western carmakers opened up sales agent points in Hungary, selling 1,000 to 2,000 cars each annually. Some of them provide consumer credit facilities to attract new customers. Now sales offices for over 20 foreign firms are already present in Hungary.

In 1993 Suzuki's share in the Hungarian car market was 25 percent as compared with Opel's 20 percent share. This is relatively low share as compared, for example, to India, where the Suzuki's share was 76 percent and in Pakistan, 66 percent.

After discussing the case study of Magyar Suzuki, let me turn now to some general observations on the motivations of Japanese firms investing in post-communist Europe.

SOME OBSERVATIONS ON JAPANESE CAPITAL IN EASTERN EUROPE

Opinions

In 1991, Jetro conducted interviews with ten Japanese firms and joint ventures in Hungary, Czechoslovakia, and Poland, asking them about their experiences in Central European markets.[10] In the following section we shall first review the reasons for directing investments into Central Europe, and then the main problems.

The reasons for investing are as follows:

- Geographically the area is advantageous. Through establishing a business center or joint venture in Central Europe, it is easy to cover the whole European market as well as the CIS markets. The Central European companies have developed long-standing connections over several decades with other Eastern markets and the Soviet market, and their local experience will aid in the market expansion of Japanese firms. In this sense, Central Europe is the best gate to the Soviet market.

- Rapid changes in Central Europe favor a Japanese foothold. In these countries, the old command-type system of distribution has collapsed, and it is the right time to set up a new sales network. New business chances are recognized also by West European and U.S. firms, which are already actively penetrating. Thus it is best for Japanese companies to establish themselves here before it is too late.

- Several market and production factors are advantageous. Japanese companies agree that Eastern markets are less competitive than those of Western countries. In some cases, the local partner companies had a unique advanced technology. In general, the technical knowledge and skill of engineers is as high as in developed Western countries, while relative wages are lower. In scientific research, the level of human networking is even higher than that of Western countries.

Companies have different opinions regarding Central Europe, depending mainly on the time of their appearance in the region. Newcomers in the financial and service sectors were positive about future perspectives. They reportedly invested because economic reforms provided new business chances. However, some companies in the manufacturing sector that went to Central Europe in the mid-1980s were not so positive about recent changes. This is because they began production under the old economic system and now, under the new condition, they are suffering from a considerable decrease in demand for their products. These companies shifting their sales from domestic markets to the Western markets.

The following main problems have arisen:

1. Forming new legislation
   - In Central European countries, the new system's legislation has been formed. The regulations on foreign direct investment are not settled completely and are not free of contradictions. Changes in the regulations are causing instability.
   - It is difficult to find out which part of the administration is responsible for certain problems. Sometimes officials of the same department decline documents that they earlier accepted.

2. Negotiations with governmental officials
   - Personal connections with influential officials are important because the usual Western business rules are not yet developed.
   - It is always necessary to obtain permission from officials, most of whom are bureaucratic (and corrupt). Negotiations are time consuming.

3. Infrastructure
   - Although the basic infrastructure (supply of water, gas, and electricity) is adequate, the telecommunications system has been outdated, making telephone and fax connections rather difficult. It is necessary to bring all the important equipment from the West.
   - It is difficult to find space for offices or warehouses. Real estate prices are increasing steeply.
   - The production infrastructure, consisting of the network of local suppliers of necessary parts, is still a problem due to low quality levels.

4. Labor force
   - Although the level of education of employees and the technical level and skill of engineers is high, it is difficult to find appropriate specialists with a good command of English or managers with market experience.
   - Japanese-style labor management is not appropriate because of the cultural differences. It is also difficult to induce cost-oriented behavior in employees.
   - Labor laws and regulations inherited from state-owned enterprises essentially remain in place and are more labor protective than in Western countries. As a con-

sequence, seniority must be taken into account when determining salary, and further, the national government strictly controls working environment conditions.

5. Other problems
   - Information in English is scarce.
   - Sudden fluctuations of the exchange rate and changes in the tax system pose difficulties.
   - The transfer of money requires more time than in Western countries.

K. Fujii, Business Planning Department Chief of the Japan Institute for Overseas Investment, characterizes the problems slightly differently in connection with the Hungarian experiences.[11] He collects the opinions into two groups, Hungarian expectations regarding Japanese investors and necessary conditions as seen by Japanese investors.

1. Expectations regarding Japanese investment
   a. Japanese investment is expected not only to alleviate the debt burden, but also to bring technology and know-how and to contribute to the modernization and restructuring of Hungarian industry. As a result, import substitution should proceed and exports should increase. Export expectations are supported by the geographic rationale that Central Europe would join the EU and EFTA, which makes Hungary the gate to these huge markets as well as to the former Soviet Union.
   b. Hungarian education and engineers' knowledge is of a high level while wages are lower than those in Western Europe, a combination which should be attractive to Japanese investors.
   c. Because of historically good social and economic relations with Austria and Germany, foreign investment is flowing in from these countries. This being the case, the 1990s is the perfect time for Japanese investment. For Hungary, as a recipient country, it is desirable to have investors from several foreign countries rather than to rely on one country. Japan's participation would be in line with this reasoning.
   d. Hungary is carrying out the privatization of state-owned enterprises and would like to see Japan buy up Hungarian companies. Traditionally, Japanese companies make an investment decision only after they have thoroughly investigated the partner and are convinced of its reliability. The mutual exchange of information and learning takes time. "Thus, to invite Japanese investors it will not suffice just to complete a list of enterprizes for sale," Fujii adds.[12]

2. Conditions necessary for Japanese investors
   a. Even if in Hungary there is a destatization, which is necessary to develop a market economy, some governmental organizations should still bear the responsibility of safeguarding capital investment. Also, a strategic policy is needed toward foreign investments concerning import regulations, exports, and taxation.
   b. The Western Countries' Coordinating Committee (COCOM) restrictions have finally been lifted in 1989, so high technology imports become possible. Still, it is not enough for technology to be advanced; it must also be the one most adaptable to Hungarian companies and training of the labor force is needed as a next step.
   c. The decision-making style of U.S. and Western European companies clearly differs from that of Japanese companies. U.S. and Western European companies have a

rapid decision-making process regarding investments, but problems occur later during the implementation. In the case of Japanese companies, decision making is slow, but afterwards there is no delay in the implementation. Therefore, Japanese investors need more time.

d. After production starts in a Japanese company or joint venture located in Hungary, the product's export competitiveness is not sufficient in Western markets. In this case, the Japanese mother company should give up a part of its EC-market share and help the Hungarian company.

e. Japanese companies initially thought that operating in Hungary would be highly risky because local parts suppliers would need additional investments to catch up in terms of quality. Now they feel this risk to a lesser degree because they can cooperate with West European–Hungarian joint ventures in local supplies.

According to an opinion from the Research Institute of MITI, Japanese business traditionally focused on Asian countries and U.S. markets. For Japanese businessmen, therefore, Central European countries seem to be a fairly remote area where the business environment and human relations are different from that in the familiar Asian domain. In regard to the gate role of Central Europe to the all-European market, Spain and Portugal are more attractive because of their relatively higher economic and political stability. A considerable problem is the lack of information on Central European countries, their development and business opportunities.

Finally, let us reiterate some observations gained by the Office of the Commercial Counsellor of Hungary in Tokyo. These can be rendered into two groups, those concerning expectations, and those on business behavior.

1. Expectations
    a. Comparing Hungary to Japan, Japanese businessmen are used to the relative stability in Japan, and when they go to Hungary, their impression is that changes there are favorable, but also very rapid, therefore they consider the situation unstable. Probably this was the reason why leading Japanese dailies misinterpreted the 1992 regulation on joint ventures located in Hungary. In 1992 the joint ventures were requested to reregister before December 1992. This was interpreted in Japan to mean that tax allowances had been abolished in Hungary. But the fact remains that the reregistered company can still enjoy a tax allowance for even as many as ten years.
    b. Japanese businessmen still think that some governmental institution should provide business guarantees as was the case under the former centralized system.

2. Business behavior
    a. Hungarian businessmen, in the hopes of establishing contacts with Japanese companies, come directly to the Japanese company's headquarters in Japan. There they are somewhat disappointed to experience a rather cool response from the Japanese. This is, however, due to the fact that the Japanese company's local offices in Western Europe have been entrusted to develop contacts with Central Europe. Therefore,

Hungarian businessmen should keep this in mind, first approaching the Japanese company indirectly through these branch offices instead of coming directly to Japan.

b. Decision making in Europe is quick; in Japan, it is slow. Before reaching a decision on investment, Japanese companies ask a research institute to prepare a study on the foreign country's development and financial system. Following a feasibility study on the project, they visit the partner company several times and establish contacts with its specialists, and only after a thorough investigation do they decide. This preparation takes several years, usually from five to six years. Changes in contact persons on the Hungarian side during this time have a negative effect on Japanese businessmen. The long decision-making time also means that Japanese companies are hardly able to buy up a Hungarian enterprise within one year, which would be desirable during privatization. Further, the long decision-making time is often interpreted by the Hungarian side as hesitation, and as a result the Hungarian company turns to Austrian and German firms. Experience also indicates that Japanese investors refrain from buying up preexisting companies, especially if there are no reliable financial records about their past performance. Instead, they prefer to establish a new company. This may be a further reason why Japanese companies might not meet Hungarian expectations in privatizing state companies. The Suzuki joint venture strengthens this impression, because the Japanese company established a new factory in spite of the fact that in Hungary two big automotive companies (buses and trucks) existed, and Suzuki began to recruit and train a new labor force instead of inviting workers with experience from existing companies.

c. Hungarian companies are slow at operative contacts, they do not respond quickly, and telephone and fax contacts are not reliable. Also, company information in foreign languages is scarce. A more recent problem is that many new small Hungarian companies without banking background have appeared in Japan, further weakening the confidence of the Japanese company regarding Hungarian firms.

CONCLUSIONS

Mutual Advantages

Further development of direct investment is to the benefit of both Central European countries and Japan. In Central European countries, these investments can substantially help privatization and restructuring. Trade and direct investments are of a relatively modest volume, though their real economic importance is far greater than their statistical share. As we can see in the case of the Magyar Suzuki project, direct investment helps through subcontracting to increase employment, modernization, and labor skill beyond the mere value of the investment itself. The same applies to Japan, but rather in the sense of trade strategy: Japan can gain a foothold in a region with a population of 120 million plus gain access to the former Soviet Union's market of 270 million people. Also, after the 3 core countries (Hungary, the Czech Republic, Poland) join the EU, Japanese firms located in these countries will automatically enter the EU market.

For Japan, Central Europe is a gate to the huge markets of Western Europe and the CIS. Therefore, it is in the interests of both sides to make further efforts.

Expectations and Realities

Japanese business is rather sensitive to political change or instability. The vague economic policy and industrial strategy of the new governments in Central Europe are not bolstering confidence, either. But even with the initial maladies of the new systems, the development aims at a democratic, market-based economy.

In Central European countries there is an expectation of greater participation by Japan in privatization and modernization. While decision making in Japanese companies is quite a long process, Central European companies and governmental agencies should provide more information. Probably these differences will result in a certain compromise, as the Central European governments increasingly realize that privatization cannot be carried out within a few years. On the other hand, increasing stability in these countries will attract more confidence and capital from Japan.

In the privatization process and while exploring new business opportunities, Japan must be aware of strong competition from Western European and U.S. firms. As discussed in the previous chapter, written by Morita, managerial skill and governmental policies are important concerning direct investments. An interesting analysis of the Daihatsu project, which failed in competition with Fiat in Poland, pointed out that as compared with Fiat, Daihatsu did not have enough managerial resources, particularly in the field of investments in Eastern European countries, and further, that the Italian government had more positive policies toward Eastern European countries than the Japanese government.[13]

Finance

In finance, the provision of credits without specification can be considered a progressive step and an important sign of confidence on the part of the Japanese. In order to promote restructuring projects, such credit policies should be in accordance with economic and particularly industrial policy in the Central European country. This would require closer cooperation between leading financial and governmental institutions on both sides.

Mutual Learning

Mutual learning thorough information exchange about business possibilities and behavior is not very developed. Exchanges of study groups from business associations and industrial associations could be of considerable help in finding effective methods of cooperation.

NOTES

1. Zs. Kapitány and L. Kállay, "The East European Motor Industry: Latest Developments, Economic Intelligence Unit (EIU)," *International Motor Business,* no. 3, 1990.

2. "Not So Swift," *Tőzsdekurir,* August 29, 1991.

3. "Shinohara úr nem pánaszkodik" (Mr. Shinohara does not complain), *Népszabadság,* August 4, 1992.

4. "Magyar Suzuki Swiftek indulnak a FAK-ba" (Hungarian Suzuki Swifts Will Go to CIS), *Népszabadság,* March 1, 1993.

5. *Inter-Japan Magazine,* no. 1, 1992.

6. *Figyelő,* no. 48, 1987.

7. *Nihon Keizai Shimbun,* Oct. 1, 1993.

8. G. Bakos, "Japanese Capital in Hungary: The Case of Automotive Industry," in *In Search of a New Relationship between Japan and Europe,* Tokyo: JAES, 1991.

9. "Az Opel motorja" (Opel's engine), *Figyelő,* July 23, 1992.

10. *Nihon Keizai Shimbun,* October 1, 1993.

11. "Hungari muke kaigai toshi ni tsuite" (On investments directed to Hungary), Newsletter-Hungari, Tokyo, 1992, no. 3–4, p. 7.

12. Ibid.

13. See also K. Morita, "An Economic Analysis of Japan's Foreign Direct Investment into Poland: The Daihatsu-FSD Case," Hiroshima University, unpublished manuscript, 1992.

PART III

CONCLUSION

13

Economic Transformation, External Imbalances, and Political Risk in Post-Communist Eastern Europe

Iliana Zloch-Christy

The analysis of the previous chapters shows that the economic transformation in Eastern Europe[1] and the external debt problems of these countries have greatly increased the interest shown by the Western business community in evaluating country risk. The former Soviet Union and its alliances in Central and Eastern Europe are regarded as a region with unstable political structure and serious macroeconomic imbalances. Since 1989 the totalitarian communist regimes in Central and Eastern Europe have been shaken up by strong democratic movements. Noncommunist governments are or were in power in Poland (until October 1993), in the Czech lands, and in Hungary (until 1994), and the noncommunist opposition (not stemming formally from the Communist party or from the renamed Communist party) despite parliamentary socialist (communist) victory of 1994 increasing its influence in the political scene in Bulgaria (where a first noncommunist government was formed in 1991–1992), Slovakia, Romania, and the former Soviet Union. The democratic movement in the former Soviet Union is gaining importance in the political life of this country, which has a serious economic crisis and nationality problems. In August 1991, after an unsuccessful coup attempt against Gorbachev, the Soviet Communist party was banned. However, the political situation there is still unclear and very unstable, as the events of the so-called Second October Revolution of 1993 indicated. Also unclear is the political landscape in Romania. All of this indicates that Eastern Europe in the mid-1990s will be different from the same region in the mid-1980s, when it was dominated by Soviet influence, communist rule, and centrally planned economies. Eastern Europe obviously will not be the region with the more than 40 years old (stable) political structure, totalitarian communist states. The process of economic and political transformation is irreversible.

The changes in Eastern Europe raise the problem of evaluating political risk in the region. Even though these countries are moving toward market economies, the political risk is still the major one. Political risk assessment should not be underestimated in business and financial circles as it was in the previous more than three decades; it should be an integral part of any international portfolio management process.

This chapter attempts to provide a preliminary basis for future research toward an analytical framework for a discussion of approaches for evaluating political and social risk in doing business with Eastern Europe, and particularly in investing in the region. Further, it attempts to reconsider methodologies of country risk assessment. The structure of the chapter is as follows. The first section briefly explores the basic changes in Eastern Europe induced by the recent economic reforms. The second section examines the external imbalances (external debt situation) of the region. The third section explores methodologies of country risk assessment to be applied to Eastern Europe. It focuses on the liquidity and structural indices and on some indicators of the debt burden and creditworthiness. The fourth section examines an approach to the question of how to assess the effects of the market-oriented reform changes in Eastern Europe. The fifth section turns specifically to an analysis of political and social risk assessment. It asks four main questions: (1) how to define political and social risk assessment in Eastern Europe, (2) what are the key aspects of political risk assessment? (3) what are the fundamental questions in political risk analysis? and (4) what are the main aspects of the assessment of social conditions? The sixth section focuses on the prospects for the economic and political changes in Eastern Europe, with an emphasis on economic development strategies. The main findings are in the conclusion.

TRANSFORMATION AND LIBERALIZATION IN EASTERN EUROPE

The present transformation aims not only at changing priorities and policies as the previous attempts did, but at changing the economic and political system. The reforms in Central and Eastern Europe in 1990–1995 and the events in the Soviet Union after August–September 1991 show this clearly. The process of transformation is, of course, accompanied by complicated and difficult-to-define developments in the region, but a consensus exists among scholars and politicians that the following can be identified as the main pillars of this process:

1. Privatization (to a certain point) of the means of production and diversification of the forms of economic activity

2. Decentralization of management decision making in the economy

3. Reducing and eliminating the political monopoly of the single party and creating political liberalization—openness (glasnost), more democratic rights, and new civil and multiparty societies

The terms "self-dependence," "self-financing," and "self-management" characterise the main directions of the decentralization of decision making in Eastern Europe. There are two major differences between the present reforms and all of the previous so called reforms. Eastern European policy makers stress that in the first place, economic reform will not succeed without political reform and therefore the two reforms must be simultaneously carried out, and in the second place, the Eastern European command economies must be restructured from "top to bottom."

The Eastern European countries and their economies are a delicately balanced web of interest and social stratas. The economic reforms require fundamental changes in the general management and macroeconomic system, and considerable shifts are required in resource allocation at the sectoral, branch, and regional levels and in income policy, a long and difficult process. The economic and political developments during the first years of the 1990s allow for the (probably premature) conclusion that the Eastern European economies are in a state of mixed economy—capitalism without profit and socialism without planning. However, a discussion of the type of economic system in post-communist Europe is beyond the scope of this chapter. (For a detailed discussion see, e.g., my 1993 study listed in References, particularly chapters 2–4.)

ECONOMIC REFORMS AND THE EXTERNAL DEBT SITUATION

The external debt situation of the Eastern European countries rapidly deteriorated in late 1980s. The large external imbalances and the "tax on GNP" to be paid abroad are serious macroeconomic constraints on the process of economic and political transformation. The total gross and net debt of the region can be estimated at the level of some USD. 169 billion and USD. 130 billion respectively in 1992. The most heavily indebted countries are the former Soviet Union, Poland, and Hungary. Bulgaria experienced serious debt servicing difficulties in early 1990 and further reschedulings of its debt are unavoidable. The debt service ratios (all interest and amortization on medium- and long-term debt as percent of one year's exports) reached alarming levels in the former Soviet Union, Bulgaria, Poland, and Hungary in 1992: 85 percent, 77 percent, 71 percent, and 65 percent respectively (25 percent is considered in business circles to be a critical level). The former Soviet Union began to accumulate large arrears to banks and suppliers in 1990 and requested a formal debt rescheduling with official and commercial bank creditors. A further increase in debt levels will be in the next years an unavoidable scenario; also, the refinancing of some of the debt repayments due will occur, given the economic chaos in this region and the trade collapse. Some estimates suggested that the combined current account deficit of the fifteen former Soviet republics will increase from $15 billion in 1992 to $20 billion at end 1993. (I.M.F., *World Economic Outlook,* October 1992, p. 20).

The policy strategies of the creditors and debtors to deal with this situation in the early 1990s are varied. Interest arrears continue to stand in the way of a normalization of creditor-debtor relations (the former Soviet Union, Poland, and Bulgaria), and commercial banks stand ready on a case-by-case basis to discuss commercially viable debt buybacks agreements (e.g., the January 1993 negotiations of Russia with Austrian commercial banks) or other forms of debt and debt service reduction. Western creditors, particularly private institutions, are reducing their exposure to the region but are interested in increasing direct and equity investment. Commercial banks are greatly reluctant to extend new trade finance to the heavily indebted Eastern European countries if there is even a slight possibility of official debt forgiveness in the future, as in the case of Poland in 1991, when the official Paris Club creditors agreed to debt forgiveness of the unguaranteed portion of bank loans for export finance. The Eastern European countries are still seeking debt relief measures (Poland, Bulgaria), borrowing from international financial organizations and official credit agencies (particularly Russia, the Ukraine, Bulgaria, Hungary, and Poland), and there have been debt reschedulings for these countries (except for Hungary). All this indicates that clearly defined strategies for how to deal with the present external debt situation in Eastern Europe are a necessity for both creditors and debtors.

An interesting question related to the assessment of the creditworthiness of the region arises: Would the process of economic liberalization in Central and Eastern Europe lead to an abatement of the pressure on the external balance of these countries in the short and medium term?

External financial problems cannot be solved without trade. Thus foreign borrowing should be considered trade across time. On the other hand, debt servicing capacity must be judged on long-term economic growth prospects rather than on gross and net debt levels, in other words, on the efficiency of the macro- and microeconomic organization, or the system that determines the principle questions in economic life: "what," "how," and "for whom." The Eastern European countries cannot solve their transfer problem with the Western nations without a long and difficult adjustment in economic policy toward a development strategy that increases the efficiency of production and toward the creation of a production base that is competitive by world market standards. However, experiences in the 1970s and 1980s in Eastern Europe and in many developing countries show that the road to economic inefficiency is paved with good intentions (e.g., in Poland, Hungary, Latin America, and Africa). What can be expected in the 1990s, the period of economic transformation in Eastern Europe? Will the self-regulating natural order of the market mechanism be achieved? What are the prospects for an economic order where "government governs best which governs least"?

It goes beyond the scope of this chapter to go into details in addressing these questions. I would suggest the following brief answers. The economic reforms are still in their embryonic period in the early 1990s. The reforms in all of the Eastern European countries lack an overall logical structure and conceptual vision (including privatization and industrial policy). It might be interesting to mention here the statement made by the Czech economist and politician V. Klaus that his country does not need a reform programme:

We do not believe in sophisticated sequencing of economic, or reform measures. We know that just as an economy cannot be centrally planned so an economic transformation cannot be centrally planned and administered. The economic transition is a process with many forces, many constraints, many policies. We have to react and react rationally. There is no computerized program saying that at the beginning, one must introduce measure one or measure two, three, four, or five. I prefer to compare reform, traumatic radical reform, with chess. One simply has to know how to play. ("Transition—An Insider's View," *Problems of Communism,* no. 1–2, 1992:72–75)

The Eastern European reformers are involved in a continuing search for better ways that the government can help (or stop hindering) economic progress. But it is obvious that no magic formulas will come to the rescue of the Eastern European governments trying to find the best policies for a mixed-market economy. And there is no doubt that it will take time—along with stability and continuity of policies—for the foundations of new states to be created and for the governments of Eastern Europe to establish the legal framework for the society and economy, to determine the macroeconomic stabilization policy, to influence the allocation of resources to improve economic efficiency, and to establish programmes that influence the distribution of income. All of this indicates that the economic reforms will not change de facto the logic of the economic system and remove all planned controls (which now can be called "state orders") and restrictions in Eastern Europe as well as effectively solve the problems of bureaucratic opposition (from the still-strong old nomenklatura), lack of financial discipline, and lack of a real price system in the medium term. And we should not forget that removing old constraints usually leads to new ones.

Another problem is creating policy-making elite and managerial groups in Eastern Europe who have adjusted to the new economic order since the reform process began. In the future, the reform process will require not only a collection of "radical" new laws, "*dekreti,*" and good rules for economic management but people—decision makers, officials, and managers—who have adjusted to these new rules. For more than four decades Eastern European countries have spoken a different economic language than Western European nations. It takes time to learn the "new" language or to eliminate old "dialects" and "accents."

All of this indicates that it would be too optimistic to expect an abatement of the debt servicing difficulties in the region in the short and medium term. However, one should stress that the main problem in the region is not the tension in the external balance and the capital gap, but the institutional gap between these countries and the Western market economies and societies.

METHODOLOGIES OF COUNTRY RISK ASSESSMENT IN LENDING AND INVESTING IN EASTERN EUROPE

Financial flows to post-communist Europe mainly involve bank lending, private direct investment (private foreign capital formation in firms, with investors' significant degree of control), and foreign aid. In my judgment, the approaches used by banks and other national and international financial institutions to measure and evaluate risk for lending money and for foreign direct investments are quite similar. That is why in the course of the discussion in this section, I will point only to the particular risks involved, for example, in foreign direct investments. From a bank's point of view, risk is exposure to a loss. Lending across national borders involves both economic risk (balance of payments difficulties, general problems in economic management, etc.) and political risks (sociopolitical upheavals, willingness or unwillingness of the authorities to meet foreign debt obligations, etc.). These risks are not easy to assess. Even if the risks of any given economic policy or political decision could be judged accurately, there would still be uncertainty over which policies should be adopted. Avramovic's (1964) appraisal of the uncertainty of creditworthiness and country risk evaluations is still valid:

> The appraisal of creditworthiness of anybody—be it an individual, a business firm, or country—is a mixture of facts and judgements. Even if we had the theory of debt servicing capacity and could satisfactorily explain the likely behaviour of major variables and their time path, we would still be facing uncertainties arising from current economic and financial policies which the decision makers in the borrowing countries may choose to adopt, be it at their own initiative or in response to all sorts of pressures. (Pp. 7–8)

The analysis of an Eastern European country's creditworthiness requires an answer to two fundamental questions: First, is the country's liquidity sufficient to cover its immediate needs (i.e., can debt service interruptions be avoided)? Second, is the economy sound, well managed, and capable of generating adequate external revenue for debt service in the future?

The first question relates to the country's immediate liquidity (foreign exchange) position, and the second to the country's ability to continue to solve its structural problems.

Potential debt service difficulties in the near term can be analysed by a liquidity index. A typical index is a weighted average of scores (varying on a scale of, say, 0 to 100 of specific indicators), some of which are discussed later. Usually an index value of 30 to 50 points is considered a gray area; 50 points and above suggest that liquidity difficulties may occur. The index might be based on developments in some, many, or all of the following basic indicators of the hard-currency debt burden:

- Total debt servive relative to exports of goods and all services (debt service ratio)
- International reserves (or Western bank assets) relative to imports of goods and all services

- Short-term, trade-related debt relative to three months of hard-currency imports (debt trade ratio)
- The country's net compressible import capacity (imports rather than raw materials, fuels, capital equipment, and food)
- Current account deficit relative to exports of goods and all services
- Interest payments relative to exports of goods and all services
- Interest earned on international assets as a percentage of interest due on external debt
- International reserves relative to short-term debt
- Large reserve losses
- Gross or net debt relative to exports of goods and all services
- Access to the international capital markets and ability to roll over debts
- Delayed payments and arrears
- Increasing level of capital flight
- Implementation of IMF stabilization programme and/or use of IMF/BIS credit lines for balance of payments adjustment
- Level of general-purpose financing
- Negotiations with official (Paris Club) and commercial bank (London Club) creditors for debt reschedulings and debt forgiveness (particularly in the case of Paris Club forgiveness agreements on bank loans)
- Negotiations for debt-to-equity swaps with the Western creditors and their interest in project lending to the debtor country
- Indications that the Eastern European debtor countries pursue a strategy to impose a so-called debtor power pressure (in the typical case of negative financial flows from these countries) on the creditors; this is particularly relevant for the former Soviet Union—Russia, the Ukraine, and other republics
- Implementation of trade liberalisation programmes associated with convertibility on the current account and their terms (fixed or floating exchange rate policy) and the probability of their sustainability over a six-month period
- Spreads over LIBOR

In the case of the Eastern European countries, it is essential to supplement an evaluation of the country's liquidity position with an analysis of its structural problems indicating the likelihood of future payments problems as well as the ability to solve existing ones.

The soundness of the Eastern European economies could be analysed by a structural index. A typical index is a weighted average of scores of individual indicators (some of them discussed later). On a scale similar to that in the liquidity index, 50 points and above is the area indicating that repayment difficulties may occur. The structural index could include the following indicators:

- Rate of growth of GNP/GDP
- Hard-currency exports relative to GNP/GDP

- Growth of real per capita GNP or GDP (recent two-year average)
- The ratio of percentage change of exports relative to the percentage change in GNP or GDP
- Hard-currency exports relative to GNP/GDP
- Net debt relative to exports of goods and all services
- Net debt relative to GNP/GDP
- Growth of total exports and of Western exports (most recent year and two-year average)
- Percentage change in consumer prices (most-recent-year and three-year average)
- Lending by the World Bank and the European Bank for Reconstruction and Development for structural adjustment purposes and for encouraging the private sector
- Composition of the inter–Eastern European regional trade (in convertible currencies) and trade practices (e.g., barter agreements, etc.)
- Trade agreements (clearing or convertible currency settlements) with the former Soviet Union and with the other Eastern European countries
- Implementation of programmes (if any) for a multilateral payment union in the Eastern European countries (indicating the potential for transferability, trade multilateralism, and full currency convertibility in the medium term)
- Programmes for privatization of the domestic economy sectors and their potential competitiveness by world market standards
- Industrial policy programmes (if any)
- Programmes for encouraging foreign direct and equity investments and levels of such investments
- Programmes for regional cooperation (e.g., Central Europe, the former Soviet Union, Asian republics)
- Standing of economic and political relations with the European Union and prospects for full membership

The liquidity and structural indexes just described are useful for comparative country risk analysis. The indicators included (by no means an exhaustive list) show different aspects of a country's debt situation, but no one indicator is sufficient. Careful analysis will review developments in many indicators before coming to a conclusion. The debt servicing problems of the Eastern European countries in the late 1980s and in 1990–1993 (particularly in the former Soviet Union, Poland, Bulgaria, and Hungary) and the changes in their economic management and economic structures suggest the following list of indicators as highly important in the analysis of Eastern European borrowers:

- Debt service ratio
- Access to the international financial markets
- Stand-by programmes with IMF and BIS lines of credit
- Multilateral clearing agreements in Eastern Europe

- Programmes in implementation phases for trade liberalisation and for introducing full currency convertibility
- Capital flight
- Foreign direct and equity investments
- Ratio of gross or net debt relative to exports of goods and all services

It is not a goal of my analysis in this chapter to discuss in detail the importance of the individual indicators. However, it should be stressed that a change in the perceptions about the creditworthiness position of the Eastern European countries should be reflected in the assessment, for example, of the intraregional trade in convertible currencies and in other settlements (e.g., primitive trade practices such as barter). This indicator is very important, particularly for the smaller Eastern European countries, which are more vulnerable than the former Soviet Union to external shocks and which have less flexibility and fewer alternatives in the shift from Eastern European to Western markets at present. All of these countries are very dependent on energy deliveries. Those countries that could continue to rely to a large extent on Russian deliveries settled on clearing bases (not a promising scenario, given the debt problems of the former Soviet Union, its internal economic and political difficulties, and its new political strategy toward its former allies) would not experience severe convertible currency balance of payments difficulties in contrast with countries that import a greater part of their energy requirements from the world market.

As regards the risks related to foreign direct investments. They involve forced divestment (nationalization, socialisation, or confiscation). Divestment ranges from formal expropriation, or forced sales to domestic subjects, to contract renegotiation. It is obvious that it involves risk that is difficult to measure. There are two principal methodological approaches in assessing risk: first, expert opinion, and second, quantitative research using past data. The two approaches involve analysis of domestic instability, foreign conflicts, and political and economic climate. As an example of the first approach, I would like to suggest the Business Environment Risk Index (BERI) and the Institutional Investor Credit Rating Index, both calculated since the 1970s. The second approach is based on quantitative research using past data (e.g., up to 400 economic and political variables), thus making an effort to achieve more objective grounds for measurement.

HOW TO ASSESS THE EFFECTS OF THE ECONOMIC TRANSFORMATION

The assessment of opportunities and risks in Eastern Europe at present requires an answer to the difficult question of how to measure the effects of changes. How successful are the introduction and the implementation of the reform changes? What is the direction of economic development, and associated with that, the main factors of economic growth—human and natural resources, capital formation, and technology? An attempt to provide specific answers to these questions obviously would be only an intellectual exercise. This section seeks to establish a basis for a better understanding of the direction in which the reform process and the economic development in Eastern European countries can be expected to move.

The central measures by which macroeconomic performance in every country (whether a market economy, centrally planned economy, or mixed economy) is judged are GNP, employment, inflation, and net exports. The main objectives of macroeconomic policies are high level and rapid growth rate of output, high level of employment, price level stability, export and import equilibrium, and exchange rate stability. The instruments used in implementing macroeconomic policies in market economies usually include fiscal, monetary, income, trade, and exchange rate policies. But these policies and instruments have different economic effects in the centrally planned economies. A starting point for assessing changes in macroeconomic policies in the reform-oriented Eastern European countries, as is obviously required for analysis in Western economic terms, is a study of the instruments these countries apply for achieving the main objectives of economic policies. In other words, what is the impact of domestic fiscal, monetary, income, and trade and exchange rate policies on the macroeconomic performance, the allocation of resources, and the adjustment to external disturbances? Do the Eastern European countries continue to rely on policies of direct control, or on market-oriented policies and instruments? Some of the interesting questions in this regard are:

How does the system for allocation of capital ''work''?

What is the role of interest rates?

How does the allocation of foreign exchange in the economy occur?

What is the role of the banking system in the economy?

What are the changes in the price system?

How many new enterprises were created?

What is the role of the bureaucracy in the economic decision making?

What targets are officials pursuing and how are they trying to achieve them?

What is the tax policy and the capacity of the new (if any) tax administration?

The transformation from centrally planned economies to market-oriented or market economies in Eastern Europe will obviously be long. How long? It is difficult to give a clear-cut answer to this question. But it seems reasonable to assume that at least the 1990s will be the transition period. In the author's view, the following basic changes are required in the transition period: (1) market clearing prices, (2) eliminating direct and indirect state subsidies, (3) import liberalisation, and (4) (last but not least), unified exchange rates and convertibility on the current account.

The assessment of the effects of the economic reforms should include a careful analysis of whether there are changes in the foundations of the Eastern European states, in their institutional gap with the West, and in the performance of the governments in Eastern Europe, particularly with respect to radical, market-oriented changes in exercizing these governments' four basic executive functions related to the economy:

- Establish the legal framework of the economy
- Determine the macroeconomic stabilization policy
- Influence the allocation of resources to improve economic efficiency (for instance, influencing the efficiency of the domestic economy through programmes for privatization or industrial policies)
- Establish programmes that influence the distribution of income

Associated with these basic changes is, of course, the expectation that the market-oriented economic reforms will be closely linked with the political liberalization of the Eastern European countries, the creation of new civil societies, and the effective abolition of the role of the former communist bureaucracy in the management of the economy. In other words, using the relatively old but still highly appropriate definition of the Hungarian economist and Harvard professor Janos Kornai (1986), the reform process should be associated with "any change in the economic system, provided that it diminishes the role of bureaucratic coordination and increases the role of the market" (p. 1688). The successful introduction and implementation of the economic reforms could be analyzed, for example, by assessing how close practice is moving toward radical changes in ownership and incentives. Further, an assessment is needed of the role of the "rules of the game" that complement, hinder, or enforce government resolution and legal regulation.

On the microeconomic level the analysis should concentrate on the following objectives:

- New company laws and accounting standards
- Fair system of company taxation
- Autonomy of the enterprises
- Accountability of the enterprises for profit and loss
- Personal profit interest of the enterprises' employees
- Enterprise efficiency as compared to the prereform period

It has to be stressed here that these objectives on the microeconomic level are, of course, associated with the existence of capital markets in the individual countries. The accountability of the enterprises for profit and loss is one of the most important indicators of the successful implementation of market-oriented economic reform in the bureaucratic Eastern European economic systems, since it gives an answer to the following two fundamental questions: (1) do the enterprises operate on the basis of "hard" or "soft" budget constraints? and (2) to what extent do firms' profits depend on bureaucratic intervention (direct corrections of prices, taxes, subsidies, etc.)?

This brief discussion of approaches to assessing the effects of the market-oriented reform process in Eastern Europe as regards changes on macro- and microeconomic levels and the role of the government undoubtedly raises as many questions as it answers. But I hope that it establishes a basis for an analysis of present and future economic performance in the region and of its fundamental goal: transformation toward a market economy.

POLITICAL AND SOCIAL RISK ASSESSMENT

The conventional wisdom in lending to Eastern Europe has been that the risks to lenders is always a country risk problem rather than a project risk problem. This concept of country risk analysis requires certain reconsiderations today. The economic reforms in the former Soviet Union and in the other countries of the region increased the autonomy of domestic enterprises and create the possibility for them to have direct access to Western markets. The new climate in East-West relations creates a positive environment for stimulating foreign direct investments to the region. These changes increase the importance of evaluating political and social risks in lending and investing in post-communist Eastern Europe.

Political risks in lending across national borders are those generated by political entities beyond one's national jurisdiction. The study of political risks in doing business with Eastern Europe is the study of national and international political processes that can influence the level of risk involved in the undertaking of a Western entity operating in an environment sufficiently influenced by political factors that they cannot be ignored. The political risks are associated with sociopolitical upheavals, the willingness or unwillingness of the authorities to meet foreign debt obligations, and many other factors. These risks are essentially dynamic and uncertain and are not easy to assess.

There are two key aspects of political risk in relation to country risk analysis in lending and investing in Eastern Europe: (1) interactions between domestic economic policy and political developments, and (2) interactions between political developments, foreign confidence, and capital inflows.

Starting from these points, the analysis of political risk in lending to Eastern Europe requires an answer to four fundamental questions:

1. What is the country's leadership and its determination in carrying out economic and political reforms?

2. What are the social conditions in the country and does social support exist for government policies?
3. What is the influence of Russia (the former main power in the region and major trading partner) on the country's domestic economic and political developments?
4. What is the state of East-West political relations?

A key starting point for political risk assessment is an evaluation of country's leadership. This evaluation may illuminate the prospects for the success and continuity of the country's political developments (democratization, new civil society, multiparty system) as well as its economic and borrowing policies and its economic management. A Western businessman considering establishing a joint venture, for example in Russia, in the Baltic republics, in the Ukraine, or in Georgia in the former Soviet Union, is keenly interested in knowing what the prospects are for the economic reform policies of these countries in the medium and long term. In the optimistic case, for example, that a Western banker is considering a provision of credit to a former Soviet enterprise, he would be confronted with this basic question. The coup attempt of August 1991, the declaration of independence of most of the Soviet republics in August–September 1991, and the recognition by the Western nations of the independence of these republics, beginning first with the Baltic states in September 1991, make clear the importance of carefully analysing short- and medium-term policies (sustainabilty and prospects) of the country's leadership. The events in Russia in October 1993 are another example indicating the importance of such an assessment.

The first questions to be asked by Western businessmen providing loans to an entity (joint venture or local business) in the Ukraine, Georgia, or Uzbekistan obviously would be how one could be sure that a particular enterprise, bank, or the government would repay debt in the medium term and who would provide guaranties—banks or national institutions—in the individual independent republics. Similar questions arise in lending to Polish, Hungarian, Bulgarian or Czech entities, although the nationality context is basically different. Although all of the Eastern European countries mentioned belonged for more than four decades to the Soviet bloc, with central planning and totalitarian communist regimes, there are in practice country-specific differences among them. No two of these countries are alike. What is important for the analyst is to understand the key developments in a particular Eastern European country and to know which questions to ask.

The most important question to be asked, particularly in the case of the former Soviet Union, is what are the chances that the countries' leadership will succeed in implementing the plans for liberalization of the economy and the associated plans for the political democratization of the totalitarian Eastern European societies? If the economic reforms fail, the result obviously would be economic and political instability in these countries and continued relative economic decline.

Interesting questions in evaluating a country's leadership in the Eastern European countries, which still have deeply rooted communist structures, are: Does the leadership consist of reformers or rather of conservative former party bureaucrats and apparatchiks? What are the professional skills of the leadership? Does it support technocrats or not? Does it understand economics? What is its programme (if any) for privatization of the medium-sized and large enterprises or for industrial policy, and what are its strategies for foreign direct and equity investments in the country? What is the managerial background of the leadership?

Associated with these questions are questions related to the political support of the leadership. Which groups support the party and government leadership? What is the basis of the leaders' control, for example, popular support? How strong are the opposition parties? The next question to ask is, What is the probability that the leadership consists of the old, although renamed, conservative guard or on the other hand, of radical reformers? In the case of the former Soviet Union, the question, for example, might be about conservatives versus the president of the Russian Republic, Yeltsin, a radical politician and Russian nationalist.

In the individual Eastern European countries, there will be a specific issue or problem that needs to be examined and then watched for future developments. Some of the questions to be asked are: Who will be the successor of a political leader, and will the transition be smooth? For example, who will be the successor(s) of the leadership that replaced the former dictators of Bulgaria and Romania, and what are the potential changes of leadership in Russia and the Ukraine? In the case of Romania, a further interesting question arises: Will the new leadership continue on the path of unsophisticated economic and debt management (almost no radical changes de facto in the centralized planning system and a ban on foreign borrowing), or will it follow the path of economic and political transformation? In the case of the former Soviet Union, the question arises, for example, What are the chances that Gorbachev will return to political activity, and what are his chances compared to some new radical reformers (e.g., from the E. Gaidar and G. Yavlinsky generation)? Other interesting questions are: Will the leadership favor more political or economic reform? Will it postpone radical economic reform measures, for example, mass privatization programmes and restrictive monetary and fiscal policy, because of political pressures stemming from parties, coalitions, and parliaments or social unrest?

Associated with the problem of evaluating the country's leadership are several interesting questions for the assessment of political developments in the individual Eastern European countries: Are the changes in the economic and political systems revolutionary, or can these developments be called a form of political decay? How developed are the institutional structures that will enable the democratic rules to work? Is there any potential conflict between political power elite and country's elite? Is the democratic transition led by the country's elite or by the masses? (History proves that elite-led transitions have better chances of succeeding.) Is a process of establishment (e.g., Russia) or of restoration of democratic traditions (e.g., the Czech Republic, Bulgaria) in the individual countries under way? What is the integrity of the state itself, and thus what are the chances that the transformation process will work? For example, consider the perestroika policy and the disintegration of the Soviet Union in 1991. Do the (new) states have close coalitions or pacts with different social groups? Are there any rebellion movements against the government, and why are people rebelling?; Is there any legitimacy crisis for the government and the new country's elite? This is obviously a serious question for almost all of these countries, with their deeply rooted communist structures. Does dual power exist, or have new political powers emerged (e.g., the battle until October 1993 between executive president Yeltzin and legislative president Khasbulatov)? Can loss of faith in the policy of the government be observed, and are there any internal riots among the ruling elite? Are the social changes in the country characterized, for example, by the replacement of the old communist ruling class by a new (non-communist) ruling class, in other words, is a de facto social revolution taking place (since there cannot be Eastern European capitalism without Eastern European capitalists)? Last, but not least, how fast is the destruction of the old institutions and their replacement by new institutions, values, and political elite taking place?

Another country-specific question that needs to be highlighted and examined is the issue of ethnonationalism and whether there are ethnic or religious disturbances in the individual Eastern European countries. It seems to me that in a number of these countries (e.g., Russia, the Ukraine, Armenia, Georgia, Romania, Hungary, the Czech Republic, the Slovak Republic, Bulgaria), ethnonationalism is emerging as a major force that engages people in politics. Almost all of these countries face potential unrest due to disturbances caused by ethnic or religious conflicts. The latter could have a major impact on domestic politics (e.g., creating a power struggle) and the economy—producing instability and, associated with this, declining production, exports, and so forth. Without going into details, I must note the ethnic disturbances and nationality movements in the Baltic states, Russia, the Ukraine, Georgia, and Azerbaijan in the former Soviet Union as well as in Romania, Hungary, and the former Czechoslovakia.

Another interesting question that arises in assessing political risk is whether there exists foreign confidence in the economic and political developments in the individual Eastern European countries. Foreign confidence in the country's development and its leadership greatly affects the state of trade and credit relations between East and West. For example, the confidence of the Western countries in the policy of Hungary in the early 1980s led to the access of this country to the IMF and the World Bank and to new capital inflows, which allowed debt reschedulings to be avoided. The liberalisation of political life in Poland in 1989—the legalisation of Solidarnosz and the election of a Solidarnosz-led government) were the main factors that led to the change of Western attitutes toward Poland and the fact that she received the first credits from the

IMF and the World Bank, in the early 1990s, as well as U.S. preferential export tariff treatment, more favourable conditions on reschedulings of Paris Club and commercial credits, and other benefits. The confidence shown by the Western countries in the leadership of Gorbachev and Yeltzin during and after the August 1991 and October 1993 events respectively were important for the provision of technical assistance and new credits to the former Soviet Union as well as for the establishment of joint ventures in the near future. Foreign confidence will also be crucial for the inflow of funds in the other Eastern European countries, such as Bulgaria (new credits, debt reschedulings, etc.).

The economic and political developments in the individual Eastern European countries can rarely be considered in isolation from regional and world events. Main trends in intraregional economic developments, such as pricing policy, clearing and cooperation agreements, and others, should be examined (e.g., the Central European regional cooperation). Some of the interesting questions to be asked are: Are there changes in the intraregional trade or pricing policy, for example, scale of barter agreements, and if so, how they will affect relations of the particular Eastern European country with the other countries in the region, the developed Western nations, and the developing countries? What are the prospects for creating a multilateral payments union in the region? What is the state of relations with the European Union and what are the prospects for full integration?

Political risk analysis requires an assessment of the relations between the individual Eastern European countries and the former Soviet Union and particularly with its main successor, Russia. Obviously the notion of the ''Soviet umbrella'' that emerged in the 1970s belongs definitely to the past, and, for economic and political reasons, no Russian assistance in case of future economic difficulties in the individual Eastern European countries can be expected. However, there are country-specific differences in the relations between the former Soviet republics and the individual Eastern European countries that an analyst should follow (e.g., Russia and the Ukraine, the Ukraine and Poland, etc.). It seems also that Russia still does not have a clear strategy for dealing with its former alliances on political and economic levels. In early 1991, the former Central Committee of the now banned Communist party and its Department for Foreign Relations argued that the Soviet Union should have a greater influence on the countries in the region, while the Soviet government and its Ministry of Foreign Affairs argued for the ''political freedom'' of the latter. As of 1993, there were clear signs that the new Russian Ministry of Foreign Affairs would pursue a strategy for increasing the influence of Russia in the former Soviet republics.

It has to be stressed that economic instability might arise in the Eastern European countries because of Russian policies. All of these countries have strong economic and trade links with Russia, and their economies can be influenced by the economic situation in the latter. Interesting questions to be asked are, for example, What will be the policy of Russia as regards the ruble debts of its former allies or its own debts to these countries? What is the Russian policy for energy deliveries, in terms of price, quantities, and time commitments, to Eastern Europe?

Last but not least, the state of East-West political relations should be one of the most important parts of political risk assessment for Eastern Europe. The East-West political dialogue determines economic, trade, and credit policies in the individual Eastern European countries toward the West. Some of the many questions to be asked are: What are the prospects for economic relations between Eastern Europe and post-1992 European Community (Union) integration? What are the effects of the Eastern European countries associated status with the European Union on their domestic economic and political developments and on their relationship with the former Soviet Union? What are the implications of a potential Eastern European membership in NATO? What are the prospects that Russia and the other former Soviet republics will receive generous Western assistance in the process of reforming their economies in the form of financial credit and direct and equity investments?

Political risk assessment also requires an analysis of the social conditions and the emergence of new social groups or classes in the individual Eastern European countries. Social tensions are less immediate in the sense that they are unlikely to apply, for example, to export payments. However, they are particularly likely to apply to long-term investment projects such as joint ventures, direct equity investments, and cooperation agreements. The analysis of the social conditions is a critical part of a country risk evaluation, particularly for countries like the former Soviet Union, former Czechoslovakia, Poland, and Hungary. The main question to be asked is: Does social support for the government policies exist? The events in Poland in the 1970s and in the 1980s as well as the implementation of the economic stabilization programme of the last noncommunist government (until October 1993) suggest that an accurate assessment of the social tensions may be of urgent importance for Western bankers and businessmen. Social tensions can precipitate political crises, change government priorities and policies, and even change the leadership. In the case of the former Soviet Union, particularly in Russia, a careful analysis of the social conditions in these countries is essential, since the improvement of the social conditions and living standards is of crucial importance for the popular support of Yeltzin's policies in Russia. The case of the Gaidar government and the Moscow October 1993 "revolution," for example, clearly demonstrated this. The strong protest and social unrest in connection with the announced price increases in the Soviet Union in May 1990 and the social discontent in 1992–1995 indicate that radical economic changes could lead to a change of government policies and even to some political tensions in the Russian leadership. The social support for Yeltzin was crucial to the failure of the coup attempt against Gorbachev in 1991. The faltering social support for the economic policy of the Russian government in 1992–1994 may also be crucial for Yeltzin's political future.

Some specific questions relate to risk assessment with regard to foreign investments. There are generally three approaches in assessing the determinants of foreign direct investment: "much politics, little economics"; "much economics, little politics"; and unstructured amalgamation of economics and politics. The principal questions posed in the discussion on assessing political and social risk apply fully to all three of these approaches. The choice of one or another approach depends, of course, on the analyst's preferences. Some specific questions to be addressed are: What is the effect of economic or political instability (e.g., in Russia) on the present value of the foreign investment? Do the government and leadership changes typical of post-communist Europe always increase the country risk? How much does social unrest (e.g., riots on the streets of Moscow) affect business activity? How much are the flows of multilateral aid (e.g., from G–7, IBRD, IFC, etc.) to Eastern Europe? It should be mentioned that historical evidence from the developed and developing countries points to the conclusion that there are two factors related to foreign investments to be seriously considered: political instability, which decreases foreign investment, and multilateral aid, which facilitates foreign investment.

This section presented a set of questions the analyst should raise when exploring political and social risk in Eastern Europe. I briefly indicated my tentative answers as well, at least to some of the questions. I do hope that even if the analyst arrives at answers different from mine, my questions are helpful to her or him in future studies.

PROSPECTS FOR AN ECONOMIC AND POLITICAL ORDER IN EASTERN EUROPE

In a broader framework, the assessment of opportunities and risk in the region, particularly for large foreign investment projects, also requires special attention to the extremely difficult question of what the prospects are for economic and political order in these countries. It is obvious that a clear-cut answer cannot be given. In this section I will try to present some observations on this issue.

The transformation process in Eastern Europe is characterised by instability and unpredictability. The countries in the region are suffering from the growing pains of overrapid changes and from the pain of readjustment from the former economic structure to the new one. But the transformation process has its own dynamics and political logic. These are based on the interaction between economic, social, and political changes. How can we explain these processes and the direction of future economic and political developments?

Ockham's razor, a principle named for an English cleric of the fourteenth century, might be helpful in approaching this fascinating but extremely difficult question. Ockham's razor stipulates that simple explanations and answers should be prefered to complex ones and that complexities should be introduced only when simple explanations prove inadequate. This principle was proposed initially as a basis for guiding philosophic inquiry, but it can be helpful also in nonphilosophical realms. This is my approach in the present section.

I would like to begin my analysis with the statement made by one of the most prominent economists of our century, J. Schumpeter, who during the Second World War published his study *Capitalism, Socialism and Democracy* (1942):

Can capitalism survive? No. I do not think it can. But this opinion of mine, like that of every other economist who has pronounced upon the subject, is in itself completely uninteresting. What counts in any attempt at social prognosis is not the Yes or No that sums up the facts and arguments which lead up to it but these facts and arguments themselves. They contain all that is scientific in the final result. Everything else is not science but prophecy. Analysis, whether economic or other, never yields more than a statement about tendencies present in the observable pattern. And these never tell us what will *happen* to the pattern but only what *would* happen if they continued to act as they have been acting in the time interval covered by our observation and if no other factors intruded [emphasis added]. "Inevitability" or "necessity" can never mean more than this. (p. 61)

This statement voices criticism of capitalism, which since the Industrial Revolution has been plagued by crisis, inequality, and depressions. The critics increased after the Second World War. Again, Schumpeter was the economist stressing that capitalism, while economically stable and even gaining in stability, would be changed—not by economic necessity—into an order of things which it will be merely a matter of taste and terminology as to whether to call it socialism or not.

These remarks reflect in a very convincing way, among other things, the eternal search for visions of a more perfect society. Philosophers have always had such visions: Plato's Republic, Sir Thomas More's Utopia, and Marx's dictatorship of the proletariat were among the most influential schools of thought. And the dictatorship of the proletariat, after more than 70 years of reality in the Soviet Union and more than 40 years in Central and Eastern Europe, proved to be a doctrine legalising one of the most oppressive political regimes in the recent history of the old continent and of the world. Its economic and political mechanisms and policies were undisputably failures. Keynes was one of the first to foresee the failure of central planning more than a half century ago, during the first years of the Soviet state, when he wrote: "How can I accept a doctrine which sets up as its bible, above and beyond criticism, an absolute economic textbook which I know to be not only scientifically erroneous but without interest or application for the modern world" (Keynes, 1963, p. 300).

Although the market economies (or, better said, the mixed economies) of the United States, Western Europe, and Japan experienced a common pattern of unprecedented, rapid growth and expanding international trade, the critics of capitalism increased when in the 1970s and 1980s inflation soared, unemployment rose, government deficits began to climb, the international financial system faced the danger of massive defaults on the less developed countries' debt, and the environment posed alarming demands. The economists in the West face again the challenge of the endless search for better ways for the government to help (or stop hindering) economic development. The Western economies have problems, and the diagnosis points to a state of sickness. Critics from Left and Right are searching for policies and schemes to revive the economies in the West.

But in the former Soviet Union and in Eastern Europe, the state of affairs is fundamentally different. Scholars and politicians both in the East and in the West agree that there are no "medicines" to revive the former centrally planned economies in the region. Their sickness is incurable, and the only way to avoid a protracted crisis in the long term is a transformation of the economic mechanism, a transformation toward Western-type markets. It should be mentioned that all of the previous (and frequent) attempts in the 1950s, 1960s, and 1970s to "reform" the centrally planned economic systems in Eastern Europe were failures because they did not attempt to change the logic of these systems. Another important failure was that they did not attempt to change the political climate for the economic reforms. It is interesting to note the statement the Soviet economist A. Aganbegyan made in late 1980s regarding the question of why there should be economic reforms in the Soviet Union: "The old economic structure, the old patterns of development, did not correspond to the new conditions both inside the Soviet Union and internationally. . . . It became very clear that it was insufficient to make minor changes in the running of the economy. New radical reform—a 'restructuring'—was needed" (Aganbegyan, 1988, p. 41).

In other words, the economies of the former Soviet Union and the countries of Central and Eastern Europe are in the process of transformation and will be changed by economic necessity. And I would like to use the phrasing (but not the contents of the quote) of Schumpeter (1947, p. 61) by saying that these economies will be changed into an order of things which it will be merely a matter of taste and terminology as to whether to call it capitalism, market economy, or neither—but it is obvious that the new order will not be called socialism.

What are the alternative economic systems?

Guided by Ockham's razor toward simple explanations and answers, one can approach this question by examining the existing economic systems in our time. But first let me define briefly the notion of an economic system. Using Samuelson's definition (1989, p. 833), the economic system is a "network of relations and organizations that: sets the laws and regulations that govern economic activity; determines the property rights and ownership of factors of production; distributes the decision making power over production and consumption; determines the incentives motivating different decision makers; and at the end determines *what* gets produced, *how* it gets produced, and *for whom* the output is produced."

As we can observe, there is a great variety in the way the countries of Western Europe, North Africa, Latin America, Africa, and Asia organise their economies.

In our century, four main economic systems have existed: the market economy, Marxism, Soviet communism, and the social democratic economic order. It goes beyond the scope of the present chapter to discuss in detail the characteristics of these economic systems. An analysis of these issues is presented in my study of the economic and political transformation in Eastern Europe (Zloch-Christy, 1994). The discussion in the first section of the present chapter justifies the conclusion that the post-communist economies are in the process of radical changes and that they will not be either Marxist or Soviet communist, but will bear to a great extent the features (in their embryonic forms) of Western European economies, the social democratic economic order: democratic governments, an expanded welfare state, nationalized industries, and planning—or, better said, government intervention—in the economy.

Another interesting question arises: What are the prospects for economic development strategies in Eastern Europe? Rostow's take-off theory, Gerschenkron's relative backwardness theory, and Kuznet's balanced growth theory give us some solid ground for thinking about this important question. At the same time, since they are not comprehensive theories that can give universal explanations for the history and the future of the individual countries, each of the post-communist European countries should be viewed individually with its special resources and needs. Such an approach requires policies that fit the particular case, considering the country's background, culture, economic resources, and political changes. Guided again by Ockham's razor, let consider some patterns of economic development in the postwar period, asking the question, Could this type of economic development be a possible scenario for Eastern Europe? I would suggest considering the scenarios of the following four countries or group of countries:

• Southeast Asian newly industrialized countries (NICs)
• Portugal and Spain (or the European Community scenario)
• Chile
• Latin America other than Chile

It goes beyond the scope of the analysis in this chapter to discuss the economic development strategies of these countries; for more detailed discussion I refer the reader again to my 1994 study, part 4. I would argue that the Eastern European countries have a good chance of following the pattern of economic development of Spain and Portugal, in other words, the European Community (EC) scenario. It is widely understood and accepted by Eastern European politicians that the future economic development of their countries greatly depends on their standing with the European Union. EU membership will speed up the reform processes on the economic and political level in Eastern Europe and the adjustment to the new realities in Europe and in the world. However, one should not be too optimistic, thinking that some of the smaller post-communist countries will soon become "second Spains" and will repeat its success story; the changes in Eastern Europe have been going on only a few years, while Spain and Portugal created market structures and made steps to restore civil society long before joining the European Community in the 1980s. But undoubtedly there is a good chance for the smaller Eastern European countries to be successful in following the path of economic development of the Iberian nations. As regards the former Soviet Union, it is difficult to speculate on this issue, given the complexity of the enormous economic and political problems of the (former) great power at present and in the near future.

CONCLUSION

This chapter presented a basis for an analytical framework for the assessment of opportunities and risks in Eastern Europe: creditworthiness assessment and political and social risk assessment. Developments in Eastern Europe in the last few years strongly suggest that the creditworthiness assessment will to some extent be misleading if it is not accompanied by a political risk assessment in order to indicate potential changes in the transforming Eastern European societies and economies in the medium and long term. Most of the Eastern European economies have embarked on a road that no one has travelled before: an attempt to liberalise, or turn into a market economy, a command planned economy. Theory and the experience of previous reforms do not suggest clearly what the optimal strategy in achieving these goals should be or what are the best answers to questions like, What is the right proportion between public and market goods, between state and market administration, and between achieving capital profitability and welfare goals? There is a strong correlation between political liberalisation and economic transformation in this region. All of this indicates that a new approach in our analysis of the economic reforms, external imbalances, foreign investments and country risk in the Eastern European countries is a necessity.

NOTES

This chapter was written during my scholarships at the Hoover Institution in Stanford and at the Department of Economics in Harvard University. I would like to acknowledge the stimulating intellectual atmosphere of these fascinating places of knowledge and reason. It was revised in February and October 1993.

1. Eastern Europe up to 2 October 1990 denoted Bulgaria, Czechoslovakia, the German Democratic Republic (GDR), Hungary, Poland, Romania, and the Soviet Union. In December 1991 the Soviet Union was dissolved, and most of the former Soviet republics joined the Commonwealth of Independent States (CIS); in January 1993 Czechoslovakia was divided into Czech and Slovak republics. More recently, Eastern Europe as a distinct geographical area with its own political and reformist identity, of course, omits the ex-GDR. The terms "Eastern Europe" and "post-communist Europe" are used as synonyms.

REFERENCES

Aganbegyan, A. (1988). *The Economic Challenge of Perestroika.* Bloomington: Indiana University Press.

Avramovic, Dragoslav. (1964). *Economic Growth and External Debt.* Baltimore: Johns Hopkins University Press.

Frey, Bruno S. (1984). *International Political Economics.* Oxford: Basil Blackwell.

Keynes, J. M. (1963). *Essays in Persuasion.* New York: Norton Library.

Kornai, Janos. (1986). "The Hungarian Reform Process: Visions, Hopes and Reality." *Journal of Economic Literature,* December, pp. 1687–1737.

Samuelson, Paul, and William D. Nordhaus. (1989). *Economics.* 13th ed. New York: McGraw-Hill.

Schumpeter, Joseph A. (1942, 1947). *Capitalism, Socialism and Democracy.* New York and London: Harper and Row.

Zloch-Christy, Iliana. (1988). *Debt Problems of Eastern Europe.* New York and Cambridge: Cambridge University Press.

————. (1989). "Programmes for Economic Liberalization and the External Balance of Eastern Europe." Mimeo, International Monetary Fund, Washington, D.C., September.

————. (1991). *East-West Financial Relations: Current Problems and Future Prospects.* Cambridge: Cambridge University Press.

————. (1994). *Eastern Europe in a Time of Change: Economic and Political Dimensions.* Westport, CT: Praeger.

14

Concluding Remarks

Iliana Zloch-Christy

This book discussed the issues of economic transformation, privatization, and foreign investment in post-communist Europe with a focus on the period after 1989. The political risk remains a major one in doing business and investing in the region. Culture and personal freedom will be important factors in the process of change in post-communist Europe. A certain danger exists that in some of these countries the increasing external and internal tensions may result in the fall of the governments implementing the radical economic reforms, and although they will probably remain on the road to transformation, they may find themselves under a new form of authoritarian government or with poorly performing market-oriented economies and emerging democratic institutions.

This explains why at one point the flows of foreign investments were directed primarily to few countries—Hungary, the Czech Republic, and Poland—in the early 1990s. But even in these countries, the average foreign direct investment remains relatively small—some $150,000. The same refers to the other countries in the region. Hungary, Poland, the former Czechoslovakia (and from 1 January 1993, the Czech Republic) have been regarded by Western business and financial circles as countries with relative political stability. Although most analysts agree that the most obvious risks involved in foreign investment—expropriation or forced divestment—are not justifiably applicable to post-communist Europe, Western businesses have concerns about increasing investment in this region. Some of these concerns are: low demand in the domestic markets, shortage of hard currencies, widespread use of primitive trading techniques like barter, long and cumbersome bureaucratic procedures in evaluating the potential projects and their subsequent realization, and limited currency convertibility. There is also concern among Western business circles that the Eastern European countries, particularly countries like Russia, the Ukraine, and Poland, insist on discussing "big" projects of "world scale" and not "small" projects.

It appears that foreign investments in Eastern Europe will be directed during the 1990s in five main channels. The first one, venture capital, appears to be the most important. As is well known, venture capital is not cheap. Even inside the Western industrialized countries, investors typically demand an annual rate of return of at least 15–30 percent for new ventures. This indicates that the post-communist Eastern European countries should offer higher rates of return if they want to be able to compete with traditional projects of this kind in the West.

Foreign direct investments by multinational corporations are a second channel for providing private external finance to the former centrally planned economies. These corporations have long-term strategies and tend to be influenced by global considerations rather than short-term profit expectations. For example, in the area of consumer goods, they are and will continue to be attracted by the large untapped markets with growth potential in Eastern Europe. Export-oriented manufacturers are motivated by the low costs of skilled labor and raw materials in the region. The multinational corporations will probably increase their activities in the region if the Eastern European countries can offer clear laws and guaranteed contracts, protection of property rights and permission for private ownership of land, provision of incentives to attract investments (e.g., tax benefits), transportation, better banking and telecommunication facilities, and investment guarantees extended by their governments. A similar list of desirable conditions drawn up by American executives was presented to the Russian president B. Yeltsin during his visit to the United States in June 1992.

A third channel seems to be the classical portfolio investment. Its scope will, of course, depend on the development of domestic stock and bond markets in the individual Eastern European countries. As at present, however, although some steps in that direction are recorded in Hungary, the former Czechoslovakia, and Poland, in many cases the domestic markets in these countries are either underdeveloped or nonexistent. And one small but important historical detail should be recalled in this regard: it took the former Soviet Union more than 70 years after Bolshevik Russia repudiated the Czarist debt to the West to be able to launch a bond issue in the West.

Foreign capital flows to Eastern Europe will be channeled also through commercial bank lending. Availability of such credits, of course, depends on the individual countries' records of servicing their borrowings, the credibility of their present policies, and also the provision of export credit guarantees and cofinancing with international financial institutions. Commercial bank lending includes trade, leasing, project financing, and very limited general purpose financing (e.g., to the Czech Republic).

A fifth channel of foreign capital in Eastern Europe consists of the financial flows provided by former expatriates. These flows have varying importance among the individual countries in the region depending on their constituency abroad. It seems that Poland, Hungary, and the Ukraine can attract foreign capital from their large constituencies abroad (e.g., in the United States, Canada, and Australia), and this will have some impact on their privatization processes.

It would not be premature to state that the post-communist countries (still) do not have a concept for their foreign investment strategy—its scope, branches, or clearly defined institutional framework. The entry of foreign firms into the Eastern European markets continues to be greeted in many instances with distrust. There are frequently heard statements that the foreign investors acquire state assets at fire-sale prices, taking advantage of corrupt and inexperienced managers and bureaucrats in the former centrally planned economies. It seems during the whole decade of the 1990s, Western investments in Eastern Europe will be directed to the production of goods and services that can be exported for hard currencies, for example, the car industry and the hotel and tourism businesses.[1] A realistic approach to the inflow of foreign investments to the post-communist countries suggests also that these flows will not represent a major net source of financial contribution to the transformation and restructuring process in the region during the 1990s. The major financial contribution of FDIs will be one of intermediation rather than of inflow. It appears also that foreign investment will in most cases follow domestic privatization. This will create a basis for relatively high competition in sales to foreign investors and will reduce the perception that foreign investment involves corruption in deals directly between the government in the individual Eastern European countries and the investors.

As history tells, foreign investment has played a major role in the economic development of many countries in the not so distant past. It was an important factor determining the development of the United States, Canada, and Australia in the nineteenth century and at the beginning of this century. The East Asian countries also partly built their economic growth strategies in the 1970s and 1980s on foreign investments; these countries achieved, however, remarkable domestic savings rates at some 30 percent. As is well known, the Eastern European nations, particularly the Central and southern East European countries, developed after World War II largely without foreign investments. The Soviet and bilateral CMEA credits provided played a minor role in their economic development. All of this indicates that at present, in a situation where domestic private savings are insufficient and foreign capital imports appear to be on modest levels, government savings will remain the alternative channel for generating investment and growth.

As is well known, economically useful employment requires capital, and labor is generally much more productive if combined with more capital. Reduced savings means reduced investments. Fewer investments means less growth and less wealth. And growth matters; it matters and will continue to matter very much in solving the many challenges of the economic, political, and social transformation in post-communist Europe, and in avoiding social tensions in the fragile democratic societies in these countries. In the long-term, however, most of the Eastern European countries have good chances of increasing the inflow of foreign investments in their economies, given their association with and anticipation for full membership in the European Union and in the emerging new security structure in post-cold-war Europe. The smaller Central and Eastern European countries can benefit particularly from such membership, and are likely to demonstrate rapid increases in foreign equity and direct investments, as the experiences of some other southern European countries—Portugal, Spain, Greece—proved during the 1980s.

NOTE

1. As discussed in Part I and Part II, the major world car producers are increasing their investments in Eastern Europe. The investments made by Fiat, Suzuki, and General Motors Europe represent some one-third of the total investments in Poland over the last few years. Volkswagen invested some $410 million in the Czech Skoda enterprises. Audi has about a $180 million outlay at a new components plant in Hungary near Györ. General Motors has invested more than $250 million in the Hungarian town of Szentgotthard. Magyar Suzuki also operates in Hungary. As recent Western reports indicate, these Japanese, American, and Western European investments in the car industry are made not only because of a long-term strategy designed to establish market shares in a potential market where the average car on the road is between 14 and 17 years old, but also because the recipient countries provide customs incentives, employment and infrastructure subsidies, and generous corporate tax benefits (*Christian Science Monitor,* 19 October 1993, p. 9).

Selected Bibliography

Bakos, Gabor. (1992). "Japanese Capital in Central Europe." *Hitotsubashi Journal of Economics*. December, Tokyo.

Balcerowicz, Leszek. (1993). "The Polish Way to the Market Economy." EBRD, London. Mimeo.

Bochniarz, Zbigniew, and Władysław Jermakowicz. (1991). "Direct Foreign Investments in Poland." *Development and International Cooperation,* vols. 7–17, June, New York.

Czech Fund of National Property Annual Reports. (Various years). Prague.

Dratch, Dana. (1993). "Russian Commodity Markets Still in Their Infancy." *Radio Free Europe/Radio Liberty Research Report,* No. 29, July.

Drysdale, Peter, ed. (1972). *Direct Foreign Investment in Asia and the Pacific.* Canberra: Australian National University Press.

East European Investment Magazine. (Various years). Budapest.

Gomułka, Stanisław. (1993). "Poland: Glass Half Full." In R. Portes, ed., *Economic Transformation in Central Europe: A Progress Report.* Brussels: Office for Official Publications of the European Community.

Hashi, Iraj. (1993). "The Polish Privatization Process and the Prospects for Employee-Owned Enterprises." *European Business and Economic Development,* vol. 1. part 4, January, Essex.

Kornai, Janos. (1992). *The Socialist System.* Oxford: Oxford University Press; *The Political Economy of Communism.* Princeton, NJ: Princeton University Press.

McMillan, Carl H. (1993). "The Role of Foreign Direct Investments in the Transition from Planned to Market Economy." Paper presented at the International Studies Association Annual Meeting, March, Acapulco, Mexico.

OECD. (Various years). *International Direct Investment Statistics Yearbook.* Paris.

Privatization Newsletter of Czech and Slovak Republics. (Various years). Prague: Charles University.

van Brabant, Jozef. (1991). *Integrating Eastern Europe into the Global Economy: Convertibility through Payments Union.* New York: Kluwer Academic.

Zhurek, Stefan. (1993). "Commodity Exchanges in Russia: Success or Failure?" *Radio Free Europe/Radio Liberty Research Report,* No. 6, February.

Zloch-Christy, Iliana. (1988). *Debt Problems of Eastern Europe.* Cambridge and New York: Cambridge University Press.

————. (1991). *East-West Financial Relations: Current Problems and Future Prospects.* Cambridge and New York: Cambridge University Press.

————. (1994). *Eastern Europe in a Time of Change: Economic and Political Dimensions.* Westport, CT: Praeger.

Index

Contributors

GABOR BAKOS, Senior Research Fellow, Institute of Economics, Hungarian Academy of Sciences, Budapest, and the Institute of Economic Research, Hototsubashi University, Tokyo, Japan.

ALEXANDER BARSKI, Senior Research Fellow, Central Economico-Mathematical Institute, Moscow, Russia, Russian Academy of Sciences.

DANIELA BOBEVA, Advisor at the Council of Ministers, member of the Foreign Investment Commission, member of the Board Center for the Study of Democracy, Sofia, Bulgaria.

ALEXANDER BOZHKOV, member of Parliament, former Executive Director of the Bulgarian Privatization Agency, Sofia, Bulgaria.

GYÖRGY CSÁKI, Institute of World Economics, Hungarian Academy of Sciences, Budapest, Hungary.

WŁADYSŁAW W. JERMAKOWICZ, Chairman of the Board of Directors, Pomorski Bank Kredytowy S.A., Warsaw, Poland, and Professor, School of Business, University of Southern Indiana, Evansville, Ind., United States.

MICHAL MEJSTRIK, Institute of Economic Studies, Faculty of Social Sciences, Charles University, Prague, Czech Republic.

KEN MORITA, Professor, Faculty of Economics, Hiroshima University, Japan.

GEORGI SMATRAKALEV, Institute of Economics, Bulgarian Academy of Sciences, Sofia, Bulgaria.

STEFAN Y. ZHUREK, Senior Research Fellow, the Institute for the Studies of External Economic Relations; former chief economist of the Russian Commodity and Raw Materials Stock Exchange, Moscow; and MacArthur Fellow, University of California at Berkeley, Berkeley, Calif., United States, 1993–1994.

ILIANA ZLOCH-CHRISTY, economist and independent consultant; faculty associate, Department of Economics, Harvard University, Cambridge, Mass., 1991–93; Senior Associate Member, St. Antony's College, Oxford, U.K., 1994.

ISBN 0-275-95212-6

HARDCOVER BAR CODE